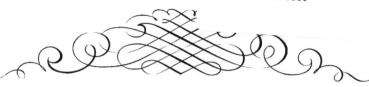

ISBN 978-1-330-14364-3
PIBN 10036488

HISTORY OF

IN ILLINOIS

Portraits and Biographies of the cultured men and women who have been liberal patrons of the higher Arts : : : : :

Edited by

SOCIETE UNIVERSELLE LYRIQUE

1904

INTRODUCTION.

So wrote the great bard in the long ago, and the years that have passed have in no way dimmed the truth of his utterance. The thought that we live by deeds not hours, that life is only worth living as it means achievement, that every day in each individual life is making history, is familiar to us all. It has been expressed again and again by philosopher and sage and poet since Shakespeare wrote the words that have become immortal.

An eminent divine once said: "If my library must be taken from me, leaving me but one class of books, give me my Biographies." This man, recognized as one of the most brilliant pulpit orators in America, realized that in the perusal of biographies one comes in touch with the realms of art, music and science, with the miracles of discovery and the wonders of research. However fascinating other studies may prove, there is nothing that can compare in variety and in scope with the study of human nature and the story of human effort and achievement.

The idea of presenting the history of the music and art of a State, or a section of country, by writing the biographies of those actively engaged along these lines or of the patrons of such enterprises, was a happy thought. It left the door of many a sanctum ajar and revealed the very self of those who have made possible the history in which all feel so laudable and just a pride. The State of Illinois has been selected as one whose history shall be thus told, and the result of the effort has been the bringing together of names illustrious and honorable, and the providing of a look into lives cultured, broad and uplifting. Into Illinois, in the beginning, came the very cream of the sturdiness and intelligence of the New England and Middle States, with the spirit of the Revolution still dominant. Then came also the culture and genial hospitality of the South, and all combined to develop the best in their adopted State. The result was one of the wonders of the century just closed, and Illinois stands to-day second to no State in the Union from any standpoint.

Business interests have developed and flourished, manufactures are large and important, educational advantages are the best, while such strides have been made in music and art as to justify the prediction that Chicago will yet become the music and art center of this country. The years have wrought great advances in the existence of a general education in art and music and of more cultivated literary tastes.

There are writers and speakers who seem to delight to revel in a sort of pessimistic rant over the degeneracy of the times and to sigh for the days gone by. Whatever has made the " rift in the lute " for them, it is a fact that the people as a whole are far more cultured than a half century ago. Then the distinction between the business and the professional man was wide, and, unless to fit her for some particular vocation, it was hardly thought necessary to inflict a thorough educational training upon the daughter of the family. To-day the demand for educated business men has been felt and met. The magazines have lent their influence to this end in presenting papers on every variety of topic—music, art, politics, religion, fiction and every sort of subject calculated to amuse or instruct the reader. The women in our homes have become earnest students, accomplished linguists, musicians and artists.

Advantages of travel, once the privilege of the rich, are

now within the reach of the multitude, and, as a result, there is a general familiarity with works of art before unknown. Men, whose days are filled with the fret and stress of business, delight in the possession of a Corot, a Millet or a Meissonier, a portrait from master-brush or a painting by Freer, Mersfilder or Chas. F. Brourn. The sonatas of Beethoven, the nocturnes and waltzes of Chopin, Listz's Fantasies and Rhapsody, and so on through the wealth of the musical world, are known even to the children of our homes, and the statues of ancient and modern times find ready recognition by the multitude. With this sort of general education broadcast, it is not strange that so much has been accomplished during even a few years. The child who once strummed with her little fingers on the window-sill, dreaming of the sweet chords that would not come, has now, if nothing more, her toy piano, from which, with tiny fingers, she brings melody. The youth who, wandering over the meadow, saw beauty in the falling leaf and springing flower, but had nothing to encourage his art-dreams, may now make his own, at least for a time, the treasures of a free institute, and learn to handle the colors he loves so well. The free library has opened to the humblest home the world of poetry and science, of history and fiction, and to-day ignorance is the result of choice, not a necessity. With all this atmosphere of research as an environment, it is no marvel that even in her comparatively short career Illinois lays claim to such an honorable history—her musical, artistic and literary life—as is unfolded in the biographies included in this volume. It is not claimed that all are found in this book who desire a place in so illustrious a roll-call. The plan of work by which this book was arranged was broad and ambitious. It attempted and has achieved much, but not all it contemplated. Reasons for this are obvious. It has been impossible for the publishers, though they have delayed the issuing of the book far beyond the original design, to reach all they desired to include.

Not entirely understanding, no doubt, the importance and the scope of the work, many have not co-operated as it was believed they would, and it has been impossible to secure the data necessary to include them in the book. Some have been abroad, others, possibly, who should have been included, have changed their residence to other States and have thus been overlooked. One cannot claim perfection even for enterprises of the twentieth century, but an honest effort has been made to represent each part of the State and each branch of work as far as possible. In looking over the list of those who have a place in this history, several general characteristics suggest themselves to the thoughtful reader. Possibly first is the comparative youth of those who have achieved so much of importance in this sort of history. No age of the world was ever more emphatically the age of youth than is the present.

The presidents of our universities, the heads of great enterprises, the artists in our studios, the greatest musicians, are found very largely in the ranks of those still in the prime of life and younger. It is said that people are living many years in one, and this may be true in a sense that brings regret, but it is also true in another sense.

Equipments for all sorts of educational work are so complete; lectures, recitals, musicales and exhibits so open the door to even the child student; that our youth make rapid strides up the hill of knowledge, and early learn to think, to do and to win for themselves. This prominence of youth is a peculiarly distinguishing characteristic of the newer States, and Illinois has not yet counted the years long enough to have lost the charm.

Possibly this might not be considered remarkable along many lines, since this is called the age of Young America, and from President down through the lines of executive officials, in the pulpit and on the forum, youth sometimes seems the most essential desideratum. But in the history of Nation or State we look for the development of its literary and art work latest, since in a way they do not represent the essentials of practical life. With us, however, the President of our great university is a man still in his prime. The directors and leaders in musical and art circles, our

Lorados, Tafts and Ralph Clarksons, our poets and our singers, are very largely young men and women, or those still on the sunny side of life. Any observer of musical and art-life in Chicago must have been impressed with this fact in attending the various entertainments given. The Mendelssohn Club, Chicago's favorite musical club, is for the most part a club of young men, with its leader, Harrison M. Wild, still in his prime. Wilhelm Middleschulte, as organist and composer, Walter Spry, as pianist, Theo. Spiering, a violinist and leader of one of the finest string quartettes in Chicago, George J. Hamlin, Charles W. Clark, Helen Buckley, Jenny Osborn, and other singers of note, are all representatives of the present musical effort. Among the studios the same truth is everywhere present, that to comparative youth in the world of achievement is given the sceptre and the crown.

One characteristic of this list which is eloquent of the times in which we live is the prominent place not given to but gained by women. Some of the most important positions have been and are occupied by them. With Mrs. Potter Palmer among the national, and Mrs. Ralph Emerson among the State representatives to the great exposition in Paris; Mrs. Warren Springer, a member of the Chicago Press Club, and among the leaders in the new industrialism of the day, and others in positions of responsibility and influence, one may well feel that women have proved their ability and fitness for most prominent and important service. In the realms of music we not only have our Thomas and our Sherwood, our Ziegfelds and others organizing and conducting musical colleges, not only our De Koven and our Neidlinger, Matthews, Bronson, the Roots and other writers of songs and ballads, Bernhard Ziehn and Carl Wolfsohn standing for the highest ideals in the musical world, but there are many women who do not suffer by comparison. Ellen Crosby, who has no superior as the interpreter of Wagner, Mrs. Gaynor, Mrs. Bond, Anita L. Owen, Eleanor Smith and other composers; Anna Shaw Faulkner, with her wonderful musical lectures and interpretations; Genevieve

Clark Wilson, Eleanor Sherwood and many another sweet
singer, take rank with the very first musicians of to-day.
In Alton, Jacksonville, Quincy, Aurora, Springfield, Knoxville, Galesburg, Rockford and many other cities are conservatories of music and musical societies which owe their existence and success entirely to the efforts of talented musical women. The same may be said of every line of artistic
and literary work In many a studio husband and wife
work together in generous rivalry, while in hundreds of
other studios scattered through the State girlish faces bend
over the easel, and girlish hands work in wood and metal.
Miss Christia M. Reade has no rival in her work in metals,
illuminated text and stained glass, and a stroll through the
Art Institute, which is doing such a great work for this section of country, is a revelation as to what women, many
young women, are achieving in various lines of art.

We have alluded to Dr. Harper, in many respects the
wonder of the age in educational circles. He has many noble
co-workers in the presidents of the various universities in
Illinois. But some of the brightest students who enter
these schools of learning go there from academies and sem-
inaries founded, taught and educated by women.

This unity of aim and effort between the intelligent
men and women on the highest plain of literary and artistic
life is one of the most marked features of this epoch, and,
perhaps, emphasizes its existence in unconscious fashion
in this history. A distinguishing feature which may appeal
to the patriotism of every loyal heart is the fact that
so largely the history of music and art in Illinois is
the history of the efforts of American men and women.
In a series of articles which recently appeared in one of the
daily papers of Chicago one of the most eminent musicians
this country boasts made earnest plea for American teachers
and American musicians. Not so very many years have
passed since American music was regarded as crude, American singers as only mediocre, and American teachers as
unable to produce satisfactory results, defying comparison
with the best instruction given in the old world. A revolu-

tion has taken place in this respect. American composers are obtaining recognition, in spite of the prejudices of education, in the old world; our singers are crowned with laurels across the water, and we have pianists who deserve a place among the best in the world.

No more realistic composition was ever written than McDowell's " March Winds;" no sweeter songs than Florence Aylward, J. G. Wison, Neidlinger, C. B. Hawley and others already named have given us; no sweeter singers than those of our own country who, whether in oratorio, opera or concert, delight and charm. Could that sweet queen of song, Maria Litta, have been spared, who shall say that we might not have given another Patti to an idolizing world? As the years pass ideals grow more lofty, standards higher, possibilities seem greater and ambition grows boundless. It is a living commentary on the change of conditions to note how the wonders accomplished in Illinois have been wrought for the most part by those who are American by birth or adoption, and gratifying to know how some of the best results have been achieved by those whose education has been received wholly in this country. As we have turned over the pages of this volume, looking into the earnest faces, each full of purpose; as we have read the story of each life, every one a history of resolve and effort, it has seemed as if these simple stories, simply told, should be the greatest inspiration, not only to those who come after to make later history, but to the readers of to-day. ·Not without honest, earnest effort have these results been reached; obstacles which seemed insurmountable have been overcome; prejudices have been met and conquered; innovations have been battled for and triumphed. Not cloudless the sky which stretches over the voyager who dares to enter unknown ports. Not rose-strewn the path that leads to fame. When the tasks of life are done by magic, when your work and mine is accomplished by wishing it was done, then will fame be won without effort and the laurel wreath without a sigh. The lives of these men and women represent self-denial, earnest conse-

cration, true ambition, untiring perseverance, the ignoring
of discouragement, and at the end—success.

Not only to the toiler, however, has result been wholly
due, but as well to the many patrons, who, by their generosity and appreciation, have opened the door of coveted
possibilities. The beautiful music-rooms in palatial homes
opened for the giving of delightful musicales, the private
art galleries where hang choice pictures from home artists,
are the evidences that these cultured men and women have a
deserved place in such a history as this.

In a careful perusal of this history of lives which have
meant so much for the various realms they portray, the
thought can but be present of the many, many who have had
a share in making achievement possible, whose names find
no place on written page. We sometimes speak lightly of
the hand which rocks the cradle, but in the utter self-forgetfulness of many a mother and the glad self-denial in many
a home was made possible the success of loved ones. Perhaps no record will ever be made even of the name of some
noble heart whose greatest boon was to live its life in the
victory of another. No picture will ever be made of many
a sweet face whose brightest smile was over the achievement
of one beloved. In many a studio, at many a desk, back of
many a sweet singer, is the memory of some dear, unselfish
life whose history is unsung save as an angel with reverent
pen shall write: "She hath done what she could." The
pioneers of yesterday—

> "Brave, stalwart men, born Nature's kings,
> True-hearted women, Nature's queens,"

made possible the artists and the singers, the educators and
the authors, the art and the music of to-day. Let their unwritten history never be forgotten in the pride and success
of the present, nor let us forget that but for their heroism
such histories as those in which we have an honest pride could
never have had existence.

That Illinois, that this middle-west, has a great future
is an accepted fact. The years will bring, no doubt, develop-

ment of present ideas, fruition of hopes now little more than dreams, improvement of what now seems perfection. Be this as it may, it is safe to predict that there can be no history embodying the lives of an equal number of men and women which has meant more to this State than this history now given to the public. Everything in the atmosphere of the times has contributed to make the years these lives represent laden with interest, full of incentive, prolific in result. These years have been wonderful years in the world's history, but most wonderful for those portions of our country which have developed like magic from nothingness to the very acme of civilization, beautified and enriched with the treasures of music and art.

In presenting this book to the public, those who have been deeply interested in it feel they should say in justice to themselves, that the work was inaugurated on a difficult plan as to its perfection and completeness. But, in spite of much delay and many discouragements, it has been the aim of the publishers, as far as possible, to make the work complete.

The *very* best in the social and artistic life of Illinois has found a place in these pages. It has been a work done with the aim of giving honor to whom honor is due, and no favoritism or personal preference has left its imprint anywhere. The pictures have been very largely taken especially for this book by one of Chicago's best artists, and every effort has been made to do justice to the face as to the character of those who have so kindly contributed to the success of the book by giving the necessary data. If it should seem as if undue prominence has been given to those in Chicago, it must be remembered that Chicago is an immense center to which many flock who desire opportunity to win success. As a result, many of our foremost men and women find a place in the great city. It has been possibly easier to impress those in Chicago with the value of such a work.

Scores of unanswered letters, others returned with the offers made declined, testify to the fact that the opportunity did not present itself as desirable to many whose names and lives would have been gladly added to those procured. Those whose judgment should be valuable have pronounced the book a marvel in the variety and scope it presents.

The book as now given to the public is much larger than the original design. In the paper employed, the type, arrangement and finish every volume is the same, the binding alone having been left to the taste of the individual subscriber.

There have been books of similar character written and published, but none which more thoroughly commends itself to the artistic eye or to the intelligence of the general reader.

The introduction to the article on the " History of Art in Illinois " was written by Rev. Austen K. de Blois, Ph. D., until recently President of Shurtleff College in Upper Alton, Illinois. As ex-President of one of the best known of the colleges of Illinois, as pastor of one of the oldest and largest churches in Chicago, it is eminently appropriate that his name should have a place in this volume.

The poem "Music," or " From Sound to Soul," which serves as the introduction to the article on the " History of Music in Illinois," was written by George Cathcart Bronson, well known as a writer, composer and most earnest promoter of the best musical enterprises in Illinois. A sketch of his life, also included in these pages, will be of interest to many.

The biographies, with very few exceptions, and historical articles have been written by Mrs. Fannie Cheney Bennett, whose writings have found place in the papers under the nom de plume " Pensèe." She belongs to a family of scholars. Her father, Rev. D. B. Cheney, D. D., was well known in the seventies as Trustee of the Chicago University, interested in its theological seminary and pastor of the Fourth Baptist Church of Chicago.

It is, therefore, a book peculiarly the product of Illinois, and is given to the public with the hope that, whatever its failures may seem to be, its merits may be found so many as to win oblivion for aught else.

beautiful thought which inspired it, not for the jingle of some rhyme which for a moment riveted the attention. A song, a symphony, is prized for the whole theme which gave it birth, not discarded for one crashing chord or treasured for some dainty trill.

So judged in its completeness, it is hoped that this volume may seem worthy of hearty recognition and endorsement as a history told by biographies of the Music and Art of Illinois.

INDEX.

14

The History of Art in Illinois.

INTRODUCTION.

Art in America has fought a long battle with two strong
foes, the Puritan and the money-maker. The New England
fathers had but little conception of the glories of art. If our
country had been peopled at first by children of the European
southland, we would doubtless have for our dowry to-day a
fairer heritage of æsthetic culture.

The ancient rock-ribbed orthodoxy tended to repress the
joyousness and freedom which the genius of art exalts, yet religion needs art as much as art needs religion. A religion that
strips the ivy from the stones of the old cathedral, drives the
song-birds from spire and turret, stills the chimes in the tower
and the music of.choir and organ within the holy place, tears
the paintings of the masters from the walls and robs the structure of every grace which the skill of the architect has devised,
is a religion that has strength without tenderness and greatness without joy. The Puritan spirit is iconoclastic, the æsthetic spirit is illuminative.

During the last half century the mammon-serving drift of
things has been even more powerful than the anathemas of a
narrow pietism. Many rich men are patrons of art, but the

throwing our monstrous office buildings into midair, transforming our marshlands into cities, and our cities into forests of stone and deserts of asphalt, darkening the sun with factory smoke, and training our fevered pulse to beat its responses only to the heart throbs of our giant engines, that we have found neither leisure nor wish to cultivate the true, the beautiful and the sublime.

The new time has already seen abundant tokens of a widespread awakening. Theology and science and materialism have filled men's lives and shorn them of their beauty. The age of culture in our land will witness a profound revival of interest in the deeper and richer qualities of life. That revival will be æsthetic, ethical, spiritual.

AUSTEN K. DE BLOIS, PH. D., LL. D.

History of Art.

The progress of art in a community may be considered, to a certain extent, the gauge of its prosperity, for its growth is absolutely dependent upon wealth and culture.

Some one has said that the golden age of painting lies in the Christian centuries, yet the history of painting is linked with that of the pyramids. The history of art is one of the most fascinating ever written. The changes in ideals with the years, the many varied conceptions of colors and their uses, the different standards which have prevailed, are indisputable testimony as to the times and peoples they represent.

In the scope of this article, it is impossible to speak of art, its history and growth, in any other phase than that indicated by the title "The History of Art in Illinois." Of necessity, the history of art in Chicago is practically the history of art in Illinois, for the State is not yet old enough to have gathered sufficient resources to admit of the establishing throughout the State of schools of art which would be worthy the name. Rather, art students from the various cities and towns avail themselves of the advantages offered in Chicago, and make them their own. In Springfield, the capital of the State, there is in the State building quite a collection of paintings, many portraits of Governors, and other distinguished men, which is probably the largest collection in the State outside of Chicago. In private homes, however, in cities and towns, may be found pictures of value from the hands of the best artists at home and abroad, and the same, in a less degree, is true of the statues which adorn many a home—beautiful souvenirs, perhaps, of some delightful trip to other lands. The progress of art in Chicago has been such as to arrest attention, and many articles have appeared at different times giving, to some extent, a review of its history. The writer has taken the liberty of quoting from Blanchard's History of Chicago, from various reports, from facts given by the Secretary of the Chicago Art Institute, Mr. N. H. Carpenter, and from a most

19

interesting article from the pen of Mr. Will *H.* Low, himself a representative American artist, which recently appeared in *The World To-Day.*

It is a remarkable fact, in spite of the idea that has prevailed and still prevails to some extent, that culture has its home in more Eastern cities, that a school of art practice, including work from the human figure, was established in Chicago in 1866, which was earlier than in any other city in the country, with two exceptions, New York and Philadelphia. This nucleus was organized into the Chicago Academy of Design, March 10, 1869, and, although the name has been changed to the Chicago Art Institute, and it has had different homes, it may be truthfully said that since that time the cause of art has steadily progressed in Chicago. Almost all such institutions embody in their history times of great discouragement and times of unexpected prosperity. There have been times of perplexity, perhaps, times when the outlook was not altogether bright, still, as a whole, the history of this institution has been exceptional in its upward and onward progress year after year. One reason may, no doubt, be found in the fact that from the beginning the institution has been practically under the same regimé; Mr. Newton *H.* Carpenter, the present Secretary, having been connected with the organization, in its various phases, from the beginning, and of Mr. W. M. *R.* French, the present Director, the same can be said. Their interest in its growth and prosperity has been such as could not have been possible with those whose identification with the work was temporary, and to them the city of Chicago and the cause of art in the Middle-West owe much.

After the fire, there was a lull in the work done by the Academy of Design for a few years, and, in 1878, after the raising of what was supposed to be its entire indebtedness, by the artists, a board of trustees was added to the artist membership, composed of business men. This experiment was not altogether a success, owing chiefly to the discovery of still further indebtedness, and, at the expiration of a year, the business trustees resigned. May 24, 1879, upon the application of Marshall Field, Murray Nelson, Charles D. *H*amill, Ferd W. *P*eck and *G*eorge E. Adams, the Art *I*nstitute was incorporated for "the founding and maintenance of schools of art and design, the formation and exhibition of collections of objects of art, and the cultivation and extension of the arts of design by any appropriate means." Its first President was George Armour, and, after one year's service, he was succeeded by *L. Z.* Leiter, who held the position two years. The first board of trustees consisted of *G*eorge Armour, S. M. Nickerson, Ezra B. McCogg, *L*evi Z. Lei*t*er, Wm. T. Baker, N. K. Fairbank, James *H.* Dole, Albert *H*aydn, D. W. *I*rwin, E. S.

*P*ike, W. M. *R*. French, G. *L*. Dunlap, E. W. Blatchford, Mark Skinner, Wil.
liam A. Bradley, J. W. Doan, George E. Adams, *H*omer N. *H*ibbard, George *G*.
Shortall and Charles L. *H*utchinson.

Of these, Charles L. *H*utchinson, S. M. Nickerson, James *H*. Dole, William T. Baker and N. K. Fairbank had been trustees through the whole history of the institution till within a short time, when the three last named
have been removed by death, a loss deeply felt.

The *I*nstitute had its first home at the corner of Monroe and State Sts.
from 1879 to 1881 A building was then erected at 10 Van Buren St., where
they remained from 1881 to 1887. This building was 54x70 feet, a substantial brick building, containing exhibition galleries and school-room; but
the growth of the organization made larger quarters necessary, and a beautiful
brownstone building was erected on the front of the same lot, facing Michigan
Ave., 80x100 feet, four stories high, *R*omanesque in design, which was opened
during Novembe*x*, 1887, and occupied by the *I*nstitute till 1893. The *I*nstitute, which had gained very much in the favor of the community, had become the possessor of valuable collections of casts of sculpture, pictures, metals,
vases, etc., and it soon became apparent that larger quarters would have to
be obtained

" By a city ordinance, passed March, 1891, permission was given for the
erection of a building upon the lake front, opposite Adams St., to be used for
the World's Congresses during the Columbian Exposition, and afterwards to
be permanently occupied by the Art Institute, the building to be the property
of the city of Chicago." Between February, 1892, and May, 1893, the present museum building was erected, after the plans of Shepley, Reetan & Cool-
idge, architects. The building which had been occupied by the *I*nstitute was
sold, in 1892, for $425,000, to the Chicago Club, which still owns and uses it,
and the Art *I*nstitute came into possession of their present permanent home,
November 1, 1893. The Art *I*nstitute thus, in effect, made a gift to the people
of the city of the money expended by it upon the building—about $450,000—
and gained a public character very advantageous for the public service, at which
it aims. An injunction, issued May 31, 1892, restraining the city from erect-
ing a building upon the *L*ake Front *P*ark, was dissolved upon a rehearing, June
23d. By this decision the Art *I*nstitute became firmly established in its
rights upon the lake front. When the Columbian Exposition made an appro-
priation of $200,000 for the building, they imposed several conditions, which
were as follows : That at least $500,000 should be expended upon the building ;
that the building should be controlled by the Exposition for the World's Con-

gresses from May 1 to Nov. 1, 1893; and that it should contain rooms and conveniences suitable for the meetings of the World's Congresses. The cost of the building at the present time has been about $785,000. It is of Bedford limestone, absolutely fireproof, in style *I*talian *R*enaissance, the details classic and of Ionic and Corinthian orders. The front is 80 feet back from Michigan Ave., and the building is 320 feet long, the wings 170 feet deep, with projections which make the whole depth 208 feet. The rear and center are not yet built. It was planned with the greatest care, not only for its service as a school of art but as a place for art exhibitions. It is not too much to say of it that in regard to light, simplicity of arrangement and intelligent, convenient classification, this *I*nstitute has no superior anywhere. The ownership of this building is vested in the city of Chicago, but the right of use and occupancy is vested in the Art *I*nstitute so long as it shall fulfil the purposes for which it was organized; " shall open the museum free to the public Wednesdays, Saturdays, Sundays and public holidays; shall make the Mayor and Comptroller of the city ex-officio members of the Board, and conform to some other simple conditions." By these provisions the influence of the *I*nstitute as an educator is widened to a degree which cannot be estimated.

Thousands of people, who could hardly afford to pay the entrance fee, thus have the opportunity to see the fine collections of pictures and statues, and even the school children become familiar with the names of great artists and their works. The value of such opportunity may possibly be appreciated when it is known that from ten to fifteen times every year the permanent collection is reinforced by loan collections of rarest worth. During the past six years the additions to the many departments have been both numerous and valuable, so that, as an Art Museum, the Art *I*nstitute of Chicago ranks among the first three or four in the country. The *I*nstitute has received much in the way of donations. Mrs. *H*enry Field, whose husband was formerly a trustee of the institution, has committed permanently to its keeping the entire collection of paintings which belonged to him. This collection comprises forty-one pictures, representing principally the Barbizon school of painters, including Millet's familiar " Bringing *H*ome the New-Born Calf," Jules Breton's " Song of the Lark," Troyon's " *R*eturning from the Market," and specimens of Rousseau, Corot, Cozin, Constable and Daubigny. This collection has its place in a separate room, known as the " Henry Field Memorial *R*oom," and is held in trust by five trustees appointed by Mrs. Field. Mrs. Field also empowered the trustees of the *I*nstitute to order from Mr. Edward Kenrys, the sculptor of animals, two monumental bronze lions, to stand upon the flanks of the

THE ART INSTITUTE, CHICAGO.

executed, and the lions were unveiled, May 10, 1894.

In 1890, the disposal of the best works of the famous Demidoff collection of works of old masters, which had not been included in a sale of a larger part of the collection in 1880, gave an opportunity by which the Art Institute secured thirteen pictures by old masters, chiefly of the Dutch school, some of them fine examples of the masters by whom they were painted. The acquisition of these pictures marked an epoch in the growth of art in Chicago. Among them are five examples of portraiture which are representative of Rembrandt, Rubens, Van Dyck, Frans Hals and Holbein; "The Guitar Lesson," by Terburg; "A Family Concert," by Jan Steen; a landscape, by Hobenna, which may be accounted among his masterpieces; "The Jubilee," by Van Ostade, and fine examples of the work of Teniers, Ruysdael and Adrian Van de Velde. By purchase or gift, the museum has been constantly accumulating rare and valuable paintings. Among the American painters represented are Chase, Hitchcock, Alex. Harrison, McEwen, Dannat, Inness, Vedder, Pearce and Davis. In 1898, a fine collection of about sixty paintings, which had for some time been exhibited in the galleries, was bequeathed to the Institute by Albert A. Munger, a life-long citizen of Chicago.

Among works of the highest merit, this collection contains Meissonier's "Vidette;" "The Bathers," by Bouguereau; "Just Before Sunrise," by Corot; de Neuville's "A Piece in Danger;" Detaille's "Reconnoissance;" Jacquet's "Queen of the Camp;" "Springtime and Love," by Michetti, and Munkacsy's "The Challenge." Gerome, Rosa Bonheur, Von Marcke, Fromentin, Vibert, Roybet, Charlemont, Zimmerman, Achenbach, Jacque, Schreyer, Troyon, Courbet, Isabay, Makart, and many other leaders of the modern world of art are represented.

The collection of reproductions of sculpture is very large and representative. A great proportion of it is the gift of Mrs. A. M. H. Ellis, who has given it the name of her former husband, and it is known as "The Eldridge G. Hall" collection. It includes only fac-simile copies of original works of sculpture, in accordance with the expressed wishes of the donor. It includes not only classical but Renaissance and modern sculpture, and the contemporary collection is the most valuable in America. Among modern sculptors represented are Dubois, Mercie, Barrias, Cain, Chapu, Falguiere, Rodin, Premier, Thornycroft, St. Gaudens, Bartlett, French, Potter, etc. The French Government sent to the Columbian Exposition, as a part of the national exhibit, an extensive historical collection of architectural casts, reproduced from collections in Paris, destined to become, at the end of the Fair, a part of the permanent collection of the Art Institute. This remarkable collection, which is unsurpassed in its kind, either in quality or extent, is now installed, as far as the room permits, in the galleries of the Art Institute, but a considerable part of it is stored, for lack of suitable room in which to place it. Another element in the sculpture collection is the gallery of reproductions of the antique bronzes of the Naples Museum, one hundred and nine of·the most famous statues, busts, tripods, statuettes, lamps, and other objects found at Herculaneum and Pompeii. This collection was the gift of *H. N. Higin*botham. They were purchased through the fine art department of the Columbian Exposition, and are certified by the Director of the Naples Museum to be perfect reproductions.

Another department which has already attained importance is that of the original Egyptian antiquities. Through the interest of Mr. *G*etty, Mr. *R*yerson and Mr. *H*utchinson, accessions have been made of typical Egyptian objects of great rarity and value, sufficient to form a collection respectable in quantity and more than respectable in quality. There is also a very carefully collected and adequately representative collection of classical antiquities, Greek vases, figurines, lamps and fragments, and marble *R*oman remains, both sculptural and architectural. Other fields of art are represented by collections of embroideries, tapestries, painted fans, textiles, etc—presented by the society of ladies called "Antiquarians of the Art Institute"—and of musical instruments, armor, etc.

In the summer of 1900, Mr. and Mrs. S. M. Nickerson presented to the museum of the Art Institute their superb private collection of jades, crystals, paintings and curios, and fitted up two galleries for the permanent installation of the collection.

On October 26, 1891, the *R*yerson library was opened by a reception to the members. This building, erected through the generosity of Martin A. *R*yerson, is most beautiful and commodious, is open at all times to both members and students, and is really a free public library on Wednesdays and Saturdays, the free days of the museum. The reading-room is a model of convenience and comfort, supplied with all the leading art periodicals of the world, and with alcoves and shelves for many books. The accumulating of books must, of necessity, be the work of time. That the three thousand books already placed are appreciated by the students is evidenced by the fact that during the year 26.509 students have made use of the library, while the total number of visitors (46,769) is said to be as large as at the South Kensington Museum Library, in

London, which contains two hundred thousand volumes. The present library has been selected with greatest care, is strictly confined to the best art, and includes many valuable works. In it is kept the great collection of large carbon photographs, known as the Braun autotypes, 16,000 in number, including reproductions of the paintings, drawings and sculpture of most of the well-known galleries in Euorpe. These are the gift of Dr. D. K. Pearsons.

During 1897, a lecture-room was built, in accordance with the original plans of the building, and presented to the *I*nstitute by Charles W. Fullerton as a memorial to his father, Alexander N. Fullerton. This room seats five hundred persons, and is a model lecture-room, as regards comfort in seating, ventilation, acoustic properties and tasteful adornment. *L*ectures upon subjects pertaining to art are given three or four times a week throughout the class year, usually in this hall, although many lectures of a more special character are given by various instructors in the class-rooms. All lectures are given late in the day in order that the student may have ample time and daylight for his technical study, and as they embrace a wide variety of topics in their relation to art, they afford a means of culture very valuable as an adjunct to technical art instruction. The various courses of lectures have gained within a year added value by the establishment of the Scammon course, the result of the Martha Sheldon Scammon endowment of about $36,000, which provides a fund for lectures upon the history, theory and practice of the fine arts, to be given " by persons of distinction or authority on the subject of which they lecture." This series was inaugurated, May, 1903, by a course of six lectures, by John La Farge, upon "The So-called Barbizon Painters." These series of lectures, together with the special lectures, are of incalculable value to all of the students, but particularly to those who have not had the advantages of a general education.

An error too often made in modern art-teaching is the absence of mental training. The technical equipment of a pupil is so difficult of attainment and so absorbing that often the student, without other special education, finds himself unable to explain to others what he knows so well. That those in charge of the Chicago Art *I*nstitute realize this danger is indicated by the following extract from the report of its Director—" It has been for many years our aim to surround our students with such influences that a young person who studies in our school three, four or five years should come out with something corresponding in some degree to a general education."

As the *I*nstitute has advanced, new departments have been added to the courses in painting and sculpture which were first established. There are now classes in decorative designing, architecture, normal and illustrative, while lately instruction has been given to more than one hundred pupils in the applied arts—pottery, china painting and metal work. This indicates the remarkably comprehensive character of art instruction given, no one art school in the country being the equal of the Art Institute in that particular. The class in decorative designing, under Louis F Millet, is especially remarkable. Mr. Millet is a pupil of Galland and the École des Beaux-Arts, is a practical decorator, to whom many public and private buildings in the West owe their interior decorations, and who is now filling the position of Director of Mural Painting and Decoration for the Louisiana Purchase Exposition, at St. Louis. Mr. Millet's success as a teacher has been such that many of his pupils are able, at the conclusion of their course with him, to begin work for which the demand of the age is most insistent, both from an artistic and commercial point of view.

Illustration also attracts many students—not only those whose intention is limited to the production of work in monochrome for illustrative purposes, but many other pupils, realizing that the struggle before them to obtain recognition as artists will probably be long and hard, give a portion of their time to this work, which may prove the most available means within their grasp to provide for their maintenance during the years of working and hoping. This class has been, for some years, under the direction of Mr. Frederick Richardson, an artist of wide reputation as an illustrator, who has, in a remarkable degree, the faculty of arousing enthusiasm in his pupils. This class emphasizes the practical, as well as the artistic, endeavor of the Art Institute, for, of the graphic arts, illustration affords by far the largest opportunities to the student at the beginning of his career as an artist.

The pupils of this Institute come from every part of the West—from Minnesota, Wisconsin, Nebraska, Montana, North and South Dakota and from the Pacific coast. They number about twenty-six hundred, with a corps of eighty teachers, almost entirely city artists. Among them may be named John H. Vanderpoel, F. W. Freer, Chas. F. Browne, Miss C. D. Wade, Lorado Taft, Ralph Clarkson, Louis W. Wilson, Frank Phœnix, and many other earnest, well-known artists. Mr. Vanderpoel, who is the instructor of drawing and painting in the life and antique classes, has been connected with the Art Institute many years. His lectures are among the most valued aids in the institution, and to his clear explanation of the structure of the human body, illustrated by bold and clearly-defined sketches in charcoal, which he executes as he talks and which are wonderfully helpful, are due much of the ef-

ficiency of his classes. The school work, so far as the technical practice is
concerned, is done on the ground floor of this great building, in rooms well
lighted, heated and ventilated. Already the growth of the school is demand-
ing more space, a necessity which will have to be met in the early future. In
every one of these class-rooms, to which the public does not have access, most
interesting work is being accomplished every day in the year. Possibly even
those who are most familiar with opportunities offered by the Art Institute
have really little conception of the magnitude of the work done by these many
pupils, the excellence of the standards attained and the reputation already honestly earned by many of the students. Some classes of work have already received mention, but the sculpture class really merits special notice. In this
class, under the scholarly direction of Mr. Lorado Taft, not only the usual
routine of study from the living model is practiced of modeling busts and full-
length figures, but work of much more ambitious scope is essayed by advanced
pupils, and groups of monumental or decorative design have been done. Their
method of work is most interesting. First, a sketch of the general composition is made, and these are modeled as separate figures on a small scale, carefully studied from life, then enlarged to the required size, and finally fitted
together to complete the composition. One of these groups, a fountain, was
temporarily placed for exhibition in the park south of the building of the
Art Institute, and attracted much attention.

When it is remembered that it was done by pupils not yet out of school,
it was certainly most creditable. Two other groups—a fountain of the great
lakes and a funeral procession—furnished experience such as is usually only
possible to post-graduate practice, and, as it is conducted under the constant
supervision of a sculptor of Mr. Taft's reputation, the advantage to the pupils
can hardly be overestimated.

By the courtesy of Mr. N. H. Carpenter, Secretary of the Art Institute,
photographs of the Institute and these groups are enclosed in this article. It
would hardly be possible, in the scope of this history, to even hint at the
various kinds of work done in the many classes of the Art Institute or the success achieved by its pupils.

A frieze, painted by one of the pupils of the Institute, has been placed
in one of the public schools of the city; the illuminated texts, stained glass and
metal work of another pupil are giving her a national reputation; another does
the most exquisite miniature work, and many of the graduates from the Institute have their own studios and their own successful classes.

The most friendly spirit prevails in the administration of the In-

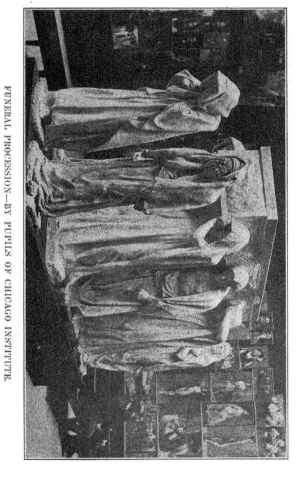

FUNERAL PROCESSION—BY PUPILS OF CHICAGO INSTITUTE.

stitute toward all who are working for the advance of art. In many cases artists striving for recognition have enjoyed the courtesy of these galleries for exhibition of their works, a help and encouragement they have deeply appreciated. To this time the Institute has been dependent for its support upon the following sources: An income of some $2,000, the income derived from membership dues, door receipts on pay days, catalogue sales and gifts from liberal, art-loving citizens. The school itself has been for a long time self-sustaining from the students' fees, which are very moderate, and expended with rigid economy; but there has been a yearly deficit in the museum expenses, a burden, with many another, most nobly borne by the Board of Trustees of the Institute. By legislation, recently enacted, the financial future of the Institute is assured, a fact which should be most gratefully appreciated not only by the citizens of Chicago and Illinois, but of the West, to whom it means so much. The following bill having been passed by the Senate, and ratified by the city, those who have watched the growth of the Art Institute from the very small beginnings feel that the future is bright with hope, and rejoice in all it portends.

Section 2 of an Act entitled "An Act concerning museums in public parks" reads as follows—"That any Board of Park Commissioners, having control of a park, within which there shall be maintained any museum or museums of art, sciences or natural history under the provisions of this act, is hereby authorized to annually levy a tax (in addition to all other taxes authorized by law) of half a mill on each dollar of taxable property embraced in said district according to the valuation of the same as made for the purpose of State and county taxation by the general assessment last preceding the time when such half mill tax shall be levied for the purpose of maintaining and caring for such museum or museums and the grounds thereof; and the proceeds of such additional tax shall be kept as a separate fund; *Provided,* The proposition to annually levy a tax, as herein authorized, shall first be submitted to the legal voters of said park district and secure a majority of the votes cast upon such proposition." This vote has been taken with most satisfactory results in Chicago, and by March, 1905, it is expected that the Institute will begin to reap the practical benefits of this legislation. This certainly marks a great change in the outlook for art growth in Chicago and Illinois. It means permanency, freedom from anxiety, a future provided for, all of which will encourage art-lovers and those who desire to encourage its progress to a still further giving.

This tax of half a mill on the dollar seems really very little for a great

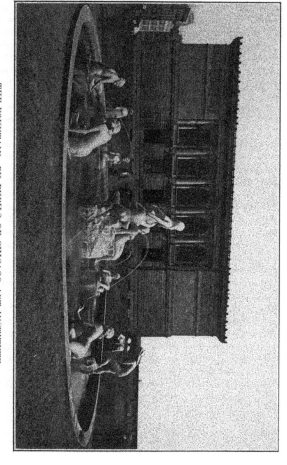

THE FOUNTAIN—BY PUPILS OF CHICAGO ART INSTITUTE.

its present accommodations. "The Art Institute is in the fullest sense an institution conducted for the public good. Without a dollar of assistance from the city, save the permission to build upon the lake front, its managers have erected a museum building, and gathered a collection which commands the respect of all competent judges, and which is the subject of pride and satisfaction to all right-minded citizens. The art-school has grown to be one of the very foremost, both in the number of students and the standard of excellence. The fine galleries are open absolutely free to the public more than one hundred and sixty days each year, and upon other days, not only the members and their families, numbering more than ten thousand, but public school-teachers to the number of four thousand six hundred, and all professional artists, are *freely* admitted." The supporters of the Institute have been most generous in many ways. Gifts of money and, as has already been intimated, of valuable works of art, together with a vast deal of labor, thought and self-sacrifice, have made possible the present; but the future, which beckons on to greater achievement, will have a surer foundation than the generosity of patrons.

To Mr. Charles L. Hutchinson, who has been the President of the Institute for more than twenty years, the Institute owes such a debt of gratitude as can never be fully known. Mr. Hutchinson is a man of wonderful executive ability, with a keen interest in the public good, with true love for art, and a deep-rooted belief in its usefulness in the widening and uplifting of civilization. In all his work he has been singularly unselfish, caring little for honor or fame, but much for the cause to which he was devoting himself, and the growth of which was so essential to the western part of our country. He has commanded the respect and esteem not only of his co-workers, but of those everywhere who, like himself, are interested in the growth of art. He has been most fortunate in having associated with him, from the very incipiency of the enterprise, a board of trustees composed of some of the best men in Chicago. They are among those to whom the city owes much of her position in the world of commerce and manufactures, and have been willing to use the same ability which has accomplished so much in these directions to aid in the establishment and advancement of a permanent Art Institute.

"The great Sculpture Hall, recently completed by the efforts of these men in giving and inciting others to give, foreshadows the completion of the present building by the erection of a new series of galleries above the Sculpture *H*all, as originally planned. Already, however, the collections stored for want of room or promised when space for their exhibition can be had, demand an extension toward the lake of another building, joined to the present one by bridges over the tracks of the *I*llinois Central *R*ailroad."

The direction of the schools and the museum, so far as art is concerned, has been, from the first, vested in Mr. W. M. *R*. French, and the success which has attended both of these departments bears testimony to his ability to fill a position unique in its requirements and which is still fraught with peculiar responsibilities. Mr. French—a sketch of whose life appears in another part of this volume—has done for the Art *I*nstitute what no other director will ever be expected to do. He has had much pioneer work to do, and in the paucity of other resources has represented to a large territory a bureau of information upon any and every subject even most remotely connected with art. It is a tribute to the versatility of his knowledge, as well as to the courteous patience of his character, that no request, however trivial, is ever dismissed without having received kind attention. Mr. Low, to whose article tribute has already been paid, has very well said—"The responsibilities of the director of a museum in older cities, or in other lands, do not, of course, include such extraneous duties as furnishing stereopticon slides for art lectures, but here a collection of some twelve hundred is classified and will soon be placed, under certain restrictions, at the disposition of responsible lecturers, and an exchange to furnish information on art subjects to women's clubs and schools is likewise maintained. "We believe in popularizing the *I*nstitute perhaps to an extreme degree," explains the Director; "but, on the other hand, in the schools the character of the work sought to be attained by Mr. French's influence, transmitted through the faculty of competent and painstaking instructors, is of the highest standard."

Mr. Newton *H*. Carpenter has been identified with the institution from the very beginning in various capacities. First as clerk, then, during Mr. French's prolonged absence, filling his place, and now as Secretary of the Institute. Mr. Carpenter is not only enthusiastically interested in all that pertains to the progress of art, particularly as represented by the Art *I*nstitute, but he is accurately acquainted with every detail of its history. While believing that honor should be paid to those to whom honor is due, and anxious to represent the growth of the *I*nstitute as glowingly as facts will permit, he is solicitous that the public should receive as history only what can be substantiated by facts in the veriest detail.

most interesting study is found in the exhibit of work done by pupils from the 8th grade down, to say nothing of that of the High School scholars. Every small town of three or four thousand inhabitants and less has at least one good drawing teacher, and the demand for such teachers in the larger cities is very great. These teachers must be trained in many kinds of drawing, for in this age the artistic instinct is strong, and outside of the schools there are many men, jewelers, carvers in wood and stone, metal workers, etc., who are anxious to receive instruction in drawing to aid them in their varied lines of work. How shall these teachers receive the necessary training except in a regular school? The Art Institute furnishes just the sort of instruction which these teachers must have, to be in any degree fitted for their work.

The management of the Art Institute is vested in the Board of Governing Members, which is limited in number to two hundred and fifty. The Governing Members elect the Trustees, twenty-one in number, who have the control and management of the Art Institute. Each Governing Member pays one hundred dollars upon election, and twenty-five dollars a year as annual dues. The Governing Members, Trustees, President, Vice-President and Treasurer give their services freely to the Art Institute. The Art Institute is greatly indebted to its many friends for their remembrance of it by bequests in their wills. A few of these have become available.

About one hundred thousand dollars have been received, all of which has been invested, and the income only has been used. About two hundred thousand dollars additional have been bequeathed to the Institute, but have not yet been turned over to it.

Illinois has reason for great pride in the record made by her school of art. When it is considered that comparatively few years have elapsed since the settlement of the State, that many of the pioneers and old settlers are still living, and remember that the establishment of an art school is not the primary movement in a new country, the present seems almost incredible. While the Art Institute stands in a large degree for art in Illinois, there are studio buildings where talented men and women are doing most excellent work and obtaining recognition in art circles in the East as well as in Illinois, as is attested by the exhibition of their pictures, not only in Chicago but in New York, Philadelphia and other cities. The Fine Arts Building is the home of many artists, and a visit to their studios is most interesting. *Here Lorado* Taft is doing wonderful work, dainty busts for the drawing-room, monumental work for the Exposition at St. *Louis.* Ralph Clarkson, in a studio which is itself a museum of curios, beautiful and rare, is making some of the best portraits seen anywhere. Martha S. Baker is winning most enviable reputation for her exquisite miniature painting, and Christia M. *R*eade and many others are doing work in marble, on the canvas or with metals in the most artistic way. Already America is taking her place in the art world. Thayer, Brush, Winslow, *H*omer, Sargent, Abbey, as painters, and St. *G*audens, French, Barnard Mc-Monnies, McNeil, as sculptors, have international reputations, and America may be most proud of her sons. Their success has not been by accident, nor by simply taking courses of lessons in the best art school. Added to natural endowment have been indomitable perseverance, unflagging ambition and mental culture. While they should be an inspiration to every art student, they should also be a reminder that only by earnest endeavor and the most consecrated zeal are such results possible. It may be said that we live in a practical age, that art itself is turned into channels of commerce, that the inspiration is lacking which made possible the results of the age of the *I*talian *R*enaissance. This is true to a certain degree, and yet the history of the work which the Art *I*nstitute of Chicago has achieved should encourage the most earnest effort on the part of those to whom *H*eaven has given a true artist's nature. In no walk of life is there the same opportunity for one's individuality to leave its impress on result as that which is offered in the artist's life. We see that for which we look in the world about us, and while the same scene would strike one as pathetic, another as absurd, and still another as most grave, the world seems almost kaleidoscopic in the variety of thought it offers to the artist as suggestive. Art is not imitative, yet the overlapping trees in the forest suggest the Gothic roof, and the poet clasps hands with the artist and sings, " The groves were God's first temples." There is no emotion of the human heart to which a beautiful picture or statue may not appeal, hardly a phase of thought which has not been painted on canvas or wrought in metal or stone. The sublime and the beautiful, the grand and the picturesque, the pathetic and the grotesque, all appeal to the artist's nature and furnish material for effort. The effect of the lovely in art upon the most uncultivated mind is eloquent testimony to its value as a silent educator. Who that has ever spent much time in art galleries has not been impressed with the effect which the silence of the rooms and the wonderful exhibitions of works of art have had upon the most careless beholders. Nature has offered the greatest possible field to painter

those battling with life's realities. This is an important truth, and most easily proved. The power of appealing to the holiest passions of the heart is the artist's opportunity, almost divine, and entails responsibility far too little recognized. At the Columbian Exposition, while pictures of grand mountain peaks riveted the admiration, and beautiful meadows and mellow sunsets charmed the eye, perhaps no picture day after day drew larger crowds of men and women, touched to the heart, than did that simple picture, "Breaking Home-Ties."

Love in its many phases—mother love, the love of home and country, the love of lovers—has furnished the theme for many a brush and chisel through the ages, and will be the inspiration of painter and sculptor for all time. This power to influence humanity, to impress a sense of beauty upon the saddest life, to make the commonplace seem full of charm, to win to laughter and merriment those unused to smiles, is a power which every artist may wield.

This thought should be one of mighty uplift and permeate every studio and every art school in the land. The highest aim of life should be to help others, to brighten the days as they come and go for those about us, to wreathe with some beauty even a bitter cross, and change the saddest tear into a smile.

For such achievement the opportunities of the artist are most abundant, and sometimes if the pinnacle of fame seems far away and hope long deferred, if the laurel wreath seems elusive and discouragements are many, the thought that a life may have been brightened by some unpretentious sketch or purified by the influence of a sweet, marble face, should be the greatest incentive to renewed and more persistent endeavor.

Viewed from this high standard, the work of the Chicago Art Institute becomes more lofty, its ideals more sacred and its ambitions of greater value than is usually realized. The history of the past has been such as to fill every heart with grateful pride; the future seems full of brightest hope and promise.

Illinois can well feel that, while the history of her brief life has given her a most enviable place in the world of commerce and manufactures, the history of the Chicago Art Institute has placed her far beyond many an older State in the world of art.

THE HISTORY

...OF...

MUSIC IN ILLINOIS.

Music.

Vibration—great and unknown force;
    Prime author of velocity—
Of budding life the pulsing part;
    Primeval cause of things to be.

Momentum—genius of the breath—
    That tacks the stars to shield of blue;
That twirls the world in safety round,
    And guides the trackless regions through.

Sound—very first born of effect,
    Result of quickening atoms' clash;
The sweep of storm, volcanic quake,
    The thunder of the lightning's flash.

Thought—the subtle, the rythmic force,
    Draws from brain the great recorder;
Shapes out the diamond from the dross,
    Sorts and lends to chaos, order.

Soul—the spark, the leavening flame
    That makes the morsel good to taste;
'Tis to the mortal, touch of God—
    The rain-drop to the pouting waste.

37

Thus beautifully has been voiced a sort of history of the birth of music. Someone has expressively called these verses " From Sound to Soul," and in a few lines great truths have been grasped and a most exquisite unfolding of what means so much to the art-loving world.

All history is interesting; every story, every tale that is told, is history of fact or fiction and enlists our attention. The history which deals in figures or statistics is the most easily told; that of the progress of events is a positive thing; but the history of music in any given locality is difficult to obtain accurately. It involves so many whose lives are unwritten, and the view-point of the historian varies so widely that the reader will, perhaps, often supply from personal knowledge events which have eluded the writer. For many facts in this article the author is indebted to various histories of *I*llinois, to Mrs. Florence French's " Music and Musicians in Chicago," and to many musicians who have courteously contributed from their own memory interesting details.

In thinking of *I*llinois as a comparatively new State, we hardly realize, with the present wealth of musical effort and achievement, that there was a beginning, even in her brief life. Seventy-five years ago, a very short time compared with that in which civilization and music and art have had their development in Europe, *I*llinois was almost unsettled. Over its prairies wild animals still roamed quite undisturbed; no waving harvests were eloquent of the richness of the soil, no busy wheel mingled with the murmur of its beautiful streams, nothing betokened the development and the growth which have been almost like magic. To-day the lives of the men and women sketched in the limits of this volume, with many another unwritten history, are testimony as to the beginning and nurturing of music and art in a way surpassed in no country and no age in a like span of years. It would be absurd to expect *I*llinois to equal *G*ermany, England, France and *I*taly in what is dependent upon centuries of experience and culture. Nothing is more inexorable than the laws of Nature. A new country does not begin its development by the establishing of Art *I*nstitutes or Conservatories of Music. In opening new territory, men are required to furnish shelter, food and raiment, and the weary toiler is satisfied for the time with the possession of such necessities. No matter how dominant art instinct and love for music may be, yet other demands must first be met, and the attainment of wealth must be assured to foster art endeavor, or its perfection is the impossible.

In the State of Illinois, where the struggle for existence has been comparatively recent, the growth of art and musical institutions since 1840 has been wonderful, and, during the past score of years, marvelous. These conditions have been made possible through the aid of those who have amassed wealth and who have had a longing for the beautiful and a great spirit of public benefaction. It is difficult to give any date of the very beginnings of musical life in Chicago or Illinois. The cradle songs voiced by many a mother with heart yearning for home and loved ones far away were, no doubt, the first songs that ever floated over the prairies which are now covered with cities and towns and villages. But the demand for music had existence, and, as the days grew into weeks and months and years, this demand grew more insistent. The lullaby and the hymn and anthem of the primitive choirs grew rapidly, till the years between the music of the early village church and the merry-makings of that time, and the present, with its Apollo and Mendelssohn Clubs, its grand opera at the Auditorium, its Thomas' orchestras and light operas at the Studebaker, seem incredibly few in the light of results achieved. It brings a realization of what the nineteenth century did, when those old settlers, some of whom perhaps sang in the earliest choirs and singing schools, live to see the perfection reached to-day. As has already been suggested, it is exceedingly difficult to positively trace the development of music in Illinois. Much of this progress had its sphere in the home life of some of these early settlers, so that only the salient points can be recorded, and only a very incomplete mention made of the many to whom honor is due.

The first piano brought to the little settlement of Chicago was the property of John Baptiste Beaubien, one of two brothers devoted to music, and leading the singing in the various social and religious " meetings " held. This piano was brought to Chicago in 1834, and was the delight of all who heard it. It is still in the possession of one of the family, Mrs. Ogee, of Silver Lake, Kansas. A brother—Mark—of this Beaubien owned the first violin of which we have any knowledge in Illinois, an instrument which became the property of John Wentworth, who presented it to the Calumet Club, and it is now in the possession of the Old Settlers' Association.

The first musical organization in Illinois was the Chicago Harmonic Society, which gave its initial concert December 11, 1835, in a Presbyterian church.

In 1848 a musical convention was held in the First Baptist Church, and

thus cited the difficulties to be surmounted by the early choir "as those who *could* sing were timid, and those who could *not* sing were unfortunately filled with ardor to serve the Lord." Possibly leaders of to-day may feel that such difficulty was not wholly confined to those early times.

In 1855 the *Philharmonic Society* was founded, under the leadership of Julius Dyhrenfurth, violinist, who was a great favorite for years in musical circles, and to him *George P. Upton,* the first musical critic of the *Chicago Tribune,* attributes the honor "of first establishing the desire for musical culture in the West."

Among those who were foremost in promoting the love and knowledge of music for thirty years following 1852 was Frank Lumbard, a genial companion, an enthusiastic artist and a fine singer. He was active in establishing early musical societies and church choirs, and when the Civil War broke out his splendid voice was heard throughout the country, the inspiration of many a disheartened soldier by the camp-fire. In those days traveling concert troupes were most gladly welcomed, and they were not infrequently named after the families who composed them. Some of the names are still familiar, as the Berger, *H*utchinson and *P*eak families. In connection with these troupes some eminent soloists made their début. Sol Smith *R*ussell, when eleven years of age, sang "Lanigan's Ball" with the *P*eak family bell-ringers; as far back as 1839 Joseph Jefferson, only a child, was a favorite singer, and McVicker, known to the present generation as a scholarly and dignified man, began his life in Chicago as a singing and dancing comedian. Ballads were great favorites with the people of that time, and some of them —war-songs and love-songs—were written by *G*eorge F. Root, and were sung and loved not only in Chicago but all over the country. Among them may be mentioned "*R*osalie, the Prairie Flower," "*H*azel-Dell," "Nellie *G*ray," "The Battle Cry of Freedom," "Tramp, Tramp, Tramp," "Just Before the Battle, Mother." To the war-songs *H*enry C. Wurk, of Chicago, contributed "Marching Through *G*eorgia," "Brave Boys Are They," "*K*ingdom Coming," etc. In 1851 Jenny *L*ind came to Chicago, with Theodore Thomas as solo violinist. In 1864 Uranus *H.* Crosby erected the first real opera house, with a seating capacity of three thousand and a cost of $600,000. It was located on the north side of Washington Street, between State and Dearborn, and was called the Crosby Opera *H*ouse, and the first season of grand opera in Chicago was opened there.

On account of the assassination of Lincoln, the opening night was postponed from April 17th till the 20th, when, under the then famous impressario, J. Grael, the opera of " Il Trovatore " was given. This was followed by " Lucia di Lammermoor," " Il Polutio," "Martha," "Norma," " Faust," " La Somnambula," " Il Puritani," " Lucretia Borgia," " Ernani " and " Fra Diavolo."

This company was from New York, and included Clara Louise Kellogg, Zucchi, Morensi, Lotti, Susini and Brignoli. This was the beginning of grand opera in Chicago, and now each year brings to our city the best talent, and a most brilliant season is opened, patronized by the wealth and culture of the city, who lend the elegance and charm of their presence to the delightful rendering of the greatest operas. The Auditorium has furnished a rarely magnificent place for the presentation of these operas, most beautifully staged and sung by the greatest artists of the world.

In 1864, a music hall was built on the site of the present Chicago Opera House, and there L. M. Gottschalk gave six concerts, the tickets being all sold in advance, and the greatest enthusiasm evinced over the opportunity given to hear the great pianist. In a letter written by him, December 4, 1864, Gottschalk gives a most interesting picture of the Chicago of that time. He speaks of the " feverish enterprise everywhere; the stores—palaces; the hotels—towns." Speaking of the Crosby Opera House, then in process of erection, he said that it easily challenged comparison with any house in New York, surpassing most of them.

Chicago had various musical organizations, but few were long-lived. In 1871 came the great fire, when Crosby's Opera House, McVicker's Theatre, Dearborn Theatre and Wood's Museum, all on the south side of the river, were destroyed, and Turner Hall and German Hall, on the north side. The winter following this great calamity concerts were held in the churches, the Michigan Ave. Baptist Church, near Twenty-second St., being the center for the south side, and the Union Park Congregational Church for the west side. In spite of all demands on time and brain and capital, music shared in the great impetus given everything at this time. Before the fire the Oratorio Society, led by Hans Balatka, did perhaps the best work done in the city. Their library was destroyed by the fire, their members scattered, and their leader, for the time discouraged, removed to Milwaukee.

Orlando Blackman and A. R. Sabin, as managers, tried to reorganize this Society, and the Handel and Haydn Society, of Boston, came to the rescue with copies of the " Messiah," " Israel in Egypt," " David," and miscellaneous

Church. On these occasions the chorus numbered about one hundred and fifty, the orchestra twenty-two, and the success attending them seemed full of encouragement. Rehearsals were had through the autumn, and a concert arranged for an evening in January, 1873, but only an hour before the time for the concert the building in which it was to have been held burned to the ground. The new library was destroyed, the members were much disheartened and, in spite of the efforts of Orlando Blackman, the society gradually became extinct.

In 1872, the Beethoven Club was organized for producing choral works. This organization was the direct result of a visit to the city from Carl Wolfsohn. Mr. Wolfsohn added to ripe musical scholarship a real enthusiasm. The key-note of the Beethoven Society was "enthusiasm for good music." This organization had an existence for eleven years, and did a vast deal of excellent work. During the first season, Carl Wolfsohn undertook the gigantic task of playing the entire thirty-three sonatas, by Beethoven, as piano solos. Ten recitals of this series were given in Standard Hall, corner Thirteenth and Michigan Ave., to large audiences. Before the fire Wm. J. Lewis, violinist, had attained prominence in the musical evenings, given under the auspices of Root and Cady. Carl Wolfsohn found in him a most earnest co-worker in his efforts to establish a demand for the best music. Soon after, Eicheim, the 'cellist, came to Chicago, and these three great artists contributed much to the delight of the reunions of the Beethoven Club. The Chicago Quintette Club, an organization for the giving of chamber music, was the most noted and longest-lived club of its kind in the city. It owed its existence to the efforts of Wm. J. Lewis and Miss Agnes Ingersoll, and was composed of Miss Ingersoll, M. Eicheim, Herman Allen, Wm. Allen and Mr. Pellage, and had always the co-operation of Mr. Lewis. Miss Ingersoll had come to Chicago from New York. She had inherited from her father musical gifts, and received her early piano instruction from an elder sister, who had been a pupil of the well-known Zundel. Later she studied in Leipsic, Berlin and Paris, under the best teachers, and became an accomplished musician. Although most widely known through her connection with the Quintette Club, she was identified with concerts and musical entertainments in different parts of the city. At this time Lewis Eicheim, Clarence

Eddy and Edward Heimendahl were associated with Carl Wolfsohn, Emil Liebling, W. ·C. E. Seebreck and Amy Fay, a sister of Mrs. Theodore Thomas, in the production of chamber music, a galaxy of scholarly musicians of which any city might justly be proud. Emil Liebling has been a most prominent factor in the production of chamber music since 1880, his series of piano recitals dating back to 1876. No one has been more closely identified with the musical education and progress of Chicago than has this genial scholar, enthusiastic musician and brilliant pianist.

The opening of the *H*ershey School led to the production of much music of a similar class. This school was founded by Miss Sara *H*ershey, famous not only as a pianist but as a scholarly artist and an excellent teacher. Born in *P*hiladelphia, and with a decided love for music, she began her professional career by teaching in Muscatine, *I*owa. In 1867, she went abroad, studying in Berlin, Milan and *L*ondon, returning to New *Y*ork, busy in concert work there and teaching in the Packer *I*nstitute, in Brooklyn, for two years. In 1875, she came to Chicago and immediately founded the *H*ershey School of Musical Art, which obtained recognition from the leading musicians of the city.

Mention should be made of David W. Perkins, pianist and instructor, who came to Chicago in 1868 and opened a studio in Crosby's Opera *H*ouse, and before the fire became a very successful teacher, with a large class of pupils, but afterwards moved to Milwaukee.

In the same building, in 1871, Charles *H*. Brettan established a school and inaugurated a series of concerts, which gave him prestige in musical circles. It is impossible to name all who, during these years, were encouraging the taste for the best music and laying the foundation for the splendid work of to-day. Many a one lives only in the grateful memory of those who received from them inspiration and encouragement to do their best work. The first music hall built down-town after the fire was the Kingsbury *H*all, on Clark St., opposite the Sherman *H*ouse. The first *large* down-town hall after the fire was McCormick's *H*all, corner of Clark and Kinzir Sts., which had a seating capacity of twenty-five hundred people. Farwell *H*all, rebuilt after the fire, proved too small, and the necessity for a new and commodious concert and lecture hall became imperative. At this crisis *G*eorge B. Carpenter undertook the personal supervision of the building of Central Music *H*all on the southeast corner of State and Washington Sts. This hall seated seventeen hundred, with room for two hundred in the boxes. It was a beautiful hall, and will ever be held in sweet memory by all music-lovers in Chicago. There

others. Central Music Hall became thus identified with the musical growth of Chicago. Here the Apollo and Mendelssohn Clubs gave their concerts, and from association this hall became sacred to the musical public of Chicago, as possibly no other hall will ever be. There, too, the lamented and "silver-voiced" David Swing charmed large audiences Sabbath after Sabbath, as hardly any other has ever done.

But of the societies which were organized soon after the fire, the Apollo Club has most bravely kept its way, and is to-day the leading club for mixed voices in Chicago. To Silas G. Pratt should be accorded the honor of the thought out of which grew this club, which has been the source of pride to the city for many years.

A meeting was held in the summer of 1872, in the store of Lym & Healy, then located on the corner of Sixteenth and Wabash, to consider the organization of a chorus of male voices. The organization was effected, and the name and constitution of the Apollo Club in Boston were adopted. The first concert was given in January, 1873, and the first conductor was Silas G. Pratt. Mr. Pratt, however, resigned this position in a few weeks, and Mr. A. W. Dohn, who had formerly been the conductor of the Mendelssohn Club, was immediately chosen his successor. The success of this society was marked from the beginning, and in connection with their concerts they gave to the public the opportunity of hearing some of the best soloists, instrumental and vocal. At the end of 1874, Mr. Dohn resigned and Carl Bergstein succeeded him as conductor, but held the position only a short time.

About this time Mr. George L. Tomlins came to Chicago. Mr. Tomlins was born in England, and early evinced a real genius for music. At the age of nine he was a choir boy, and at eleven was organist; two years later he became choirmaster, and at seventeen conducted his first oratorio. He combined with a passionate love for music a rare gift for conducting, and his name became the synonym for success in whatever he attempted. He had rare opportunities for study, and in 1870, when twenty-five years of age, he came to New York. While making a concert tour he visited Chicago as conductor of the Richings-Bernard Old Folks' Concert Company. He came just when the change in the conductor of the Apollo Club was pending. He was offered the position, and accepted it, a connection which proved most advantageous in every way, and from that time he became identified with the musical progress of Chicago. With him the thought that a ladies' chorus should be added and made permanently a part of the club became conviction. A number of ladies were trained, and their first appearance was made at an extra concert given for the benefit of Mr. Tomlins, June 8, 1876. The next day the *Chicago Tribune* made this comment: "Mr. Tomlins has succeeded with this mixed chorus exactly as he has with his male chorus, namely, in perfect enunciation, fine phrasing and shading, promptness of attack, steadiness in time and development of power. The enthusiasm of the chorus was unlimited, showing a very remarkable magnetism and inspiration on Mr. Tomlins' part." From that time the success of this club has been assured, and to-day the Apollo Musical Club is one of the largest, as well as one of the most popular, musical organizations in the city. A review of its progress and a detailed history of its programs would be most interesting, but the society is so well known as to hardly need this sort of introduction to the public of Illinois. April 21, 1898, this club held the closing concert of the season. This concert had memorable interest from the fact that it marked the retirement, after twenty-three years of continuous service, of William L. Tomlins as conductor. The chorus was unusually large, four hundred and fifty strong, augmented by a portion of the Chicago Orchestra. Mr. Tomlins was succeeded by Harrison M. Wild, who is to-day the conductor of the society. While still a comparatively young man, Mr. Wild is a man of great versatility of talent, an unrivaled director, a superb organist, an able writer on musical topics, and a most successful teacher of both the piano and organ. His ideals are the highest, his demands upon his choruses are large, and his rules are rigorous, yet he wins not only the respect but the affection of those under his tuition or leadership. He directs the music at Grace Church, and has elevated the music there to such a high standard that the church often will not accommodate the many who long for the influence of this beautiful service. Under his leadership the Apollo Club has made great strides in the finish of its work, but the ambition of their leader is not yet satisfied. He is a man of quick decisions, rare judgment in musical matters, and indomitable perseverance, and the public may expect a great future for this club under his management.

Contemporaneous with this club was the Beethoven Club, already alluded to as the first large mixed chorus in Chicago. This club had a membership of over two hundred of the best voices in the city, which fact indicates the sort of work done by them. As before mentioned, this club owed its existence to Carl Wolfsohn, a man of great attainment, personal magnetism and

benefit of its influence is still felt in the higher musical circles of Chicago.

The Mendelssohn Club, an organization of sixty male voices, is one of the older musical clubs, and would be an honor to any city. Harrison M. Wild is its director, and in its work he feels he has succeeded in nearing the realization of his ideals. The club gives three concerts during the season, and they are among the greatest musical treats given to the public. Their singing is marked by the most exquisite shading, and so perfectly do they sing together that one can hardly realize that there are sixty voices. It is like one great harmony. The greatest enthusiasm prevails among its members, and there is a marked freedom from the petty jealousies which so often retard the work of musical organizations. At each concert a soloist assists in the program. This season they have been: George Hamlin, who is recognized as a leading American tenor, and who is a great favorite with Chicago audiences; Glynn Miles, a magnificent baritone, who has been winning many laurels of late; and for the last concert, Mrs. Maud Fenlon Bollman, of Rockford, Ill., whose brilliant soprano voice is making her a place among the best singers of Illinois. Mr. Wild feels a great pride in the work of this club, and is ambitious for its future.

While these clubs were at work for the attainment of the best possible in chorus work, those interested along other lines were not idle. The Chicago Quintette Club, already mentioned, for years did most excellent work and achieved an enviable reputation. Various attempts were made by different conductors to organize a home orchestra. Notable among these were Silas G. Pratt, Adolph Rosenbecker, Dr. Ziegfeld, and others, but the orchestra led by Theodore Thomas so completely eclipsed all others that it has absorbed them to some extent, and they have become extinct.

Possibly the World's Fair contributed towards making Theodore Thomas a permanency in Chicago. Although his name had been identified at various times with the musical history of Chicago, since 1891 he has been permanently associated with the Chicago Orchestra, which closes its twenty-third season this year, 1904. Theodore Thomas was born in Essen, Hanover, and came to America when but a ten-year-old boy. Dependent upon himself, he obtained a musical education, and in 1855 became the leader of the Thomas-Mason chamber-music concerts. For fourteen years this celebrated quintette worked together, and made a lasting impression upon musical circles far and near. In 1866 he became the leader of an orchestra which gave a series of summer concerts in New York, and later symphony concerts in the winter. In 1870 he made a tour of the country with his full orchestra, his May festivals in Cincinnati attracting the attention of the musical world. Since coming to Chicago his programs have been remarkable for their wide range of music and the excellence of its rendition. Mr. Thomas is a natural director, exacting in his requirements, yet of courteous, gracious manner, never imposing upon others what he is unwilling to attempt himself. The music given by this orchestra has been a great source of education to the Chicago public. Liszt, Wagner, Brahm and others have thus become familiar, and through various lectures, given as incidental to the work of the orchestra, the audiences have come in a degree prepared to enjoy intelligently the programs prepared for them. It seems now as if the dream long cherished will have realization, and that this orchestra, with its distinguished leader, will have a home of their own.

In the midst of many financial and other discouragements, Theodore Thomas has stood immovable for all that is high and ennobling in music, and he has gained the confidence not only of musical circles but the respect of the community and the esteem of those who have been under his leadership.

The organization of the Spiering Quartette has given to Chicago a first-class string quartette. Its success is eloquent of the musical taste of the present Chicago, for these accomplished musicians play nothing but the highest class of music, and their concerts are always attended by enthusiastic audiences.

As has been mentioned, various schools have been established during the years. Among them may be named the Chicago College of Vocal and Instrumental Music, Chicago Conservatory, Chicago Music College, Chicago National College of Music, Balatka's College of Music, the Hershey College of Musical Art, the American Conservatory, the Chicago Conservatory and the Sherwood Music School, which this year (1904) does conservatory work. We can only give a brief resumé of the work done by the largest of those still in existence. Some facts suggest themselves in this glance at the work done by the leading musical schools of Chicago, for it will only be possible to write fully of those longest established and most largely patronized.

The standard set before the youth of to-day is so very high that some years ago its attainment would have seemed the impossible. In many a home the daughter plays the piano, organ or violin with a skill that once would have been found only among professionals. There must be a knowledge of harmony, of the theory of music; the aim of every musical composer must be understood to enable the player to give a correct interpretation, and not

of the larger institutions supplies their demand. Every possible incentive is offered to pupils in every department to do their best work, and recognition of their efforts is given in medals, diamonds, gold and silver, presented in addition to the usual diploma and certificate. The army of youth in Chicago and through the State engaged in the earnest study of music on the highest plane would, no doubt, surprise even those comparatively familiar with the facts. The very best talent is engaged in teaching. Artists like Bernard Ziehn, Carl Wolfsohn, Emil Liebling, Wm. *H.* Sherwood, Fannie Bloomfield Zeissler and others, are teaching, and the result must necessarily be the accomplishment of much which not long ago seemed the impossible. They are giving to the world some of its finest pianists, (Fannie Bloomfield Zeissler herself having been a pupil of both Carl Wolfsohn and Bernard Ziehn), some of its favorite singers, violinists and composers. We have already alluded to the Chicago Music College as one of the oldest music schools in *I*llinois. For facts connected with the history of this college we are indebted to Mr. George P. *U*pton, for many years the musical critic of the *Chicago Tribune.* The history in its entirety appears in the catalogue of the college, and is used by the courtesy of Mr. Wm. K. Ziegfeld. The college was organized in 1867 by Dr. Florence Ziegfeld, who is still the President. Chicago was then a city of two hundred thousand people, and the college has kept pace with the growth of the great city, and is now a musical and educational center of a city of more than two million inhabitants. Its first home was in the Crosby Opera House, then the musical center of the city, and its beginning compared with its present magnificent equipment was humble. From the Crosby Opera House it moved to more commodious rooms at 253 Wabash Ave. Then came the great fire, "when the daughters of music were brought low." It might seem that music would be the last thing to receive attention at a time of such disaster, but in a short time the college resumed its work, first at 800, later at 493 Wabash Ave., where they remained till Central Music *H*all was erected. In that building it seemed as if its accommodations were large enough to satisfy any possible demands, and from those quarters thousands of graduates went out, equipped with the musical culture and the gracious influences received there. But their rooms proved too small to gratify the ambitious plans of the founder for improved and additional facilities for their work, and to-day the home of this college is in their own building, on Michigan Boulevard, where they may boast the most elegant structure devoted exclusively to musical purposes in the United States, if not in the world. The location itself may be said to be artistic, for it stands facing the lake, almost opposite the Art Institute, not far from the Public Library adjoining the Fine Arts Building, that hive of music and art. The building is large and elegant, six stories high, and no expense has been spared in so equipping every department that all material requirements shall be met in the prosecution of their work. During thirty-seven years this college has been a center of musical inspiration, and has achieved more than can be estimated in figures. Dr. Florence Ziegfeld is, and has always been, the President of the college, and every department receives the benefit of his advice and long experience. He is nobly aided by his two sons, Carl and Wm. K., the former as secretary and treasurer, the latter as manager, and their united efforts can only crown with greater and still greater glory this—Chicago's—oldest college of music. The faculty has many members of world-wide reputation as artists or as teachers, and no teacher is selected without the utmost care. Proof of the results achieved by this college may be gathered from the fact that several pupils from Berlin and London are now studying at this school. Not only is instruction given —both vocal and instrumental—on every instrument which can be named, but there are also classes in harmony, counterpoint, canon, fugue, in composition and ensemble playing, and so on through every line of study that can benefit the most ardent pupil. In connection with the college there are schools of opera, of acting; instruction is given in fencing, stage or fancy dancing, and in foreign languages.

Some of the most prominent citizens give each year diamond medals to those competing for excellence in the various departments, and commencement night at the Auditorium, when hundreds are graduated, is a marked event. Concerts and recitals are given with frequency, thus aiding the pupil in self-poise and confidence. This college has about two thousand pupils.

Dr. F. Ziegfeld has done much for musical growth in Ilinois. He was born in Jever, in the Grand Duchy of Oldenburg, where his father had an official station at the Royal Court. He began the study of music in his sixth year. Among his instructors and, later, his friends were such masters as Mascheles, Plaidy, Popperitz, Wenzel, Richter and David.

. He was a friend of Liszt, Wagner and other musicians, and corresponded with them for years. He keeps in close touch with musical affairs in the Old World, and visits Europe at least once a year. He made the selection of the

country of Abt, Strauss, Bendel, Peschka-Leutner and other contemporaneous artists. He has been for nearly forty years a resident of America, and is a prominent figure in its musical history. Not long since he was awarded the gold medal and diploma of the Bellini Royal Society of Letters, Art and Music, of Italy. His latest decoration is that of the Chevalier of the Legion of Honor, of France, conferred by the French Government, sent him by the President of France through the French Consul, of this city. So far as we know, he is the only musician in America on whom this honor has been conferred. But among all his decorations none is more prized than a diamond-studded cross inscribed "To Dr. F. Ziegfeld, from the citizens of Chicago," presented to him Feb. 23, 1891, on the twenty-fifth anniversary of the founding of the college. Aside from his work in the college, Dr. Ziegfeld has been prominent in public affairs, and was chairman of the jury of piano and organ awards at the World's Columbian Exposition. He merits marked recognition in the history of music in Illinois.

The Balatka Musical College is next, probably, in age to the Chicago Musical College. It was founded in 1879 by Hans Balatka, whose name it bears, and a sketch of whose life may be found in another place in this volume. It was called at first the Balatka Academy of Musical Art, but under his supervision its growth was constant and its work done on broader lines, and it became a leading school. Like other schools established in the earlier years, it has had many homes, having been located in the American Express Building, Kimball Hall and the Isabella Building. For some years now it has had its quarters in the Le Moyne Building, on Randolph St., near State St. While less pretentious in some respects than many other schools, in point of musical instruction and desired result this school occupies an enviable place among the music schools of Chicago. For twenty-one years Hans Balatka was the head of this institution, and his artistic instincts and cultured mind were an inspiration to every department of the school. Many musical affairs conducted by Mr. Balatka form part of the musical history of Chicago and America; they gave him prominence before the public, and have enshrined his memory in many hearts throughout the land. He was a busy man, an enthusiastic lover of music, devoted to his profession. His death, April 24, 1899, after more than fifty years' labor in the field of music, was a great loss to musical circles in Chicago, for he was a gifted artist and consecrated to the best advancement of the work he loved. The end came suddenly, as the result of heart-failure, so to the very close of his most useful life he was able to pursue his

known as a courteous gentleman, of gentle presence, a most scholarly musician and a composer of merit. He was very enthusiastic in his ambitions for the conservatory, and its advancement was the source of greatest gratification to him. Patiently for years he had borne the burden of failing health, and at last, after a brief illness, the useful life came to a close while still his hand was guiding the work he loved so well.

One more school deserves special mention, since it began its first year's work as a conservatory this year. It is the Sherwood Music School. This school was organized in 1897, and has had a most remarkable growth, having now five hundred pupils. Its quarters are attractive and commodious in the Fine Arts Building, which is perhaps the finest edifice in the world given up entirely to music and the arts. The school suite is so arranged as to be available for smaller recitals, while in four halls, varying in size, in the building larger recitals and concerts are held. The teachers are well fitted for their respective duties, using the best methods and understanding American needs and character. Mr. Wm. H. Sherwood, the director, has a world-wide reputation as a pianist of the very first rank, and has been a rarely successful teacher, some of his pupils being recognized in the professional world both in Europe and America.

Realizing how much advantage accrues from hearing the best artists, frequent opportunity is given the pupils to hear the members of the faculty and other artists. Among the faculty are such favorite soloists as Mr. Walter Spry, Arthur Beresford, Mrs. Genevieve Clark Wilson, Adolph Rosenbecker and Holmes Cowper, and this school is certainly doing excellent work for the youth of the city and State.

There are very many smaller schools and newer schools scattered through the city, doing work which would challenge comparison with that of any of the larger conservatories, but it is impossible to review them at this time.

Among them may be mentioned Mrs. Regina Watson's school, the Bush Temple Conservatory, the Columbia School, the Tomasso Mandolin and Orchestra School, and many others. Enough has been written to show that even in her comparatively brief history Chicago has attained very much in the establishment of the very best grade of music schools.

Recognition of the efforts of Maurice Grau in giving to the people of Chicago season after season of grand opera should find a place in any history of its musical life. He has given the city opportunity to hear the best artists in their favorite roles, and has had a pride in having every presentation of opera as far as possible above criticism. That he has succeeded in attaining his ambitions in a marked degree is evidenced by the enthusiasm and numbers of the audiences which have availed themselves of the opportunities thus offered. No more honest expression of appreciation could be given.

While the grand opera has been presented at the Auditorium, Henry W. Savage, at the Studebaker, has been providing entertainments which have been a delight and an education to the public. He had two aims—first, the production of standard operas, both grand and light, in English and at popular prices, and, second, a plan of promotion which should encourage American singers. In both of these experiments he has been remarkably successful.. He opened with the Castle Square Company, which soon became a favorite with the public. The outgrowth of this was the Savage English Grand Opera Company, which plays annual engagements here with a repertoire of seventeen operas.

Last year " La Tosca " was produced for the first time in English, this year " Othello," and Mr. Savage expects next year to give " Parsifal " in English with a company distinct from his grand opera company. His scheme of promotion has proved a powerful incentive to earnest work, and almost all his principals had their beginning in the chorus, and are great favorites with the Chicago public. Between the regular seasons of grand opera he has produced several light operas, " King Dodo," " Sultan of Sulu," " Peggy from Paris " and " The Sho-Gun," being presented now. Of these " King Dodo" and " Prince of Pilsen " are by Frank Pixley and Gustav Luders, and the other three by George Ade, of Chicago, with the music of the " Sultan of Sulu " by George G. Wathall, " Peggy from Paris " by Wm. Lorraine and the " Sho-Gun " by Gustav Luders. They have all had long seasons, and Mr. Savage has the unusual record of having brought out seven new musical attractions without a failure. The orchestra of the theatre, led by John McGhie, is well trained, so that the orchestration is an added pleasure to those attending performances at the Studebaker. The house is home-like and attractive, seating fifteen hundred and seventy-three. It is the largest producing center for musical plays in the West, and has done much for the education, as well as the entertainment, of the music-loving public of Chicago and Illinois.

That Chicago is the home of so many musicians of international reputation is indisputable evidence of their estimate of the work to be done here and the possibilites of the future. We have already alluded to some of them, as Theodore Thomas, Carl Wolfsohn, W. H. Sherwood, Emil Liebling and others, but a few more deserve mention, although a complete list is quite impossible.

chosen work. After his death his son, Christian F. Balatka, succeeded to the directorship. He had been associated for years in the affairs of the college as assistant director and head of the piano department, and had had the advantage of the companionship of his illustrious father. He has with great care and thought gathered about him a competent corps of instructors, many of them soloists holding high rank in their profession. Some of the prominent members of the Thomas' Orchestra are members of the faculty, and honest, competent instruction on all orchestral instruments is assured. This college quietly, but conscientiously, is doing good work, and its graduates obtain recognition and endorsement in the best musical circles.

The American Conservatory of Music is an American institution, fully equipped to teach the art of music in the most practical and scholarly way. More and more, American parents are recognizing the fact that their children can receive the best advantages in their own homes, and the American Conservatory is a home institution particularly designed to meet the requirements of American musicians and appealing to our national spirit. The President and faculty of this school are men and women of liberal culture and advanced ideas, in sympathy with American life and its demands and devoted to their profession.

The American Conservatory was founded and incorporated in 1886, with John J. Hattstaedt as its President, and endorsed by some of the most prominent citizens of Chicago, well known for their liberality and devotion to music. Its name was intended to be significant of its design, for it was organized especially to give to the American student the opportunity to receive a thorough education along whatever line he may select. The faculty consists of between fifty and sixty teachers, carefully selected, many with a national reputation, and all with wide experience as educators. The success of this conservatory has been assured from the beginning, and some musicians well known in this part of the country have been graduated from this school. It was for years a sort of belief that Chicago could not vie in any respect with New York either in the magnitude or excellence of its musical enterprises, but the time when that was true is long since past. The standard of musical attainment is higher every year, and the student may have as many advantages in Chicago as in any of the musical centers of the country. It is to the music colleges and conservatories that this remarkable condition is to be ascribed. No less an authority than Wm. H. Sherwood has said that he believed Chicago was destined to become the musical center of this country, and the work done by the schools and colleges is hastening that possible time. The American

lecture-room, with a fine two-manual organ and the use of its recital halls, which are in the building. Emil Liebling, who is connected with the Normal Department, not only gives lectures pertaining to the piano but the most valuable "conversations" before the students of the conservatory. It has been said, "In catholicity of musical culture, practical experience and felicity of expression Mr. Liebling is surpassed by no living American." Mr. Hattstaedt, Mr. Wiedig and others also give courses of lectures to the students. With Wilhelm Middleschulte, Mad. Ragna Linnè and others of like enviable reputation members of its faculty, it is safe to predict for this comparatively new conservatory a brilliant future.

The Chicago Conservatory was organized in 1884 for the purpose of giving opportunity for the highest class of instruction, and the standard established then has been maintained during the years of its history. The large faculty embraces some of the ablest instructors and most scholarly artists to be found in this country or Europe. The work of the conservatory has been such as to win the confidence of the public and the musical world to such a degree that it is easily recognized as one of the leading institutions of the kind in America. The school averages about fifteen hundred pupils in actual attendance, the number enrolled being somewhat larger. It is fortunate in having its home in the Auditorium Building, one of the famous buildings of the world. It is within easy reach of the Art Institute, Public and Crerar Libraries, and convenient to all the leading theatres and opera houses. Opportunity for the pupils to make public appearances is afforded by the beautiful Auditorium Lyceum Theatre, of which they have the use. Every branch of music receives the most careful attention, and, as many of the rooms were planned especially for the conservatory, many advantages accrue which would be impossible in an ordinary structure. The Hinshaw Schools of Opera and Drama, which are a part of this conservatory, afford the best instruction for those desiring to lead a professional life. Quite an unusual feature in such a school is a fine arts department, where oil painting, water-color, china painting, etc., are taught. There is also a department for the teaching of foreign languages, and physical culture receives special attention. Particular thought is bestowed upon the little ones, and children's music forms no unimportant part of their curriculum. The conservatory has sustained a great loss during the year 1903 in the death of its director, Frederic Grant Gleason. Mr. Gleason was well

To Mrs. Caroline Scott, a gentle woman of musical attainments, belongs the honor of compiling the first anthem book ever published in Illinois and of doing much musical work in the earlier years.

A master better known in Europe than America is Bernard Ziehn. To him Von Bulow advised the musicians of Europe to go for instruction, calling him "the greatest theorist of music in the world, whose judgment was beyond question." The critics of Germany said of his book on harmony that it was "the work of a genius that can be recommended to any master and disciple, teacher and pupil." One cannot be in his presence without recognizing the fact that he is a master worthy of mention with those we are taught to revere. He is exceedingly retiring in disposition, but his success has been such that some of the great artists of this country feel pride in naming him as their instructor.

W. S. B. Mathews must be recognized as a prominent figure in the musical history of Illinois. It has been said of him that no other man has been so successfully and extensively a teacher through the medium of the printing-press. His text-books for both advanced and elementary pupils have obtained recognition throughout the country as standards, and are in general use. Besides these text-books he is the author of various books on the history of music and kindred subjects valuable to the general student. He has been one of Chicago's leading pianists and organists, and for years was associated with various daily papers in Chicago as their music critic.

Clarence Eddy, of wide reputation, was at one time Chicago's favorite organist, and has had a moulding influence on the musical life of Chicago and, it might be said, of the West. He is a scholarly musician, a successful teacher, and an accomplished artist, and some of his pupils have attained most enviable reputation.

Ledochowski, a pianist and teacher, whose playing may be said to be that of a virtuoso, and who studied under one of Chopin's pupils, has identified himself with Chicago and become part of its musical history.

Hundreds of cultivated teachers are doing most artistic work in their various studios, who rarely receive the public recognition they deserve save as the world may learn of them through the success of their pupils. Scores of notable men and women have lent the value of their influence to the development of the musical life in Chicago and Illinois, but it is impossible even to name all those who most deserve such distinction.

So far we have written only of the history of music in Chicago, and to a degree it is also the history of music in Illinois, they are so interdependent, but mention should be made of some of the more prominent of the many flourishing schools throughout the State.

For this wonderful progress, of which the foregoing is but a suggestion, has not been confined to Chicago, but in every city, town and village under the inspiration of the love of what is artistic and beautiful, men and women are, through individual and concerted effort, seeking for the uplift of the community in which they live. They are striving also to bring into their own lives the refining and elevating influences of the best productions of musical art.

In Alton, Miss Katherine V. Dickinson has been identified for several years with " music-education " in connection with Shurtleff College, and a list of her pupils and graduates will show that many of them are holding responsible positions as singers and teachers in churches, conservatories and schools. The Alton Conservatory, with Ruth C. Mills as director, takes rank among the first schools in the State, as do the music schools in Jacksonville, Aurora, Knoxville, Springfield, Joliet, Galesburg, Quincy, Freeport, and many others of equal excellence scattered through the State.

The Moline Conservatory of Music, founded in 1902, by Mrs. Ella Carter Bryant, enrolled more than one hundred pupils the first year, and its subsequent growth has been amazing. This conservatory has the advantage of the co-operation of Emil Liebling. The school in Sycamore has as a member of its faculty George J. Lewis, who has a studio in the Auditorium, in Chicago, and is an artist as well as a successful and popular teacher.

Rockford has possibly the reputation of being as musical as any city in Illinois, if not the most musical. Its Mendelssohn Society, composed of ladies organized for the study and rendering of the best music, has become well known in the musical circles throughout the State as doing the most unusual work. Mrs. Chandler Starr, for many years the President of this club, and its accompanist, is not only a fine pianist and organist but a woman of superior musical scholarship, of devoted love for music and great executive ability. She is well known outside of Rockford, having been accompanist at presentations of the Persian Garden and miscellaneous programs in other cities. She has also received honors for her musical work in large and important gatherings. Twice a year the Mendelssohn Society gives to Rockford a program by the best artists procurable, and twice a year concerts which shall show the public who are deeply interested in their work what they have accomplished during the season. Of comparatively recent organization is a chorus of young ladies identified with this club who are under the direction of Harrison M. Wild. He goes to them every week and feels great pride in their work. He feels that it will soon bear comparison with that of the Mendelssohn Club of Chicago, a very great compliment from this conductor, whose requirements are of the highest order.

Choral societies and various singing clubs in different cities attest to the desire for musical advancement all over the State, and cheap transportation and commutation rates make it possible for those near Chicago to avail themselves of its concerts, operas and other musical advantages.

The Elgin Choral Society gave the " Messiah " this season with great success, and similar societies elsewhere do as excellent work. Sacred music has not been neglected in the years during which the musical history of Illinois has been made. In no city, excepting possibly New York, will fine music be found in so large a proportion of the churches as in Chicago, while throughout the State the traveler is impressed with the excellent choirs, quartettes or choruses which are the rule in the churches. Sacred concerts and organ recitals of the highest order are given on Sabbath afternoons, so that opportunity is afforded to all who desire to embrace it to hear the choicest sacred music rendered in the most artistic and impressive way.

Chicago and Illinois have furnished more than would have been expected in the way of composers. Dr. Geo. F. Root, Reginald de Koven, Max Heinrich, Emil Liebling, F. G. Gleason, Mrs. Jessie L. Gaynor, Eleanor L. Smith, Carrie Jacobs Bond, and many others have made reputations for the excellence of their compositions which are used everywhere.

Not without many struggles and much self-sacrifice have the results of the present been attained. Pioneer life of any sort is only poetic in the retrospect, and pioneer effort in the musical development of any State is like all other pioneer work; it means the brave facing of obstacles which seem insurmountable and the overcoming of ignorance and prejudice, the introduction of new ideas, the expenditure of individual monies, and a vast deal of labor for which no remuneration is received or expected. The work that has been done so well in the past is being prosecuted in the present under different conditions and from a higher vantage ground, but it is still the work of uplift and education. Chicago to-day is the musical center of a vast territory, her schools and colleges receiving pupils from the coast to the sound, and from all over the States which have more recently sprung into existence. Of those who laid the foundations many have passed to the great beyond, but others remain to rejoice in the results of small beginnings, to feel a pride in the wealth of musical resources in Chicago and Illinois.

The men and women whose faces and lives find place in this volume have

the development in others of the gifts which have made them
the past, so in the future we may hope for the best in the
Illinois, and hope confidently, believing that realization, not·
will be the history of the years yet to come.

William Rainey Harper.

William Rainey Harper

William Rainey Harper.

William Rainey Harper, President of the University of Chicago, was born in New Concord, Muskingum county, Ohio, July 26, 1856, son of Samuel and Elizabeth (Rainey) Harper. His education was begun in the United Presbyterian College, of his native village, in which the course of study covered six years, two being given to preparatory work, four to college studies proper. When eight years of age he entered the Preparatory Department, and, in 1870, when fourteen years of age, he graduated with the degree of Bachelor of Arts. As the college was largely a school of preparation for those who intended to enter the ministry of the United Presbyterian Church, the study of the Bible in Hebrew, as well as in English, was a prominent feature in the work. The proficiency of the youthful student in this language was such that when he graduated he delivered his oration in Hebrew, an incident which, probably, had more to do with the shaping of his life than, at the time, he or his friends imagined.

After three years spent at home pursuing favorite studies, in 1873 he went to Yale University, where he became the earnest student of philology, under Prof. William Dwight Whitney. His completion of this period of study was marked by the conferring upon him of the degree of Doctor of Philosophy, in 1875, when he was nineteen years old. Soon after this he married Miss Ellen Paul, daughter of Dr. David Paul, then President of Muskingum College. In the fall of 1875, he became principal of the Masonic College, in Macon, Tenn. From this position he went to Granville, Ohio, to become a tutor in the preparatory department of Denison University. Here he at once attracted attention by his enthusiastic devotion to his work. He proved himself an excellent drillmaster, enlisting the interest of his students to a marked degree and arousing their ambitions so as to secure great results in the quantity and thoroughness of the work accomplished.

The zeal displayed by him, and its attendant enthusiasm among the students, led to his selection as principal of what soon became Granville Academy. The President of the University was Dr. E. B. Andrews, and these two progressive teachers worked together in great harmony and secured from their students remarkable results.

While in Granville, Dr. Harper united with the Baptist Church, and after three years of successful teaching, on the recommendation of Prof. Andrews, he became Professor of Hebrew and Cognate Languages in the Baptist Union Theological Seminary, at Morgan Park, Ill. At this time two thoughts seemed to dominate him, one the belief in the value of the inductive method in teaching languages, the other the desire to awaken fresh interest in the study of Hebrew. These ambitions led to the joint authorship of a series of Latin, Greek and English text-books on the inductive plan, and to the publication of a series of text-books in Hebrew, the organization of Hebrew correspondence and summer schools and the publication of a periodical called the *Hebrew Student.*

The work of promulgating was carried on, not alone

through the correspondence schools, the summer schools and the *Hebrew Student,* but also by means of Bible lectures delivered in various places, which made Dr. Harper's name familiar to all those interested in Bible study. Large sums of money were required for the circulation of literature connected with the work, and they were often secured by him, at great personal sacrifice. One result of his work was the organization of the American Institute of Hebrew, which was succeeded by the American Institute of Sacred Literature.

In 1875, he became Principal of the Chautauqua College of Liberal Arts, and six years later of the Chautauqua System, which position he held till 1898. In 1886, he became Professor of Semitic languages in Yale University. Here he aroused great enthusiasm among his students, and, by means of lectures in New Haven, New York, Boston, Chicago and other cities, and at Vassar, Wellesley and other colleges, created widespread interest in Bible study. In 1889, he had the great honor of being elected by the authorities of Yale to the Woolsey Professorship of Biblical Literature, thus holding two full professorships in the institution at the same time.

In 1891, he was elected to his present position as President of the University of Chicago, and it is interesting to note how his previous experiences influenced him to the organization of a new university on a broad basis. One feature of this work which has attracted widespread attention is the University Extension Division, whose threefold plan of instruction by means of lecture studies, correspondence studies and class studies in the afternoons and evenings was only the developing of plans previously tried by him.

In like manner the *Hebrew Student,* which differentiated

sity of a series of journals devoted to special departments, and designed to furnish contributions to these several branches of study.

While perhaps it may be too early to consider the influence of President Harper in connection with the University of Chicago, it must be apparent that he stands as one of the foremost educators of the century. We must take into account his widespread influence in the University, in the many-sided Chautauqua work, in the public school work of the city of Chicago, in the editorial work connected with some of the University publications, in his frequent public lectures in various parts of the country, and in the suggestion and advice which he is constantly asked to give to those who, like himself, are struggling with the great problems which confront the educators of to-day.

Mrs. 'Potter Palmer.

MRS. POTTER **PALMER.**

Mrs. Potter Palmer.

Mrs. Potter Palmer is a representative woman of America as well as of Chicago and Illinois.

Twice, the distinction of her birth, social position and remarkable ability have won for her the highest honors among women of the world.

When Congress, in 1891, created a Board of Women Managers for the World's Columbian Commission, Mrs. Palmer was unanimously chosen President. This unprecedented step towards the advancement of women in art, literature, science and the industries found an invincible and wise leader in their President, whose report upon the work accomplished by this Board is a marvelous history.

The responsibilities of such an office, unique and untried, demanded an intelligent, comprehensive knowledge of the mental, moral, social and physical well-being of women, as well as the customs and laws that affect their lives from every standpoint.

Mrs. Palmer's record as President of this Board has made history for all time, so vital and masterly was her grasp of this epoch-making period.

Three times did her personal influence with the powers that be in Washington and in Springfield, the State capital of Illinois, gain concessions so gratifying to all that the whole

67

Columbian Commission presented Mrs. Palmer with a resolution of thanks for her brilliant success.

Several visits to foreign nations, personal interviews with royalty and the leading minds of different governments, brought instant recognition which worked colossal reforms in the advancement of women, and placed Mrs. Palmer's name as the foremost among women for all time.

Through her untiring efforts, skilled labor, so long hidden behind capital, found "honorable mention" in the awards to both men and women during the Exposition. Those who had the privilege of being present at the meetings of this great body of women, representing the minds and ideas of the great nations of the world, will never forget those occasions.

They will recall with pride the infinite tact, marvelous memory for names and faces, the perfect poise and great personal beauty, as well as the wisdom and diplomacy of this highest type of an American woman.

Force and integrity have been shown in every act, both public and private, of a life which has borne the fiercest light of public scrutiny.

When Mrs. Palmer's name headed the list of eighteen commissioners whom President McKinley appointed and whom Congress confirmed to represent America at the Paris Exposition of 1900, it was an official recognition of Mrs. Palmer as the foremost woman in America. It was a notable fact that her's was the only woman's name among the national commissioners.

Bertha Honorè, of most distinguished ancestry, was born in Louisville, Ky., but came so early in life to Chicago that Illinois claims her as her own. Here she married Mr. Pot-

ter Palmer, now deceased. He was a retired merchant, whose
sterling public and private character was most brilliantly
proven. He stood one of the prominent men of America for
brains and an ability which gained for him a second colossal
fortune, after the great fire swept away a princely income in
a few hours.

Both Mr. and Mrs. Palmer's civic pride was shown in
their encouraging their sons to enter a public life in their native city.

In their superb home, with rarest tact, Mrs. Palmer
has given to talent opportunity to come in touch with appreciative audiences, opening her beautiful rooms for musicales
which have marked epochs in the history of music in Chicago. The art gallery in this home holds one of the finest
private collections of pictures in the land. Near by are priceless specimens of jade, ivory and crystals, the result of years
of study and research for the beautiful in art.

Socially, Mrs. Palmer reigns supreme. Charming in disposition, loyal to those dear to her, sympathetic and ready
with words of encouragement and cheer, wealth, political and
social distinction have failed to change this womanly woman,
and she is devoted to the friends of long ago, effacing every
thought of comparative position and opportunity. Personal
aggrandizement seems ever to be the thought most remote in
all her plans, which are made on a scale which indicates the
largeness of her views and the manner in which she grasps not
so much individual as world-wide demands.

The history of music, art and literature, not only of Illinois but of America, will place Mrs. Palmer's name at the head
of those brave, notable women it was her proud privilege to

To be in Chicago and keep herself free from the myriad claims made by society, art, charity and a thousand demands made upon her time and attention, seemed the impossible. Quiet and rest from all importunity seemed imperative, and since Mr. Palmer's death Mrs. Palmer has spent most of her time in Europe, where she has been a most highly honored guest in every place she has visited. She has been so many times abroad that she is thoroughly at home in the principal cities of the old world, and is so accomplished a linguist that she enjoys conversation with the most cultured people of every land.

Like many another who has risen to greatness, she seemed born for a time of special need, and early began a career of usefulness, waiting opportunity. Most truly has it been said:

"For a web begun the gods find threads."

A RESUME OF MRS. POTTER PALMER'S REPORT TO CONGRESS, AS PRESIDENT OF THE BOARD OF LADY MANAGERS OF THE WORLD'S COLUMBIAN EXPOSITION.

In the important Congressional enactment authorizing and providing for the administration of the Columbian Exposition, the provision creating a Board of Women, and assigning to the same unwonted duties, glides so quietly and unobtrusively into place that no warning is given of the momentous innovation it inaugurates.

On re-reading the words, however, they arrest attention. Becoming conscious of their unusual import, one tries to discern the intention lying behind them, the altered attitude of the Government which they indicate and the changes which they forecast.

The silence of centuries regarding women is broken by this unprecedented utterance of the Congress of the United States.

It would seem to furnish conclusive proof of quickening perceptions on the part of the Government; to give evidence of its discovery that there exists a large and responsible class of citizens, heretofore excluded from participation in national affairs, which may on occasions be profitably called into service. In thus decreeing official administrative participation for women, and in specifically stipulating that they appoint jurors to judge the handiwork of their sex, Congress has in effect accorded to women the right of direct representation as well as the further right to be judged by a jury of their peers.

These vital admissions once having been formulated by the Government, and action upon them having been put into successful, even though temporary, operation, their underlying truths may be regarded as accepted; a striking precedent has been created and placed upon record which will facilitate their further application and their liberal extension into broader fields of equity.

In studying the phraseology of the act, it is noted that the unaccustomed privileges embraced not only work produced *wholly* by women, but embraced exhibits produced *in part* by women.

This signal from the Government, which indicated a faint recognition of the anomalous and unnatural position into which industrial women have been forced, together with freshly awakened desire to be just and helpful to her, elicited a wonderful response from women all over the world. It was a response which revealed the existence of an entirely new and, hitherto, unappreciated altruistic force in every community: As a result of its efforts, the Board of Lady Managers of the World's Columbian Exposition found itself at the head of the most remarkable and powerful international organization of women that the world has ever called into being, and acting under high sanctions that have never before been accorded them.

The Woman's Board created by the Government of the United States had co-operating with it thirty royal and imperial women commissions, formed at its request by the Governments of Austria, Belgium, Brazil, Cape Colony, Cey-

lon, Cuba, Denmark, France, Germany, Great Britain, Guate-
mala, Holland, Italy, Japan, Mexico, New South Wales, Norway, Sweden, Russia, Siam, Spain, and thirty-two State
boards of American women, authorized and maintained by the
Legislatures of the various States.

Behind this official phalanx stood unnumbered hosts of
women laboring in various industries, more or less organized
in various groups and associations. There were from thirty
foreign countries two thousand four hundred and two voluntary organizations, having a membership of one million two
hundred and twenty-eight thousand three hundred and three,
expending annually $4,103,400, and from forty-six of our own
States and Territories, three thousand three hundred and sev-
enty-seven organizations of American women, with a membership of three million four hundred and eighty-one thousand
seven hundred and thirty-one, expending annually $11,889,-
938.40, all endeavoring to promote the ethical end of civilization. These unofficial organizations, only a part of the great
total that existed, knew little or nothing of each other, having
formed themselves in every part of the world, in obedience to
a spontaneous impulse, to accomplish ends manifestly desirable, and were themselves astonished at the showing they
made.

The Woman's Building was the first completed. Their
dormitory was the largest ever built by women for women,
and was entirely managed by them, and, although many hotels
failed, their restaurant closed with a surplus in its treasury.
Twelve hundred guests were housed daily, twelve thousand
two hundred and ten women found a home there, and no sick-
ness nor death occurred there. The invention or re-discovery

lin, of Cincinnati, through the efforts of this Board of Managers, obtained recognition, as well as the re-discovery of applying gold upon porcelain (Japan art), by Miss A. Healy, of Washington.

These may be reckoned among the most important artistic events in American history.

Space forbids more than a glance at the important things accomplished by the united efforts of this wonderful band of women, at this time.

Even more important than the discovery by Columbus, which we were gathered together to celebrate, is the fact that the general Government has just discovered woman. Having revealed themselves in response to a call from the Government, and having done their utmost to forward its intentions while organized under its sanction, this great army of women stands waiting a second message of helpful import.

May they not reasonably hope for such a call?

George Mortimer Pullman.

6

In Brow
Lewis Pulk
March 3, 18
builder, a tl
labor-saving
ventor, he d
mother was
a noble wor
has been se

The fi
daughters,
success.
possible t
more in t
have thou
vantages
cal rather
partly, su
ceived fo
his broth
that hun

George Mortimer Pullman.

In Brockton, Chautauqua County, N. Y., lived James
Lewis Pullman, of whom George Mortimer Pullman, born
March 3, 1831, was the third son. The father was a house-
builder, a thoughtful, reserved man, who had invented some
labor-saving appliances, although, like many another in-
ventor, he did not reap much financial benefit from them. The
mother was the daughter of James Minton, of Auburn, N. Y.,
a noble woman, serene, cheerful, loving and brave. Of her it
has been said:
"She met hosts of sorrow with a look
That altered not beneath the frown it wore."

The family consisted of eight children, six sons and two
daughters, whose lives are full of interest and crowned with
success. Ambitious for their children, the parents did all
possible to aid them in the best self-development, expending
more in this way than many, in their circumstances, would
have thought they could. George had all the educational advantages available. He was persistent and teachable, practical rather than brilliant. At the age of fourteen he, at least
partly, supported himself working as clerk, for which he received forty dollars a year. A year later he was employed in
his brother's cabinet shop, in Albion, N. Y. Who can say but
that humble beginning indirectly led to the great results he

achieved? for in the Pullman car we find the very acme of
devices for indoor comfort.   In 1853, his father died, not having been able to hoard any resources for the loved ones he was
leaving.   As the oldest unmarried son, he assumed the support of his mother and the younger children, who needed care,
and most cheerfully he carried this burden.   His mother lived
till 1892, and for the forty years of her widowed life he was
her support and stay.

With increased responsibilites came the necessity for increased resources, and he began the business of house-raising
on the banks of the Erie Canal.   A few years later he was engaged in the same business in Chicago, having maintained the
family and accumulated six thousand dollars as the beginning
of a fortune.   Some of the largest building jobs ever attempted, not only in Chicago but in the world, were attempted
and successfully accomplished by him, and their record furnishes most interesting history.

But the great achievement which made him famous was
the invention of the sleeping-car system.   For three years
he was in Colorado, attracted by the wonderful gold dis-
coveries made at that time.   As he traveled he was greatly
impressed with the discomforts of journeying at night.   Cars
were then being introduced which were an attempt at furnishing a better place to rest than had been known heretofore.
The berths were, however, little more than shelves, and in the
narrow cars poor ventilation and crowded quarters were inevitable.   As he often told the story, one night, while making
a most comfortless trip, great possibilities dawned upon him.
After his earnest solicitation, the Chicago and Alton R. R.
gave him two old passenger cars to experiment on and an old

shed to work in, and there he spent his time and his own money till the first pair of " sleepers " was put on the night train between Chicago and St. Louis. These were fairly satisfactory to those who used them, but did not realize the anticipations of their builder. Lured still by hopes of gold, he returned to Colorado, but the thought of a possible sleeping-car was ever present, and, returning, he went again to the Chicago and Alton R. R., who gave him the opportunity to again try, which was all he asked or needed. After a year's time and the expenditure of eighteen thousand dollars he had built a traveling palace. He named it the " Pioneer," and to-day it is carefully preserved at Pullman, an interesting and valued memento of the perseverance and the genius of the man whose reputation this invention made world-wide. This car was part of the funeral train when the remains of the martyred Lincoln were brought back to the State which had so proudly given him to the nation. From this time there was no question as to the demand for their general use, and to-day they are everywhere, a comfort to the traveler, a perpetual monument to George M. Pullman.

Mr. Pullman's name is connected with many gigantic enterprises, such as the New York Elevated Railway, the Nicaragua trans-isthmian canal, and others.

The great industrial experiment at Pullman—a prosperous manufacturing town, full of the spirit of enterprise and content—was regarded first with curiosity, almost distrust, but later with admiration by those who from the beginning watched its development and success.

Outside of his business life, Mr. Pullman was a patron of art, a lover of books, enjoying with zest the best social life.

afterwards that no fund was ever more sacredly handled,
a dollar being diverted from its original purpose.

In 1867, he married Miss Hattie A. Sanger, daughter
an honored citizen of Chicago, and their family consisted
two daughters and two sons, who were twins.

His death was a great loss, not only to those who lo\
him but to the financial world, for his integrity was prov
bial, as was his shrewdness and his ability to manipulate gr
enterprises.

Mrs. George M. Pullman.

Mrs. Geo. M. Pullman

Mrs. George M. Pullman.

Mrs. George M. Pullman bears a name of international importance, one which royalty has honored. Harriet Sanger Pullman was born in Chicago, and is a descendant of Sir Richard Sanger, of England. Her grandfather, David Sanger, and her father, James Y. Sanger, were fine types of American men. Her father was famous for projecting ways of transportation. The first railroad from Sacramento to Marysville, Cal., the Illinois canal and the Ohio and Mississippi Railroad are monuments to his energy. It seemed only poetic justice that Mrs. Pullman, with such ancestry, should share in the decoration and title of nobility conferred upon her illustrious husband, George M. Pullman, by King Humbert of Italy, who regarded him as a benefactor of the human race. His marvelous inventions have revolutionized the entire system of travel. An audience from Queen Margarete was expressive of her appreciation. Mrs. Pullman's private car furnished transportation for Eulalie during her visit to America. Mrs. Pullman is a great traveler, and generally shares this pleasure with her friends. While in Mexico she was entertained by President Diaz and his wife.

Shortly after their marriage, in 1867, Mr. and Mrs. Pullman built their present Chicago home. They spent their summers on Pullman Island, in the St. Lawrence, in their lovely home at Long Branch, N. J., or in foreign travel. In their elegant Chicago home many distinguished guests have been made welcome, among them Prince Leopold, Queen Victoria's son. In return for this courtesy Mr. and Mrs. Pullman were entertained both at Buckingham Palace and Stafford House during the life of the first duchess. Gen. Grant and family, Gen. Sheridan and other army people formed a house party given by Mr. and Mrs. Pullman on their island in the St. Lawrence. Pullman, that city of miracles, lying on the banks of the Calumet, was the scene of a most unique entertainment, characteristic of the hospitality of Mr. and Mrs. Pullman, nearly one thousand guests being entertained at dinner. In their Chicago home, filled with all that wealth and taste can suggest, art and artists have been welcome. Near this house stands a statue presented to Chicago by Mr. and Mrs. Pullman, commemorating the massacre of Fort Dearborn. While Mrs. Pullman was one of Chicago's acknowledged belles, she never courted social notoriety, but her generous patronage of all art is well known. Her intense love of music and art has filled her home with means of gratifying her taste. A magnificent pipe-organ, fine piano, old tapestries, ivory carvings and paintings, create an atmosphere in which artists delight to revel. To Mr. and Mrs. Pullman were born two daughters and two sons. Mrs. Pullman's character is best revealed in her devotion to her husband, children and mother, and in the love with which she is regarded by those who have been in her service many years.

rs. Marshall Field, Jr.

Mrs. Marshall Field, Jr.

To make a home radiant with happiness, to so direct her children that they shall be equipped for life's experiences, to keep herself in touch with what is loveliest in music and art, and be an inspiration to those she loves best, are some of the purposes which are moulding the life of Mrs. Marshall Field, Jr.

Mrs. Field, whose maiden name was Albertina Huck, was born in Chicago, in 1873. Her mother, Clara (Kenkel) Huck, was of German descent, a fact in which Mrs. Field has the most loving pride. Mrs. Huck is remembered by many in this city for her beauty and versatility of talent. Practical, a model housekeeper and devoted mother, she was gifted with a lovely voice, and sang with exquisite charm. Her life, of which the memory is tenderly cherished, closed when her daughter Albertina was fourteen years of age, but she has still lived in the hearts of her children, an ideal to be attained. From her mother Mrs. Field inherits both the practical and the artistic thought of life. In her home she is conversant as to every detail, not in a superficial way, but intelligently, because under her mother's supervision she was taught to do each task herself. After her mother's death she was educated abroad, and it was on the steamer, when en route to devote herself to the study of art, that she met Mr. Marshall

Field, Jr. As many another time, Cupid laughed at the plans of the girlish student, and (1890) she was married to Mr. Field. Since her marriage she has lived much of the time abroad, although she has repeatedly returned to this country. She has three children, two sons, the older ten years of age, and a little daughter still in her babyhood.

To these children and her home she is giving the best hours of her life; in them she finds her greatest happiness, and for them she cherishes her highest ambitions. Social duties necessarily claim her attention, but it is not Mrs. Field's ambition to be in any degree a leader of society. She devotes some time to music, which she studied under Mad. Marchesi in Paris.

She is very fond of both painting and drawing, in which she received excellent instruction in Dresden. She is particularly interested in portrait and miniature work, and is about to resume her studies in this direction. Mrs. Field's two sisters are both married and live abroad; one, Baroness Kunowski, lives in Germany, the other, Marquesi Spinola, in Italy. Her only brother is living in the West.

Mrs. Field is a great favorite in Chicago society, which would gladly accord her a prominence which she does not desire. She is a beautiful woman, yet apparently unconscious of her charms; a womanly woman, gracious in her hospitality, devoted to the claims of home, feeling that the noblest crown a woman can wear is that of a consecrated wifehood and motherhood.

Austen K. de Blois, Ph.D., LL.D.

AUSTEN K. de BLOIS.

Austen K. de Blois, Ph.D., LL.D.

Austen K. de Blois was born at Wolfville, Nova Scotia, thirty-seven years ago. He is a descendant of an old French family, which gave its name to the castle and city of Blois, near Paris. His immediate ancestors resided in England, and he is nearly related by marriage to the late Lord Wm. Kennedy, the Marquis of Ailsa, Admiral Austen, of the British Navy, and Jane Austen, the celebrated novelist. Dr. de Blois has been a devoted student from boyhood, and was graduated from the various schools with which he was connected at an exceptionally early age. Graduating from Horton Academy at the age of fourteen, he entered Acadia College, N. S., from which he was graduated in 1886. After traveling abroad, he entered Brown University, Providence, R. I., from which institution he received the degree of Master of Arts, in 1886, and that of Ph. D. in 1889. His theological studies were prosecuted, first at the Episcopal Divinity School, in Philadelphia, and later at the Newton Baptist Theological Seminary. In June, 1900, he married, and, with his bride, again visited Europe to study and to travel: At the University of Berlin he was a student of Paulsen, Ebbinghaus and Zeller, in philosophy, and of Harnack, in church history. Immediately upon his return to America, Dr. de Blois was called to the Vice-Principalship of the Union Baptist Seminary, St. Mar-

91

tins, New Brunswick, and a few months later became its Principal.

In 1894, Dr. Kendrick resigned the Presidency of Shurtleff College, Upper Alton, Ill., and so great had been Dr. de Blois' success in the management of the Seminary at St. Martins that at once, by a unanimous vote of the governing body of the college, he was tendered the position, an offer he accepted. This invitation was a marked recognition not only of his scholarship but of his executive ability, which, in view of the fact that he was but twenty-seven years of age, was a most exceptional compliment. For five college years he held this position, and then accepted the pastorate of the First Baptist Church, Elgin, Ill., where he remained about four years. The record of his pastorate there was one of such achievement that, in the early part of 1903, he was invited to become the successor of Rev. P. S. Henson, D. D., as pastor of the First Baptist Church, of Chicago, a position he still holds. While it is too early to speak of what he may accomplish in this field, during the brief year he has so endeared himself not only to the members of the church but of the community, that it is safe to predict that the future will only emphasize the history of the past.

Dr. de Blois has written two books, " Bible Study in American Colleges " and " The Pioneer School." He has traveled extensively, having made four long visits to England and the Continent.

Franklin College gave him the honorary degree of LL. D. Few men in so few years have accomplished so much, his versatility of talent giving him great opportunity for achievement.

Mrs. A. A. Sprague.

Nancy A. Sprague

Mrs. A. A. Sprague.

Among those well known in the best social circles of Chicago, no one is a greater favorite than Mrs. Albert Arnold Sprague. Shunning notoriety, she is still always the cordial, gracious hostess and a guest welcome everywhere.

Nancy Atwood was born in Barnard, Vermont, the home of her parents, Ebenezer Atwood and Elvira (Tucker) Atwood. She was educated in the common schools and in the Royalton Academy, Vermont. September 29, 1862, she was married to Mr. Albert Arnold Sprague and came to Chicago, where her home has been ever since.

Fond of music, she devoted herself to its study in her earlier life, and her home has always been a favorite rendezvous for musical people.

Mrs. Sprague is in no sense of the term a club-woman. She is a Colonial Dame, but not an active member of the organization. She has a bright and appreciative intelligence, is intuitive in her judgments, practical in her occupations, with unusual capacity for details. She is lofty in her ideals, with conscientious discrimination between right and wrong, fastidious in her tastes, with a keen sense of humor. Loyal in her friendships, tender in her affections and sympathies, Mrs. Sprague's greatest pleasure lies in ministering to those about her, helpful to those whose lives come in touch with

had exceptional advantages of travel, having been abroad repeatedly. A lover of the beautiful, she has collected many lovely souvenirs in this country and in the old world. These she has arranged in her home, where they are objects of interest to those whose privilege it is to see them.

Keeping pace with the trend of the age, Mrs. Sprague aims to wield an influence for the upbuilding of right, and stands as a lover and promoter of music and art and all the enterprises which make for cultivation and refinement. Her most coveted distinction, however, is to excel as a homemaker, and those who know her best accord her this honor.

Mrs. Sprague is one of the most modest of women, and nothing is more distasteful to her than to know that she is the subject of public notice even in the most friendly way.

Happy in her home, helpful to those about her, Mrs. Sprague is an excellent example in the various walks of life of the best type of American womanhood.

Ralph Emerson.

RALPH EMERSON.

Ralph Emerson.

Among those connected with the industrial history of Illinois none are more honorably known than Mr. Ralph Emerson, of Rockford. Old citizens remember who rescued the infant industries of Rockford when they seemed likely to be crushed out, in the fifties, by wealthy rivals of other places.

Mr. Emerson was born May 3, 1831, in Andover, Mass. His father belonged to a distinguished family, his father and the father of Ralph Waldo Emerson being cousins. When only twenty years of age he came to Bloomington, Illinois. He soon moved to Beloit, Wis., and in 1852 to Rockford, where he now lives. He became a partner of Hon. Wait Talcott, who, with his family, had settled on the shores of Rock River in 1838. In 1858 he was married to Adaline E. Talcott, daughter of above, and from their home have gone forth some of the most beautiful and helpful influences of Rockford social life. Ralph Emerson is the only survivor of those engaged in the famous J. H. Manny and McCormick case. He was a member of the firm of the defense which paid Abraham Lincoln his first large cash retainer. Edwin M. Stanton, later made Secretary of War by Lincoln, was the leading lawyer employed by the defense, and it was during the progress of the trial that the two men became acquainted.

99

He has been prominently connected as President, Vice-President, Trustee, sole owner or otherwise, with the organization and working of over forty manufacturing, commercial, agricultural, educational, financial and other enterprises, some of national reputation. These enterprises include such interests as the manufacture of agricultural implements, knitting machines, cotton goods and woollen goods, the development of two insurance companies, two national banks, two electrical companies. Of some of the most important enterprises he still retains active control. His insight, dispassionate judgment and quick perception render his advice valuable, while his devotion to his gifted wife reveals a warm heart.

The name of Ralph Emerson will occupy a foremost place in the permanent history not only of Rockford but of Illinois.

line Elizabeth (Talcott) Emerson.

MRS. EMERSON.

Adaline Elizabeth (Talcott) Emerson.

Quiet and unobtrusive, a womanly woman, a loyal wife and devoted mother, possessing a quick sympathy with the aspirations, the achievements, the sorrows of others! Such is the subject of this sketch.

Few women in Illinois have had more honors bestowed upon them, or have been more closely connected with the leading social, literary and public achievements of the State, than has Mrs. Ralph Emerson, who has made Rockford, Ill., her home since 1857. Mrs. Emerson was born October 12, 1837, in Vernon, Oneida County, New York, and is the daughter of Hon. Wait Talcott and Elizabeth Ann (Norton) Talcott. Her ancestors extend back to Alfred the Great, Charlemagne, and, through the Nortons, to the French ancestor De Norvile, who married into the house of Valois, and came into England with King William the Conqueror, and was his Constable.

When nineteen years of age she graduated in the class of 1856 at Rutger's, New York City, under the chancellorship of Rev. Dr. Ferris, President of Columbia College, and Dr. Van Norman, President of Rutger's. She was a student of music under the late Prof. George F. Root and Prof. Daniel N. Hood, but in later years she has devoted more time to literary research and various kinds of literary work.

Married on September 7, 1858, to Mr. Ralph Emerson, at
that time a partner in business with her father, the Hon. Wait
Talcott, she has been prominently identified with him in all
the social and great industrial development of Rockford for
practically half a century.

The rearing of a family of six children occupied her
closely at home for many years, but even these family cares
did not prevent her being a companion of her husband in his
many travels and excursions all over America and Europe.
In the principal cities of England, France, Germany, Switzerland and Italy she feels very much at home, having spent
months in Paris, Florence and Rome, and over a year at one
time in Munich.

This life abroad familiarized her with many peoples, and
as she was brought in touch with various public enterprises,
having daughters with her studying music and painting, it
was in some sense to her as well a student life.   Intensely interested in every line of literary and art achievement, not only
in a general way but in its detail, she returned to her native
land greatly enriched in thought as the result of her observa-
tions.   The clubs for whom she has outlined courses of study
and to whose interests she has devoted herself have been
greatly indebted to her for the fund of information thus
gained.

Of an enthusiastic nature, feeling a pride in the success
of her husband and interesting herself in the best enterprises
of the city, delighted with everything which means advancement, whether in musical work or the encouraging of young
artists, or lending the benefit of her experience to aspirants
for literary fame, she has gladly interested herself in all such

efforts. Among such enterprises as she has helped to sustain may be mentioned the Mendelssohn Club, of Rockford, a club which has won for itself a widespread reputation for the rare excellence of its work. She has also been connected as a patron with the Art Institute, of Chicago, from its beginning; nor is her affiliation one only in name, for she is most thoroughly cognizant of the work done and is ambitious for its future.

The family, consisting of five daughters and a son, inherited much talent from their gifted parents. One daughter, Mrs. Belle (Emerson) Keith, is an artist, who has studied under the most able professors in New York City, also for years with Professor Carl Marr, in Munich, and Professor Lazar, in Paris. Mrs. Keith's sketches and paintings have been uniformly accepted, and are favorably known in art exhibits both in Chicago and in New York City.

A son, Ralph Emerson, Jr., when only twenty-three years of age, was instantly killed while heroically protecting from the ravages of fire his father's property in Rockford. As a young man he had already shown a rare executive ability. Mrs. Emerson prepared a " Memorial " for her son, a work of love which was grief's solace. Some years afterwards she published a second volume, " Love-bound and other Poems." These books have attracted much attention and widespread commendation, and may be found in some of the best public libraries in our land. While busy with her pen, with family cares and myriad social obligations, Mrs. Emerson has still found time to be identified with many of the best organizations of the nation. She is a member of the Society of American Authors, of New York City, The Fortnightly, The Twen-

Dames of America in the State of Illinois, Society of May-flower Descendants, and Colonial Governors, Founders and Patriots.

By reason of her culture, catholic spirit and rare executive ability, Mrs. Emerson has been called upon repeatedly to occupy for long periods of time positions of great importance in philanthropic, patriotic and social organizations, not only in the city but in the State and national societies, representing some of them as delegate at international conventions in America, Paris and London.

At the time of the organization of the Army and Navy League, during the late Spanish war, Mrs. Emerson received appointment from the Governor of Illinois to a responsible position. In 1900 she was appointed by Governor Tanner, of Illinois, as an Associate Commissioner to the Paris Exposition.

Notwithstanding the fact that she has held so many prominent positions, Mrs. Emerson is never more happy than in her own home circle with loved ones about her, enriching all with the brightness of her intellect, the breadth of her thought, the culture of her mind. Such a life blesses and inspires all who come in touch with it.

W. M. R. French

W. M. R. French.

· Prof. W. M. R. French is the Director of the Art Institute of Chicago, the most important art institute of the West, taking rank with the Boston Art Museum and the Metropolitan Museum, of New York. It was founded in 1879 as the result of Mr. French's efforts, and he has been its only Director. It includes a museum of art and a school of art, occupying a fine building on the Lake front.

The museum includes extensive collections of paintings and sculpture and decorative objects, while the school offers instruction in drawing, painting, sculpture, decorative drawing and architecture, and last year had eighteen hundred and three students and sixty-five instructors.

Mr. French is curator of the collection and principal of the school. He is a lecturer of the University Extension courses of the University of Chicago, and has been known as a popular lecturer for twenty years. He was born at Exeter, N. H., and educated at Phillips' Academy and Harvard College, graduating in 1864. In 1867 he removed to Chicago, where he has been ever since, except for trips to Europe or the East. Until 1875 Mr. French was engaged in the practice of civil engineering and landscape gardening.

As a lecturer his success has been phenomenal. The peculiar and attractive feature of Mr. French's lectures is their

109

abundant illustration by large extemporaneous sketches, drawn on paper before the audience, in color and crayon. Among the subjects of his lectures are the following: " The Wit and Wisdom of the Crayon," "An Hour With the Caricaturists," " Conventional Art in Pictures and Decoration," "A Knack of Drawing, Natural or Acquired;" " The Value of a Line " and " The Innocency of Vision."

Possibly " The Wit and Wisdom of the Crayon " is as popular as any of Mr. French's lectures, and may be taken as an example of his method. It treats of the analogies between literature and art with such readiness of address, such swiftness and profusion of illustration, that even every child listens, watches and understands. In it he draws thirty or forty pictures, including faces, figures, animals, landscapes, etc. He has lectured in almost every city, large and small, from New York to Kansas City; before Chautauqua, Lakeside, Round Lake, and other assemblies; at Cornell University, New York, and always holds his audiences so delighted and interested in what he says and does that they are reluctant to have him close. Wherever he has been, the press notices have been most flattering, giving him, without question, the foremost place as an art-lecturer. His quick wit, fascinating manner of presenting and elaborating propositions and his marvelous use of the crayon unite to make him one of the most instructive and entertaining lecturers of the day. Mr. French belongs to a well-known family. He is a brother of Daniel C. French, whose " Minute Man," at Concord; group of " Death and the Sculptor " and " Colossal Statue of the Republic " at the Columbian Exposition, are widely known.

Mrs. Warren Springer.

Marguerite Warran Springer.

ff

No w n...
has attempted
has Mrs. W...
dalas and w
not widely !

Art as R
—that is her
that doctrine
expressing h
the eloquen
her readers
prowess. ...
ark Ohio,
the North
proudest fa
pason, a gr
Set six in
Cincinnati,
an Indian.

Mrs.
a girl beg
She is on
Daughter

Mrs. Warren Springer.

No woman of her age in Chicago, probably in America, has attempted and achieved so much along so many lines as has Mrs. Warren Springer, whose work in literary and art circles, and whose championship of the new industrialism are most widely known.

Art as Ruskin thought it out, work as Carlyle preached it—that is her doctrine. Someone has said—"Mrs. Springer *is* that doctrine." A lecturer of note, a most versatile writer, expressing herself with the strength of conviction, yet with the elegance of culture, she impresses her audience and wins her readers to admiration of her ability and belief in her utterances. Mrs. Springer was born, March 27, 1871, in Newark, Ohio. Her father, John V. Maginnis, was a native of the North of Ireland, a descendant of one of the oldest and proudest families of Ireland. Her mother was Mary F. Ferguson, a great-granddaughter of Major Ferguson, one of the first six in Pennsylvania to sign the membership roll in the Cincinnatus, of which he was a promoter. He was killed by an Indian, near Fort Recovery, Ohio, in 1791.

Mrs. Springer was educated in a convent, and when but a girl began to be interested in the great problems of the day. She is one of the board of managers of the National Society, Daughters of the Revolution, as well as State Regent of the

Illinois Society, and is identified with general club work. Her keenest interest, however, centers in industrial reform, and for its success, as editor of *The New Industrialism,* and in other ways, she has been, and is, most actively engaged.

Dr. Oscar L. Triggs, of the University of Chicago, has dedicated his book, " Chapters in the History of the Arts and Crafts Movement," to her, on account of her devotion to the cause. She holds membership in the Chicago Press League, and is one of the active organizers of the " Fields and Work-shops Society," which is international in its scope, and has on its membership lists the strongest minds in the country.

Mrs. Springer is one of the most beautiful of women, as has been written—" with the sort of beauty of which Ruskin dreamed when he thought of the queen in the queen's gar-den;" yet no air of self-consciousness reminds one that she values her beauty. She has a fair, youthful, patrician coun-tenance, large violet eyes and hair of silvery white. Her sweetness of expression and charm of manner win for her the admiration of those who meet her, the love of those who know her. Exceedingly original in her thought, it is a delight to hear her speak either from the platform or in private life, for she always has something to say well worth saying. While the most gracious courtesy is ever present, she has no hesi-tancy in voicing her most positive convictions.

With charming presence and pleasant voice, she is a most fascinating lecturer, and her audiences realize from the time she begins to speak the treat in store for them. While so deep-ly interested in questions which are claiming the most seri-ous attention of the *savants* of the day, Mrs. Springer is an intensely womanly woman. Her dainty satire and keen wit

give zest to her most ordinary conversation, but she is interested in the beautiful, rare and the unique, and covets its possession. Her dining-room is the most artistic in Chicago, and
teems with riches in ancestral pewter, priceless china, matchless homespun linen and antique copper and silver vessels, the
accumulation of centuries. There are few women so well
versed in all things antique as Mrs. Springer, and it is an education to listen to her as she talks of colonial times and customs, while her own fancies lend a charm to history.

"I like to think," she said, "that those dear old grand-
mothers of ours wove their own integrity into these linen
cloths. They have the sterling endurance of those pioneer
women." Among her treasures is an old-fashioned cabinet,
crowded with willowware, with ancient blue dishes, etc., all
heirlooms from her great-grandmother. Three pieces of early
Delft, for which she paid fifteen hundred dollars, are con-
tained in this wonderful collection. A mahogany table, with
a century or two of years its dower, and a collection of all sorts
of rare curios, are Mrs. Springer's delight. Possibly her most
valued possession is an immense four-posted bed, on which
George Washington slept, and to reach which she climbs steps
placed by the side of the bed. Revering the antique, her
thoughts constantly recur to the great questions of life, and
to their elucidation she is devoting herself. Proud of her ancestry, her greater pride is in the possibilities of the present
and their achievement, and she has written and spoken with
so much wisdom that one can hardly realize that such utterances are those of a woman still in her youth.

She is recognized as a generous antagonist, firm in her
own convictions, yet believing in absolute freedom of thought.

and her merry laugh is often heard to the discomf
opponents and the delectation of her adherents.

The history of her short life is replete with i
when the records of what this century has wrou
manity are gathered up, no name will be more hc
that of Mrs. Warren Springer.

Mrs. James R. McKay.

Elizabeth Mears McKay.

Mrs. James R. McKay.

One of the most delightful studios in Chicago, with its many artists and many studios, is that where Mrs. James R. McKay works, quietly bringing out of shapeless clay forms instinct with beauty—we had almost said life.

Mrs. McKay is the daughter of Nathan Mears, of Massachusetts, who came to Chicago in 1850. She graduated from St. Mary's School, in Burlington, N. J., and finished her school training at Mrs. McAuley's, in New York City. She was married June 19, 1867, and has five children—Mrs. McKay LeRoy, Mrs. Albert W. Goodrich, Mr. James M. MacKay, Robert M. MacKay and Nathan M. MacKay. She has always been deeply interested in all forms of art and in the study of languages. Having spent much time abroad, she has had fine opportunity to study the best in the realms of art and to perfect herself in the study of languages.

She has devoted some attention to painting, having studied with Laurence Earle, Miss Ella White, of Pasadena, Cal., and others. Modeling, however, appealed to her most strongly, and in it she has achieved her greatest success. She has studied this line of art with Leopold Bracony and August Rodin, of Paris. Her work impresses one at once as most artistic and conscientious. In her studio are plaques bearing the faces of her father and mother, busts of her h s an , two of her sons and her daughter, Mrs. McKay Le Roy, whose recognized beauty she has most exquisitely reproduced.

Her work, while stamped with the individuality of the subject, has a daintiness of finish and a grace of pose which bespeak the artist.

Statuettes—a French maid, another of a Carlsbad milkmaid, and a third of a golfer—are all wonderfully well done, and evince the versatility of talent which produced them, the characteristics of each being carefully preserved and every detail made effective.

Among other work one easily recognizes Mrs. Peter Dunne, and the pose in a small head of John Drew is marvelously lifelike.

Mrs. McKay does not, however, confine herself to work in the studio, much as she enjoys it. She is the President of the Reception Committee of the Cercle de l'Alliance Française, and gave the first entertainment for the Salon Française.

She is also Hon. Vice-President of the Dante Alighieri Society, and very few scrap-books of an American woman in private life contain as many cards and letters of illustrious foreigners as do Mrs. McKay's. While receiving honors from those who represent other nations, Mrs. McKay is proud of her American ancestry, and is a member of the Daughters of the American Revolution.

Such women as Mrs. McKay are an inspiration to the best womanhood of any land. Crowned with silvery hair, with queenly presence and gentle grace, she lives her artist life in her studio, yet home and society are enriched by the results of her rare experience and study.

Ferdinand W. Peck.

Ferdinand W. Peck

Ferdinand W. Peck.

No one man in the city of Chicago has done more for the advancement of music, art and literature than has Ferdinand W. Peck. While he has always contributed liberally of money, time and energy to works of benevolence and public interest, the advancement of music and art has also been pronounced in his lifework. He conceived and carried to a successful conclusion the Chicago Opera Festival, which gave for the first time in Chicago the presentation of grand opera fully and elaborately at popular prices. Out of this success came the thought which, realized, produced the Auditorium. This building was designed and constructed under Mr. Peck's personal supervision, and he alone financed the colossal undertaking.

For twelve years he was its President, till the pressure of other public and private affairs induced his retirement. He was one of the founders of the Illinois Humane Society, and for many years its President, and he introduced in Chicago the horse ambulance. He has served as Vice-President of the Board of Education, and as President of the Union League Club. He was one of the founders and, for several years, the President of the Chicago Athenæum, which has steadily grown, and now holds a prominent place in educational work. He was exceedingly active in the efforts early put forth to secure for Chicago the World's Columbian Exposition, and was appointed as a member of the commission sent by the United States Government to Europe in behalf of the Exposition. He was First Vice-President of the Corporation, Chairman of the Finance Committee, and a member of the Board of Reference and Control. He was prime mover in the erection of the Confederate monument at Oakwoods Cemetery, which did so much toward bringing about a fraternal feeling between the North and the South.

In 1898, he was appointed by President McKinley U. S. Commissioner to the Paris Exposition of 1900. To this work he brought the valuable experience acquired during his various connections with the Columbian Exposition. There is no doubt but that to the organization under his control and personal supervision is due the marked success which attended the participation of the United States in this great exhibit. Mr. Peck has, in connection with these large undertakings, been associated with many movements which have stood for the advancement of his native city and the amelioration of its needy ones. He is a man of wide sympathies, and no deserving object appeals to him in vain. A busy man, grappling ever with most practical problems, he is known as a patron of art and a lover of music. He has never sought for, neither will he accept, a public position for emolument. The public good and the advancement of those objects which speak for the higher things in life have been the motives prompting his every effort.

Mrs. H. O. Stone.

Mrs. H. O. Stone

Mrs. H. O. Stone.

In every community there are women, as well as men, whose names we come to recognize as identical with uplifting effort and fresh aspiration in the realms of art, literature, music and science.

Often they do not covet such heraldry, yet so ever-present and so potent is their support and patronage that, without it, failure and dismay would overtake those who are most active in the organizing of such enterprises.

History, in this age, centers more than ever about individual lives, and is now, as always, a mosaic of people and events, in which, however, the latter seem often the subservient. Into this sort of history, women, the leaders in society, the most charming mothers and wives in our homes, are being woven more and more conspicuously. This is not by accident, but is because of their persistent influence for the great advancement of all pertaining to art, literature and science, and the happy results they have achieved. Quite fitting, it seems, that to such women should be accorded a sort of leadership in establishing a demand for the best which the world of music and art can offer, and wonderfully have they risen to the requirements of a position which is, perhaps, more often admitted than expressed.

Among such women in the city of Chicago, it is a pleas-

127

ure to recognize the right of Mrs. H. O. Stone to a place in the foremost rank.

Mrs. Stone was formerly Miss Elizabeth Yager, of Clifton Springs, New York, but ever since her marriage to Mr. H. O. Stone she has made Chicago her home, identifying herself with its interests and progress. She is a most devoted lover of music, and has not been contented with being able to gratify her own taste in this direction in her beautiful home, but has been specially interested in having the best artists come to Chicago with their best work.

To this end she has been a generous supporter of everything which reached the highest standard of musical excellence, and has lent the charm of her cultured presence for years to all the finest operas and choicest concerts. Not only is she a lover and a patron of music, but all forms of art appeal to her most strongly. She has surrounded herself with art treasures from every land, with curios rare and exquisite, with lovely and dainty souvenirs of her travels. She has also in her home works of great masters, which are silently eloquent as to her taste and her knowledge of what is most to be desired in the realms of the artistic and the beautiful.

Mrs. Stone may not, perhaps, recognize the extent of her influence in music and art circles, but it is potent in many a studio, recognized in many a concert room in this city, destined to become an art center.

Charles Chauncey Curtiss.

Faithfully Yours

Charles Chauncey Curtiss.

Charles Chauncey Curtiss was born in Chicago, July 31, 1847. His father, Hon. James Curtiss, was a lawyer, much engaged in public affairs and twice Mayor of that city. In 1854, he purchased three thousand acres near Champaign, Ill. This became a model country estate, and was visited by many distinguished men from abroad. It was here that Charles Chauncey Curtiss spent his childhood, receiving impressions which have influenced his life. The death of his father, in 1859, with financial affairs so involved as to necessitate the selling of the farm, brought the boy face to face with life's realities. He moved, with his mother, into Champaign, and attended the public school for two years, when he was obliged to begin work. He obtained a place as messenger in the local telegraph office, receiving twelve dollars a month. Studying at home, he cultivated a literary taste and gained general knowledge. Presently he secured a clerkship in a dry-goods store. When the Civil War broke out, he was anxious to enlist, but his youth prevented until, in 1864, when less than seventeen years of age, he enlisted in Company B, 135th Illinois Infantry, organized for one hundred days' service. Afterwards he obtained a clerkship in the Ordnance Department, at Nashville. In April, 1866, he returned to Chicago, was employed in a dry-goods store, and later secured a position as bookkeeper with Lyon & Healy.

After the Chicago fire, in 1871, he founded a music publishing house (Chandler & Curtiss), and soon was elected the first secretary of the Apollo Musical Club, of Chicago, of which he was one of the organizers. Ill health, in 1881, compelled his retirement from business. In October, 1881, he organized the firm of Curtiss & Mayer, managers of the Weber piano business in Chicago, for whom was built " The Weber Music Hall Building," the first exclusively art and studio building in the city, from the success of which grew the plan of the Fine Arts Building. Meantime the firm of Curtiss & Mayer was, in 1890, dissolved, and Mr. Curtiss organized the Manufacturers' Piano Company, of which he was President until 1895, when, for three years, he devoted his splendid energies and abilities to perfecting this scheme until the great Fine Arts Building was completed. This wonderful edifice created a new art center. It is the *magnum opus* of its founder, whose devotion to art is thus crowned in a brilliant manner.

In private life Mr. Curtiss is a valued citizen and cherished friend. Four visits to Europe have broadened and quickened a mind alive to the best in art and literature. A domestic rather than a club man, he is still a member of the Loyal Legion, Chicago Literary Club, Chicago Historical Association, American Historical Association, American Archæological Association, " The Players," of New York, and the Glen View and Edgewater Golf Clubs. Everywhere he has secured the respect and esteem of associates.

Mrs. Charles H. Deere.

MRS. CHARLES H. DEERE.

Mrs. Charles H. Deere.

In a lovely home in Moline, Ill., with the pleasantly suggestive name " Overlook," is a cultured, home-loving woman, whose influence is felt in that city for all that means achievement of the beautiful and good.

In Newbury, Vermont, August 9, 1841, Mary Little Dickinson was born. Her parents were Gideon Dana and Judith Tappan (Atkinson) Dickinson. She was very early taken to Boston, Mass., which was her home till her eleventh year, when she moved to Chicago, where she resided till her marriage. There is no question but that in early childhood the most indelible impressions of life are made. No doubt those years in the New England center of culture had a potent influence upon the tastes and character of the child, whose later life has revealed her aspirations for the best in the realms of music, art and all forms of beneficence as well.

Her school life was spent in Chicago, where she received the best educational advantages the city afforded, and was a member of the first class graduated from the Dearborn Seminary, of that city. After leaving school she devoted much attention to the study of music under the tuition of Paul Becker, who, at that time, was considered the finest teacher of music in Chicago. Later she married Charles H. Deere, one of the most prominent manufacturers of Moline, Ill., and moved to that city, where she still resides.

135

the best work done by them, and is a member of the Fortnightly.

Her ancestry was represented in the war of the American Revolution, a fact in which she has a natural pride. As a result, she is interested in the perpetuation, through their descendants, of the memory of those heroes of the long ago. For the past eight years she has been Regent of the Moline Chapter of the Daughters of the American Revolution, and State Regent since February, 1901.

Mrs. Deere is interested in all the social enterprises of Moline, and is conscientious in the discharge of the duties devolving upon her in her church relations. She is very fond of travel, and has greatly enjoyed the unusual opportunities she has had for making wide observation and research in many lands. She has been abroad three times, and to her beautiful home has brought many rare and exquisite souvenirs of her extensive travels. A modest and retiring woman, feeling that her home is her kingdom, she is a great favorite in social circles, and, if she could be persuaded to accept them, would be given many official honors in the various societies of the city where she lives.

As it is, her influence is felt in all enterprises—art, educational, social or charitable—and her quiet endorsement is a recognition most highly valued.

Edward Jarvis Parker.

Edward Jarvis Parker.

Almost identical with the progress of the best enterprises of Quincy, Ill., is the name of Edward Jarvis Parker. Endowed with financial genius, rare executive ability and absolute integrity, his counsel, opinions, as well as his services, have been valuable in affairs of magnitude and importance. It is impossible even to name all the organizations with which he has been associated in any brief sketch of his life. He has had extensive affiliation with large banking concerns; with the City Bank of Hartford, Conn.; in 1863 with L. & C. H. Bull's Bank in Quincy, Ill., and later with the following banks in the same city:

In 1865 he was Director and ex-Assistant Cashier of the Merchants' and Farmers' National Bank; 1873-1878 connected with the bank of E. J. Parker & Co., which, in 1878, was consolidated with L. & C. H. Bull; in 1892 Director and Cashier of State Savings, Loan & Trust Co.; and 1903 Director, Cashier and Secretary of the same corporation. In connection with the banking business, he was, for many years, a director and the Treasurer of the Quincy Paper Co., afterwards absorbed by the American Straw Board Co.; Treasurer for years of the Quincy, Omaha and Kansas City Railway Co.; Chairman of the Committee on Public Improvements of the Board of Commerce. He has been President

rying Co., and the Quincy Gas Light and Coke Co.

Mr Parker is the Vice-President of the Chamber of Commerce, on the advisory board of the National Business League of Chicago, a member of the Chicago Club. He was Vice-President for Illinois at the second session of the Indianapolis Monetary Conference, and has done work in connection with the State Bankers' Association of Illinois and the American Bankers' Association. But not alone to the world of finance has Mr. Parker devoted his energies. Religious and philanthropic enterprises have greatly interested him. He has held several ecclesiastical positions, and assisted in the division of the Episcopal Church in Illinois. Since its incorporation, he has been the Treasurer of Blessing Hospital, and is Trustee and Treasurer of the Lindsay Church Home. For many years he has been the Senior Warden in the Church of the Good Shepherd, Quincy, and Director and Treasurer of the Woodland Cemetery Association.

In 1888 he married Miss Elizabeth Goodwin Bull, a native of Quincy, and their home is a delightful center of culture and generous hospitality. Mr. Parker's widespread influence is always for the upholding of the right, and he is beloved and respected by the community which has given him such prominence and bestowed upon him so many proofs of its confidence.

Mrs. Hugh Taylor Birch.

Marie Root Birch

Mrs. Hugh Taylor Birch.

The great influence wielded by Mrs. Hugh Taylor Birch upon the highest musical life in Chicago is well known. For years her home has been the center of notable musical events. None have exceeded her in generosity or fine judgment in presenting great artists and their work. Her superb music-room has also always been open to rising young artists who wished a hearing before the best audience that wealth and fine social position could command. Carreno, Harold Bauer, Marteau, Bendix and his string quartette, are among those who have charmed society in these ideal surroundings.

Frequently, with exquisite taste, she has arranged these programs with such skill as to call forth the approbation of Theodore Thomas and other experts in this difficult task. Her personal contributions to the entertainments of the Amateur Club have been in fine taste and of importance in creating the high standard of that club.

Herself devoted to piano music, Mrs. Birch has gathered about her the great pianists, violinists and 'cellists with whom she has played for years, keeping in touch with all the finest music.

Mrs. Birch was born in Buffalo, N. Y., her maiden name being Maria Root. There she was educated until 1875, when she went to Europe to pursue her study of music. In Berlin

143

she had the rare advantage of private lessons from Theodore Kullak, who was then at the head of his famous conservatorium, in that city.   During her residence in Paris and her visits to Bayreuth, London, Vienna and other cities, it was her good fortune to meet and hear the world's great artists in their own homes, where, restraints being thrown aside, days and hours never to be forgotten were perhaps the inspiration as well as compensation of her efforts to develop music as an art in Chicago.

The close friendship it has been Mrs. Birch's privilege to enjoy with Mr. and Mrs. Theodore Thomas has been fraught with most gratifying experiences, both in Mr. Thomas' summer home, in the White Mountains, and in Chicago.   No greater proof of Mrs. Birch's impress upon musical life could be given her than the voluntary dedication to her by Theodore Thomas of his orchestral arrangement of " Rheingold."   It reads, "Fragments from Wagner's 'Rheingold,' arranged for the Chicago Orchestra by Theodore Thomas for the special delectation of Mrs. Hugh T. Birch.   Felsengerten, 1901."   This is indeed a compliment the finest musician in the land might covet, and is a distinction enjoyed and appreciated by Mrs. Birch.

Mrs. Birch has two children, a daughter and son.   The daughter, Miss Helen Birch, has already shown such wonderful talent for composition that some of Chicago's best musicians predict for her a future as one of the great woman composers of the age.   Though but a young girl, her songs, which belong to the distinctly modern school, are impressive and artistic to a marvelous degree.

Jessica Haskell Fuller.

Jessica Gaskell Fuller

Jessica Haskell Fuller.

Unsurpassed in method, style and musical gifts, by instinct classic in her tastes, Mrs. Jessica Haskell Fuller's wonderful achievements place her in the front rank of Chicago's artists. Miss Haskell was born in Toledo, Ohio, but came to Chicago when quite young, and became identified with its best musical effort. Her first public recognition was won in Verdi's opera, "Il Trovatore," when she sang the role of Leonora with great success. For three years she was the leading soloist of the Beethoven Society, which, under the leadership of Carl Wolfsohn (one of the most poetic and masterly interpreters of Beethoven) presented the best classic music, and elevated the tone of musical study in Chicago, and was the inspiration of a reverence for the great masters. Miss Haskell next became a pupil, in Paris, of Mad. Pauline Viardot Garcia, renowned for her unfolding of great roles, particularly those of Mozart. She was the teacher of Mme. Pauline Lucca, whose never-to-be-forgotten role of Marguerite made her famous. In teaching Miss Haskell the same part, she called her the "American Lucca," so closely did their talents and personal appearance resemble each other. With Viardat this gifted young singer gained that purety of method and highly finished interpretation which at once placed her among the first American artists. A remarkable example of her perfectly accurate musical ear was her singing from memory and without accompaniment that long and difficult coloratura aria, " Bel Raggio," from " Semiramide," ending this wonderful musical feat absolutely upon the key. Theodore Thomas, for whom Mrs. Fuller was singing, pronounced this " the greatest proof of musical ability and perfect intonation." Her exquisite and musicianly renderings of Beethoven's "Ah Perfidio," Handel's " I Know That My Redeemer Liveth " and " Oh, for the Wings of a Dove," Schumann's " Woman's Love and Life," Schubert's " Erl-King," Listz's " Lorelie," and countless other works in her tremendous repertoire, have won for her the highest praise. Rémenyi was enchanted with her beautiful voice and art, and used every effort to secure her for his famous concerts. During Mrs. Fuller's residence abroad, she studied Italian singing with Luigi Vanuccini, in Florence, oratorio with Shakspeare, in London, and the Wagner roles, in Dresden. In 1876, Miss Haskell married Mr. Edward M. Fuller, of Madison, Wis., where she now resides. Professors from the university, artists of international reputation, and life-long friends enjoy the gracious hospitality of her beautiful home. Her art, which has improved with the years, is now a charming accomplishment which her family and friends associate —and ever will—with her fine music room, and the gorgeous sunsets and moonlight over the forests and lakes and all nature about her delightful home, which Verdi and Wagner called the " Divine Teacher " of music.

Looking out on the loveliness about her, well may she say,

"In woods aglow with warm sunlight,
From them I learned my singing."

rs. Greenberry L. Fort.

Clara B. Fort,

Mrs. Greenberry L. Fort.

In one of the newer States of a new country, it is a distinction worthy of note for one to be still living, after a lapse of years, in the house where one was born, reared and married. Such a distinction belongs to Mrs. Greenberry L. Fort, of Lacon, Ill., who, while a woman of extensive travel, and for some years a resident of Washington, D. C., has known but one home, and that in the city and house where she was born.

Miss Clara Boal was the daughter of Dr. Robert Boal, one of the earlier settlers of Lacon, Ill., her native city. He was eminent in his profession, beloved, as well as respected, in the community where he lived, recognized as a man of remarkable force of character and a well-balanced judgment. His life was one of sterling worth, his loyalty to his country unswerving, his integrity unquestioned. He was one of the founders of the Republican party, and was most vitally interested in important State and national problems. Miss Boal was married in Lacon, to Greenberry L. Fort, and both her husband and father were actively engaged in State politics. Her son, Col. Robert L. Fort, seems to have followed in the footsteps of both father and grandfather, as he is now (1903) a member of the State Legislature.

For years Mr. Greenberry L. Fort was a member of the Congress of the United States, and with him Mrs. Fort enjoyed official life in Washington, D. C. In addition to her delightful experiences there, Mrs. Fort has had the advantage of frequent trips abroad, and these united influences have, no doubt, done much to develop in her that *savoir-vivre* and cosmopolitan ease which are among her most marked characteristics. Mrs. Fort is in many ways a remarkable woman. Keenly and intelligently interested in the questions which have so absorbed the lives of father, husband and son, she is fond of all music and art, and aids their advancement as far as possible by her influence. She has a charming presence, and preserves a figure noticed and remembered for its symmetry and grace. She is as agile and lithe in all her movements as a young girl, erect and dignified in her carriage.

She is of a frank nature, and appreciative of every courtesy and kindness. In no place is she happier than in the home endeared to her by many associations, and she feels a pardonable pride in the results achieved by those dearest to her. While her position has given her marked prestige, she is free from arrogance, affable in her manners, thoroughly companionable at all times and in all places.

George Cathcart Bronson.

George Cathcart Bronson.

Descended from peculiarly musical ancestry, it is hardly strange that George Cathcart Bronson should have inherited the varied talents which have gained for him a wide reputation as singer, musical composer and writer, as well as promoter, of the best musical enterprises. His father, James Cathcart Bronson, organized and directed the first brass band in Indiana, in 1847. This band consisted very largely of musically inclined relatives, eight of them being brothers. They used to come to the village of Chicago to give concerts, and the " ra-ta-ta " of the, then, wonderful band was most enthusiastically welcomed there. In 1849, they crossed the Continent, and for a long time retained their organization in the mining-camp of Placerville, Cal. This was the first band that ever crossed the Continent, and marked the introduction of concerted music in California. While there Mr. Bronson married Miss H. M. Pennington, a Philadelphia singer of note, who had made the long and tedious trip around the " Horn " to see the " wonderful gold fields " and the land of sunshine and flowers.

Their son, George Cathcart Bronson, was born in Placerville, Cal., in 1869. The family moved later to San Francisco, where the boy began his musical studies with his father. His progress was such that before many years he had sung all over

the West with various concert organizations, and in 1889 went
to Berlin, Germany, where he was graduated in musical history, harmony and voice. After most successful operatic engagements abroad, he came to Chicago, and ever since that
time has been engaged in promoting musical interests there.

He organized the Chicago School of Opera, and was
elected its President. The Cable Company appointed him its
assistant manager and director of all their educational concerts, which have been exceedingly popular. While abroad,
he met Miss Maude Wellings, a gifted and brilliant singer
from Lansing, Mich., and since his return to Chicago she has
become his wife. Mr. Bronson has published quite a number
of books which have received most flattering endorsement
from the press and public. Among his books there are " Letters from Musicians," "Ab Inter," " Soul Immortal " and
" Thou Shalt Waken," the latter invading the field of psychology. His poem, " Music," or, as he has sometimes styled
it, " From Sound to Soul," is a rare gem, worthy of a wider
reading than it has hitherto obtained. Through his kindness,
it furnishes the introduction to the article on the " History of
Music in Illinois," in this volume. As a musical composer,
he is known by many songs and operettas, the latter having
been used mostly at private musicales. Mr. Bronson is a man
enthusiastic in his profession, of real poetic instinct and practically interested in the encouragement of the loftiest musical
ideals. His influence for musical progress is universally conceded to be as intelligent and uplifting as it is potent.

Ellen Crosby

Mrs. William Spencer Crosby.

Genius is a term which can rarely be truthfully employed. A century, as it passes, holds but few who merit that designation. Talent is everywhere, and may be cultivated, but that subtle, intangible gift we call genius is Heaven's rarest boon, and nothing less than Heaven can bestow it. Of no one is this distinction more true than of Mrs. Ellen Crosby, the well-known and marvelous interpreter of Wagner. The press abroad and in America has exhausted itself in trying adequately to describe her work.

Royalty has welcomed her again and again, fascinated by her presentations of what before seemed only mystery. Society in New York, Chicago and other large cities has deemed it a privilege to add to the laurels already won by this gifted American woman; the savants of Boston have sat at her feet enchanted, and everywhere she has had the homage of artist, music-lover and culture. And yet, it has left undisturbed the serenity of this home-loving woman; she moves among it all, appreciative, modest still—a genius.

Ellen Conkey was born near Syracuse, in Onondaga Valley, New York. She has no memory of a time when she could not play the piano. When about eight years old she had three terms of lessons, two with E. C. Phelps, one with John Becker, and this comprises the tuition received by one of the greatest pianists in the world.

159

Coming to Chicago when only a girl in her early teens, she played for nearly three years the masses in St. Mary's Cathedral. Mozart, Haydn and all the great masters were thus familiarized to her, and once a month she played the service with an orchestra with the most remarkable choir in the city. Who can tell but that then, in that girlish heart, throbbing with delight as the grand strains rose at her touch, there was the dawning of the wonderful inspiration which has made her famous. From the first day that Prof. Swing preached in Music Hall she played the great organ there, adding to the dignity and influence of those services which have become historic.

At one time, wishing the advantage of studying the two Bach Fugues, she took nine organ lessons from Clarence Eddy. She has played accompaniments for the greatest artists in the world, herself their peer.

But it is as the interpreter of Wagner that Mrs. Crosby has shown the wonderful genius which is her birthright. At every appearance, she has met with the most favorable press notices and opinions from the world's recognized critics. The press notices represent such papers as the *Boston Evening Transcript,* the *New York Mail and Express,* and the *Elite,* and various Chicago papers. From the other side of the water, the *London Times, London Court Circular,* and many papers of Paris, and other Continental cities.

Mrs. Crosby has met the great Wagner conductor, Hans Richter, and received his endorsement of her work. She was the guests of Mme. Wagner, at Baireuth, where Siegfried Wagner was most gracious in his encouragement.

Herself a worshipper of Wagner, she brings to her work

of interpretation not only intelligence but a real love for every theme which reveals itself in voice and touch. From the first to the last word spoken by this distinguished woman, she holds her audience entranced, and, giving the key-note of Wagner's wondrous aim, mysticism vanishes, and a great humanity is revealed in works which may have seemed incomprehensible. Mrs. Crosby, while she plays Wagner, talks Wagner, and her recitation simply gives words to the master's chords. Mrs. Crosby plays and talks entirely without notes. A most remarkable example of her phenomenal memory, showing as well something of her repertoire, occurred at the home of Mrs. Daniel Lord Lawrence, N. Y. Musical and fashionable New York had gone wild with enthusiasm over the Wagnerian recitals given by Mrs. Crosby. Mrs. Lord had before opened her magnificent music-room to Mrs. Crosby, but she determined to give a musical treat to a very few of New York's most musical people, among them Havemeyer.

Her music-room is one of the most beautiful in America, hung with priceless tapestries, lit by curious lanterns, with every environment which exquisite taste can suggest. The windows look out, beyond the lovely grounds which surround this palatial home, upon the salted meadows which stretch to the sea. As Mrs. Crosby said—" When I played, nothing between me and the old world." It was late in the summer's day, and the birds were singing their evening hymn. " What music-drama shall I give?" Mrs. Crosby had asked. " May the little audience select whether it shall be ' Rheingold,' ' Siegfried,' ' Tristam,' ' Walküre,' ' Götterdämerung ' or ' Parsifal?' " and Mrs. Crosby assented. Few artists would be willing thus to meet an audience without one moment's prepa-

reply. Not one of that little circle will ever forget that ho
when this charming artist, with her magnetic presence, s
before them and opened to them a new world of poetry and
music.

Mrs. Crosby possesses great personal charm and ma
netism; a light, quick, but forceful, touch, a voice dramat
but so musical that the effect is often almost that of singing.

Her daughter, Grace Runyon, now Mrs. J. W. Wass
is one o the most gifted composers of the day. Her son
are being sung by the greatest artists, while her instrument
compositions are being orchestrated and played by the b
orchestras of the world. Competent critics, among who
may be mentioned Bernard Ziehn, prophesy that she will
one of the greatest women composers in America, if not
the world.

George Stephens.

GEORGE STEPHENS.

George Stephens.

Among men distinguished in the business world, no one has enjoyed a more enviable reputation than George Stephens, late of Moline, Ill.

George Washington Stephens was born in Westmoreland County, Pa., February 22, 1819, and was so christened from the fact that his birthday was the same as that of the "Father of his Country," but he early dropped the use of the name. He was the great-grandson of Capt. Alexander Stephens, a follower of Prince Charles Edward, who fled from Wales to America in 1746, served under George Washington, and, for gallant service, was awarded a large tract of land in Westmoreland County, Pa., which has been in the possession of the Stephens family ever since. His father, Randall Stephens, served in the war of 1812; his mother was Martha Boggs, of English parentage. Mr. Stephens' education was limited to that received in the private schools near his home, but he was a great reader, and investigated the latest scientific theories as they were advanced. Thus he received a broad view of the practical world. Mr. Stephens came West in 1841, without a dollar, having, with characteristic generosity, given his share of his father's estate to a brother, who was married and whose needs were greater than his own.

As he left his home to seek a fortune in the West, he stood

on the mountain, and, looking back, pledged himself never to return until he had earned a thousand dollars. He returned before many years, and often related this incident in his life as an illustration of what a man of determination could do.

It was not, however, until 1843 that he came to Moline, Ill., then in the beginning of things, now called "The Lowell of the West." Several enterprises engaged his attention, but it was in 1870 that the Moline Plow Company, with which his name is so identified, was incorporated with a capital of $240,000, which has increased to $5,000,000. Mr. Stephens was its first Vice-President, and held the position till 1885, when he resigned and made a trip to Mexico. Later he was elected President, a position he held till his death. To his energy and ability the factory owes the success which has made it one of the largest in the world.

In 1846, Mr. Stephens was married to Mary A. Gardner, a notable woman, of remarkable character. Pre-eminently a lover of home and family, his domestic life was full of charm. To them eight children were born, of whom six survive.

Mr. Stephens was a man of most noble character. Aiming at success and achieving it, he scorned any ostentatious display of wealth, and endeared himself to the laboring class, who are quick to recognize true worth and manliness. This was touchingly shown after his death, when, among the wealth of flowers, was found an exquisite wreath, one of the pieces sent by the workingmen of the factory, inscribed "Our Friend."

For a year before his death his health had begun to fail, and on July 12, 1892, he entered into rest.

Mrs. George Stephens.

MRS. GEORGE STEPHENS.

Mrs. George Stephens.

A woman of distinguished ancestry, noble character and tender heart, Mrs. George Stephens was a worthy companion for the man whose name is so deeply engraved on the history of Moline, Ill.

Mary A. Gardner was born near Utica, N. Y., March 14, 1830, daughter of Ebenezer and Mary Wilkinson Gardner, her mother being a member of the Wilkinson family, the founders of Providence, R. I. She was also a descendant of Stephen Hopkins, the signer of the Declaration of Independence, and of Ezek Hopkins, the founder of the American Navy. Her ancestry is given in " Browning's Americans of Royal Descent." The family came West when she was a young girl, and settled in Rock Island County, Ill., but very soon removed to California.

When not quite seventeen years of age she was married, November 4, 1846, to George Stephens, then a competent, industrious young millwright, in the beginning of his wonderful career. Possibly this experience made them both so full of sympathy for those who were toiling day after day, and gave them the rare tact to endear themselves to those who had been less fortunate than they in the amassing of wealth.

Mrs. Stephens was known as an ideal wife and mother, giving to each member of her large family all the helpful coun-

sel and loving care which they needed. But her generous
nature could not be satisfied with simply meeting the demands
of those in the home circle. Throughout the community she
was recognized as an angel of mercy to those in need, those
in sorrow or suffering from any cause. She was a woman of
most sterling character, of a religious nature, yet with the
broadest and most tolerant views, and endeavored to imbue
the minds of her children with the loftiest ideals and the highest ambitions. From their earliest childhood she urged them
not to make money the standard of judgment, or to give to
its possession undue value, but, rather, to use it as a means
of self-education and benefaction to those about them.

Her sweet face and sunny smile, her rare judgment and
sincere sympathy, made her most beloved, the friend alike of
the rich and the poor, mourned universally when, February 4,
1888, her gentle spirit passed away. For a year and a half she
had been seriously ill, suffering greatly from heart trouble,
but she bore it all with a heroism and submission peculiarly
her own.

Although her loving presence is no longer the inspiration of the home-life, still she lives in the hearts of her children, who love her memory, in the thoughts of many to whom
she was a kind and valued friend, and in the gratitude of others who more and more, as the years pass, " rise up to call her
blessed."

The George Stephens Family.

It is a remarkable fact that in a single community are settled the entire family, the six children, of so distinguished citizens as the late Mr. and Mrs. George Stephens. These sons and daughters are, without exception, living lives which are not only creditable to themselves but an honor to the parents who are so closely identified with the progress and uplift of Moline, Ill.

A brief sketch of each life is all that is possible in the scope of such an article as the present, but these histories are such as should encourage parents to cherish the most lofty ambitions for their children, and incite children to emulate the examples of parents whose lives have been full of achievement.

George Arthur Stephens, the oldest of the family, was born, May 2, 1851, in Moline, as were they all. He was educated principally in eastern schools and academies. In earlier life his ambition was to become an artist, and under instruction, he painted quite a little, but later this ambition was relinquished, although he has always been an enthusiastic lover of art and its liberal patron. When only twenty-two, he was married to Miss Mary Frances Haynes, a girl beautiful in character and appearance, who died, leaving him with two children.´ The daughter, Gertrude, was gifted with a fine

171

voice, and became a favorite in social and musical circles. She
married John Hassock Porter, of Ottawa, Ill., at present
stockholder and manager of the Buffalo Steel Co. Mr. Stephens later married Miss Nancy Stewart, of Corine, Ill., a descendant of the North Carolina Stewarts, a woman of most
attractive personality and greatly beloved. Her hair is snowy
white, which, in contrast with her young face, gives her a most
charming appearance. Mrs. Stephens is exceedingly hospitable, and is never more happy than when entertaining her
friends. They are just completing a new and very handsome house. She belongs to many clubs, and has held offices
in them all. Not, however, contented with the distinction of
being a leader in social circles, Mrs. Stephens is most charitable, and is at present the President of the Associated Charities of Moline, a position she fills with great dignity and rare
tact. Mr. and Mrs. Stephens have one daughter, Dorothea.

After leaving school, Mr. Stephens came to Moline and
engaged with his father in work connected with the Moline
Plow Company, of which he is the President. He is interested in all that pertains to the business life of Moline, and
has holdings in various other undertakings. A man of great
nervous energy, quick to decide and act, he is also a man of
tender heart, hardly recognized at first by those who meet him.
He aided in the successful establishing of the free kindergarten school, which is now merged into the public school system.
Possibly no passion of his life is more dominant than his love
for children. The little ones recognize him as their friend,
and have abundant reason to remember his generosity. One
after another, he has been called upon to give up three beautiful boys, in whom his love and pride were centered, and in do-

ing for other children he seems to find much happiness. He
is President of the Moline Hospital, has served as Alderman,
and in all business and literary, social and benevolent circles
occupies a position second to none, while his unbounded popularity speaks for his kindly heart and generous impulses.

Mary Stephens Huntoon, the oldest daughter, is a handsome woman of distinguished appearance. She was educated at Mt. Carroll Seminary, and devoted not a little attention to the cultivation of an excellent voice. She married Mr.
George H. Huntoon, who belongs to the old New England family of that name. He is one of the officers and stockholders
of the Moline Plow Company, First Vice-President of the
Henney Buggy Co., of Freeport, Ill.; and Second Vice-President of the Mandt Wagon Co., of Stoughton, Wis. Mrs. Huntoon is a most philanthropic woman; it has been said of her
that the mantle of her sainted mother rests upon her. She is
deeply interested in the needs of the working classes, and
is most eloquent in pleading for the redress of wrongs, where-
ever they are found. She is President of the Fortnightly
Club and of the Woman's Club, which, although only a year
old, has grown wonderfully, and has achieved much good
through its various departments. Mrs. Huntoon has three
children. Grace is very musical and has studied whistling
with Bain with such success that were she thrown upon her
own resources she could easily have a successful career. Her
son George was educated chiefly at the University of Illinois,
and has devoted much time to travel, while Helen is a sweet
school girl of fourteen. George is now at home and engaged
with the Moline Plow Company.

The second daughter, *Minnie Stephens Allen,* was edu-

cated at Smith College. She belonged to the class of 1883, and
has devoted much attention to music, having studied with
some of the best teachers in America. · Her love for music is
such that she keeps herself in practice, as is too rarely the case
with American girls after they assume the duties and responsibilities of later life. Emil Liebling still directs her musical studies, and counts her one of his most advanced pupils.
She married Frank Gates Allen, son of Hon. E. R. Allen, of
Aurora, Ill. Mr. Allen was educated for a lawyer, was graduated from Ann Arbor, and enjoys the distinction of being
a Sigma Phi. He practiced law for five years of their married life, when their home was in Ottawa, Ill. He is now Vice-
President of the Moline Plow Company, President of the Moline National Bank, President of the Mandt Wagon Co., and
also of the Henney Buggy Co.

While living in Ottawa, Mrs. Allen organized its first
musical society, which is still flourishing, and of which she
was the President while living there. An enthusiast in whatever she undertakes, endowed with rare executive ability and
blessed with superb health, it is not strange that she is called
upon to fill more positions than would seem possible for one
woman to fill. Yet she has no desire to be considered simply
a club woman, but finds her greatest happiness in her beautiful home, while pride in her home, husband and love for their
only child predominate in her thought. This daughter, Mar-
jorie Stephens, is being educated at Smith College, the Alma
Mater of her mother. While Mrs. Allen's modesty has made
it difficult to obtain perhaps a complete record of her various
offices, the mention of a few will indicate her busy life. She is
Recording Secretary of the State Federation of Women's

Clubs, Corresponding Secretary of the Moline Woman's Club, was President of the Beethoven Club, of Moline, for ten years, and is at present Vice-Regent of the Moline Chapter of D. A. R. Through her efforts the Woman's Club was organized, and she is deeply interested in all philanthropic, literary and social enterprises, and has written not a little under various *noms de plume.*

Charles Randall Stephens was named for one of his grandfathers, and is a most enthusiastic and successful business man. That his ability in this direction is marked is shown by the fact that, although a comparatively young man, he is Secretary and General Superintendent of the Moline Plow Co., President of the Acme Steel Company, Vic-President of the Mandt Wagon Co., and connected with various other business ventures. His life is still before him, but with the indomitable perseverance, business instinct and general ability which he inherits from his father, it is not too much to predict for him a brilliant future as a financier and far-seeing business man. He is exceedingly fond of outdoor sports, and is quite an athlete. He married Catherine Law Bayne, of Anthony, Kan., although the family formerly lived in Illinois. They have a beautiful home and two lovely children—Mildred and George Bayne.

Mrs. Stephens is greatly beloved by all circles of people. Although not in robust health, she devotes much time to visiting among the poor, and does very much good in a gracious, gentle way. Their home is full of happiness, and that happiness they delight to share with others.

Ada Stephens Jordan was a girl in her 'teens when her mother was taken from the home where she seemed so much needed. Although'so young, she at once assumed the care of father and home, a care she never relinquished during her father's lifetime. Self-forgetful, she lived her young life for others, making the home still the place for all family re-unions, her father's companion in his travels and in his home-life, laying aside all plans for her own pleasure to minister to him. Her life has been one of those, rarely seen, of cheerful self-abnegation, of absolute unselfishness and devotion to those she loved. Deprived of the wife who had been so many years his companion and helper, Mr. Stephens was, in many ways, peculiarly dependent upon this brave, sweet life, and it was a dependence which never failed him. As a writer, she is most successful, but has never had much opportunity to do work along this line. In February, 1903, she maried Mr. Jordan, a journalist of ability, who, for a time, owned and edited one of the daily papers of Moline, and is now the principal stockholder and manager of the Moline Printing Co. They have recently returned from a winter in California, and are living in the old home.

Nellie Stephens Lippincott, the youngest of the family, was educated at the Northwestern University. She is exceedingly fond of music, and is a fine pianist, having studied with the best teachers, among whom perhaps Emil Liebling has done as much for her as any. Some six or seven years ago she married Charles Howard Lippincott, descended from the well-known Lippincott family of Philadelphia. They have two winsome little children, Mary Stephens and Gardner Pennington. While Mrs. Lippincott is prominent in social and literary circles, the demands of home occupy most largely her heart and life.

Henry Wade Rogers.

HENRY WADE ROGERS.

Few men, (
lines and in his
loved the effort
educator.

He was bor
and received all
ambitious schol
at the age of
versity of Mic
ceived that of
daughter of Jo
ton, N. Y.

Meantime
perseverence
earlier effort
profession, t
From 1882 to
of Michigan
law, profess
connected w

At this
some the Pr
ton, Ill. It

Henry Wade Rogers.

Few men, of his age, have achieved along educational lines and in his professional career such success as has followed the efforts of Henry Wade Rogers, jurist, author and educator.

He was born in Holland Patent, N. Y., October 10, 1853, and received all possible educational advantages. An earnest, ambitious scholar, he so devoted himself to study that in 1874, at the age of twenty-one, he was graduated from the University of Michigan, with the degree of A. B., and in 1877 received that of A. M. In 1876, he was married to Emma, daughter of John Ogden and Sarah Jane Winner, of Pennington, N. Y.

Meantime he was pursuing, with the same indomitable perseverence and enthusiasm which had characterized his earlier efforts, the work which should fit him for his chosen profession, the law, and was admitted to the bar in 1877. From 1882 to 1885 he was professor of law in the University of Michigan. The years 1885-1890 found him professor of law, professor of Roman law, and Dean of the Law School connected with his Alma Mater.

At this time he received a most urgent invitation to become the President of the Northwestern University, in Evanston, Ill. It was a most flattering tribute to the reputation he had made his own, and yet he was deeply interested in the work in which he had made such rapid strides. After careful consideration, he accepted the position offered, and from 1890 to 1901 he was President of the Northwestern University. While there he greatly endeared himself to the students, and his helpful influence was appreciated by the community in which he lived. His resignation, to become professor of law in Yale University, in September, 1901, was accepted with great regret, and many kind wishes followed him to his new field of labor.

During the past few years he has occupied some of the most important and prominent positions in the gatherings of representative men in his profession.

The years 1893-94 he was chairman of the American Bar Association, and in 1893 was chairman of the World's Congress on Jurisprudence and Law Reform at the World's Columbian Exposition, in Chicago. In 1898, he was the general chairman of the Saratoga Conference and the Foreign Policy of the United States. Thus he was brought in touch with the leading lights in his profession, not only of this country, but from abroad, and gained a reputation as a fine presiding officer and a man of executive ability.

The honorary degree of LL.D. was conferred upon him in 1890 by the Wesleyan University, Conn. Dr. Rogers has added to his routine work quite a little literary work, and is the author of " Expert Testimony," published in 1893, and of many articles on law and other subjects which have appeared in miscellaneous publications.

rles Wesley Leffingwell, D.D.

C. W. Leffingwell.

Charles Wesley Leffingwell, D. D.

A literary man engaged in important church and educational work, the life of Charles Wesley Leffingwell has been replete with much good accomplished. He was born December 5, 1840, his father being Lyman Leffingwell, his mother Sarah Chapman (Brown) Leffingwell. He is descended from Lieut. Thomas Leffingwell, prominent in the Norwich, Conn., Colony (1636), and a leader in the Indian wars. He was married in 1862 to Miss Elizabeth Francis, a native of England. He began early in life to give others the benefit of his literary research and the influence of his own aspirations.

From 1859-1860 he was Principal of the Galveston Academy, and Deputy-Surveyor of the city and county. In 1862 he was graduated from Knox College with the degree of B. A., and in 1875 received the degree of D. D. From 1862-65 he was Vice-President of the Military Institute of Poughkeepsie, N. Y. In 1867 he was graduated from the Washotah Seminary, and the same year was ordained deacon and priest, being assistant minister of St. James Church, Chicago.

In 1868 he founded St. Mary's School at Knoxville, Ill., and has conducted it ever since.

He became the editor and publisher of *The Living Church* in Chicago in 1879, and retained this position for

was divided, he represented it in the General Convention (1877), and has been elected a deputy from Quincy for every subsequent convention. He has been President of the standing committee of his Diocese most of the time from the beginning, and has twice been elected Bishop by the Clergy. His heart was still in the work of educational uplift for the young, and in 1890 he founded the St. Alban's school for boys in Knoxville, Ill., a school over which he is still presiding. Bringing to the work not only intellectual training, but also a consecrated life, success was assured.

Dr. Leffingwell is the Rector of St. Mary's and St. Albans' schools, and the prestige of this position is felt in the school work to which he is devoted. While school duties and those connected with his parish work absorb to a great degree time and thought, Dr. Leffingwell has still done some important work with his pen. He is a scholarly man, an able writer, and his contributions to the press are highly valued by thoughtful readers. He has completed a " Reading Book of English Classics," which has been published by Putman Sons, of New York, and " Lyrics of the Living Church," published by A. C. McClurg & Co., of Chicago. Useful days, consecrated aims, devotion to his chosen work and a deep desire for the uplifting of those about him, characterize the life of this eminently earnest man, whose influence in the community in which he lives is felt as a benediction.

Cecil Clara Harvey.

CECIL CLARA HARVEY.

Cecil Clara Harvey.

There are uncrowned-heroes in this world of ours living lives so beautiful in their unselfishness, so full of sweet deeds, yet so unobtrusive and so quiet that comparatively few know their merit. Such a life was that of Cecil Clara Harvey, who was born in Elgin, Illinois, July 12, 1845. Her father was George P. Harvey, who, with her mother, M. L. (Burr) Harvey, was a pioneer in the city of her birth.

Miss Harvey was educated in the Elgin High School, and for eighteen years was a successful teacher in the public schools of that city, for four years Principal of one of them. In 1881 she became Librarian of the Gail Borden Public Library, which position she held until her death, a period of twenty-two years. Every hour possible she spent in study, and thus became familiar with the literature of the present and the past. Always ready to place her knowledge at the disposal of others, children perplexed over school tasks and members of literary clubs availed themselves of her services. She was an honorary member of the Elgin Woman's Club, and an active member of the Every Wednesday Club, the oldest literary club of the city. More than her conscientious performance of the duties of her responsible position or her rare literary attainments, it was her unselfish life, a life of self-abnegation and devotion to others, which impressed all who knew her.

The story of her life presents no dramatic incidents or startling events. Rather it is a history of what is far better, a steady course over a narrow way, with many an obstacle to overcome, many a test of patience and endurance, yet pursued uncomplainingly to the end. For her the toil and anxiety of many a weary day, but for her loved ones lives of comfort and freedom from care. Her life of self-forgetfulness was lived cheerfully; her presence was one of sweet influence, and her devoted friends were myriad. She delighted in encouraging high aspirations in those with whom she came in daily contact, and although often weary, she was content in her home, in the happiness she had provided for the dear ones there.

As bravely and sweetly as she had met the problems of life she met death. Her chief anxiety seemed to be to spare those about her sorrow. It was characteristic of her unselfishness that she would not distress them by reference to the end, but after she was at rest a little note found under her pillow expressed her wishes.

Truly *she* was one of earth's uncrowned heroes, and of no one could it be more emphatically said:

> "None knew her but to love her,
> None named her but to praise."

Bertha Couzelman.

Mrs. W. J. Conzelman.

One of the most prominent of the women of Pekin, Ill., a leader in social functions, identified with its musical effort, foremost in church work, is Mrs. W. J. Conzelman. Bertha Herget was born in Pekin, Ill., December 19, 1870, and has lived her life in her native city. Her father was John Herget, a well-known distiller, of that city, and her mother was Ernestine (Schreck) Herget, both being natives of Germany. Her education was received in the public schools of Pekin. On October 21, 1891, she was married to Wm. J. Conzelman, who came to Pekin that year, established himself in business and was soon elected Mayor. As wife of the Mayor of the city, she was prominent in all social functions, and soon became a leader in local society affairs. She became identified with the various musical and literary societies of the city, and deeply interested in the work done by them. She is a member of the Pekin and Peoria Woman's Club, of various social clubs, and of the " Litta Society," a musical organization, named for the gifted young artist whose early death was so deeply mourned.

In many ways she has contributed to the growth and development of musical and literary enterprises, and is ambitious for the attainment of the highest possible results.

Mrs. Conzelman has not, however, been allowed to remain

191

simply known and beloved in the city of her birth. As the wife of Col. Conzelman, for her husband is Colonel on Gov. Yates' staff, she has been prominent in social life at the capital and throughout the State, and is well known for her charming presence and gentle grace. She is active in all church work and a most generous donor to all worthy charities.

If, however, Mrs. Conzelman was questioned as to where she finds her greatest happiness, she would not speak of social triumphs, of musical achievement, or even of her church work, which she holds most sacred, but of her home and her life there.

Mrs. Conzelman's home, recently built by her husband, is one of the most beautiful in the city. Into it has been placed everything which wealth and taste could suggest for its adornment. The family consists of Mr. and Mrs. Conzelman and their two sons, bright boys of nine and six years of age. In this lovely home, with her husband and her children, Mrs. Conzelman counts herself most happy, and enjoys the beauty of her home and the companionship of her loved ones more than anything else. Those who know her best have called her home life idyllic, and she covets such distinction more than any honor which can be conferred upon her. To create a beautiful home-life is a true woman's most womanly work, and its achievement is too often lightly considered.

While Mrs. Conzelman must prize the social distinction which is hers, and enjoy the environment of the culture in which her life is passed, above all she counts herself most blest in her beautiful home-life, most happy in making others glad.

Wm. J. Conzelman.

William J. Conzelman.

In this age of materialism, it is with pleasure a life is reviewed which, while it is synonymous with material success, is also identical with interest in art, literature, the best political effort and church work.

Such a life is that of William J. Conzelman, of Pekin, Ill. He was born in St. Louis, Mo., May 20, 1865. His father was Dr. John Conzelman, a native of Germany, his mother Louise (Graf) Conzelman, born in Switzerland. From them he inherited the indomitable energy and untiring perseverance which have been such important factors in his success. In 1881, he began his business career, working first seven years for the Simmons Hardware Co., of St. Louis, and later for E. H. Linley, of the same city. He was ambitious and anxious to work independently, and in 1891 moved to Pekin, Ill., and engaged himself with the Star Distilling Co. His success has been constant. He has commanded the confidence and respect of his business colleagues, and occupies many positions of responsibility. He is one of the managers of the Standard Distillery and Distributing Co.'s plants at Pekin, is President of the Tazewell Hotel, President of the Peoria Oil and Mining Co., Director in the American Truss Fence Co. and of the Pekin Library.

Politically he is a staunch Republican, and has been active in campaign work, doing much to secure the nomination of Gov. Yates, in Tazewell County. He is Colonel on Gov. Yates' staff, and is interested in projects which are engaging the attention of the Chief Executive of the State. While positive in his convictions and loyal to his principles, Mr. Conzelman is a man of broad views and great liberality of thought. Thus, while maintaining his own individuality in all that he does, he does not antagonize those who differ from him in opinion. As he has kept in touch with business and political life, he has not ignored the claims of society, of art and literature, of benevolence and religion. He is a member of St. Paul's Evangelical Church, and of other religious and charitable organizations. He has built for himself and family one of the most elegant homes in and about Pekin, and has no greater pride than its adornment, no greater happiness than in the society of his beautiful and accomplished wife. Such men as Mr. Conzelman are an honor to any community, and certainly the people of Pekin have shown their appreciation of his integrity, executive ability and sound judgment in every possible way.

Too rare are the instances where a business man, a man immersed in political affairs, recognizes higher claims and makes opportunity in his crowded life for church work and kindred demands.

Mr. Conzelman has been twice elected Mayor of Pekin, the second time with the largest majority ever given a Mayor in that city.

Theodore Thomas.

THEODORE THOMAS.

Theodore Thomas.

Theodore Thomas—the name means much to music in merica—was born in Essen, Hanover, and came to America hen ten years of age. He is, therefore, in every real sense the word an American musician and, in the minds of a large ajority of American people, he is the foremost in his proession. His father, who was a violinist, gave him instruction when very young, and at the age of six he played the olin in public most creditably. When the Jenny Lind, Sonng, Grisi and Mario companies gave their concerts in this untry, Mr. Thomas was the first violinist, playing as well in e Italian companies, with whom they sang, often conducting e performances. An able critic writes: "It is due Mr. omas to say that he has established a new ideal of orchesal work, and throughout his long career he has continued to intain the highest standard his musicians could achieve, ising it as fast as the ability of the orchestra could follow."

It was in 1866 that he engaged himself for orchestral rk on a large scale. The orchestra organized for the sumr concerts at Terrace Garden, and after two years removed Central Park Garden, saw the beginning of a movent destined to create a new epoch in American musical his-·y. All lovers of high-class music will remember the first

199

tour of the Thomas' Orchestra, in 1869.   Neither this nor the
second, nor the third, tour paid expenses, but, in spite of all
discouragements, Mr. Thomas was determined to build up
among the American people a good and lasting taste for orchestral music.   In him the public soon recognized a graceful
and masterful conductor, and felt the force of his personality.   Men and women of culture discussed the merits of the
new era in music, and sent the current of appreciation in all
directions.   During the following tours through all the leading cities, it became apparent that the orchestral innovation
had grown into a great educational power and an inspiration
in art.   People traveled scores and hundreds of miles to its
concerts in the cities of the Eastern and Western States.

The present knowledge and appreciation of the great masters in the United States are certainly largely owing to his
work.   It was he who taught the people to love Beethoven and
appreciate Wagner; and he was also the first to play the
works of Berlioz, Saint-Saens, Dvorak, Richard Strauss,
Tschaikowsky, and many others.   He was among the first to
bring out the works of American composers, and has always
been a leading spirit in every progressive movement.   Some
important questions were, in consequence, understood earlier
in this country than in Europe, owing to his catholic spirit,
which kept him abreast of the most modern European thought
and often in advance of its practice.   He established in this
country the low pitch of the orchestra, and introduced uni-
form bowing.   In 1891, he left New York City and moved to
Chicago, where he became the Musical Director of the World's
Columbian Exposition, and of the Chicago Orchestra, which
last he has developed till it is now universally ranked with

the best existing. Not the least of his labors has been the conducting of great biennial musical festivals in Cincinnati for a period of more than thirty consecutive years.

It is impossible in a brief history to give any real idea of the immense work done by this wonderful leader and musician, but a partial list of enterprises with which he has been connected will be a suggestion of what he has accomplished since 1864, when he founded the Thomas Orchestra. That same year he began a series of symphony soirèes, which he continued till 1867. He was the Musical Director of the Cincinnati College of Music from 1878 to 1880, and of the Brooklyn Philharmonic Orchestra in 1863, 1866-67-68, and from 1873 to 1891, continuously. He was Musical Director of the New York Philharmonic Orchestra from 1877 to 1891; of the American Opera Company, 1885-87, and, as is well known, of the Chicago Orchestra since 1891. He has been also, at various times, Musical Director of the following choruses, New York Mendelssohn Union, New York Chorus Society, New York German Liederkranz and Brooklyn Philharmonic Chorus.

In 1870, Mr. Thomas made a tour with his entire orchestra through the country, and since that time his name has been familiar to every lover of music.

The innumerable May festivals throughout the country may be legitimately counted among the fruits of Mr. Thomas' labors, and, with the many other festivals given under his direction, have attracted the attention of the musical world. It is a notable fact, worthy of mention, that he has repeatedly given works simultaneously with their first performance in Euorpe, and often compositions have been played here before they had been publicly produced in their homes across the water.

Mr. Thomas possesses in a marked degree those qualities which would have made him a leader in any walk of life.

He is systematic, thorough, a strict disciplinarian, yet courteous and gentle in manners. He never imposes conditions on his men which he does not accept for himself, and he shows the same consideration for their comfort as for his own. As an educator and a musician he ranks among the greatest men of the day.

Possibly few realize the tremendous financial difficulties with which Mr. Thomas has had to contend in establishing and maintaining the work of the Chicago Orchestra. In spite of such discouragement Mr. Thomas has persevered, and Chicago is justly proud of this institution and its famous leader.

Genevieve Clark Wilson.

Genevieve Clark Wilson

Genevieve Clark Wilson.

One of the most pleasing concert and oratorio singers of the West, a favorite wherever she is heard, is Mrs. Genevieve Clark Wilson, of Chicago. She was born in Galesville, Wis., into an artistic environment, for both her parents were musical. Her early training was under their supervision, and was of the strictest kind, thus laying the best foundation possible for future instruction. This home education was followed by the best tuition which the location afforded. Her progress and her talent seemed to warrant her making music her profession, and demanded the best equipment for such work. The really serious preparation for her professional life was begun in Boston, under J. C. D. Parker, for piano, and Frank Morse, for the voice. While in Boston, she was also particularly fitted for teaching, and later filled several prominent positions with credit to herself. She was, for some time, head of the vocal department of the Illinois State Blind Institution. In 1896, she studied oratorio, for which she is particularly well adapted, with Henschel, in London, and returned to America unusually well trained for this difficult line of musical work. Since her return she has sung with most of the prominent musical organizations of the country. Among them may be named the Handel and Haydn Society, the Cecilia and Apollo Clubs and the Symphony Orchestra, all of Boston.

In Chicago she has appeared many times as soloist with the Thomas' Orchestra and Chicago Symphony Orchestra, and with the Apollo and Mendelssohn Clubs. In addition to these, she has sung in connection with nearly all the smaller orchestras and musical clubs of Chicago and vicinity, and has won the highest encomiums wherever she has appeared. Mrs. Wilson has a most delightful voice. Clear, and of wide range, with great volume, it is full of expression and the sympathetic quality which brings the listener at once *en rapport* with the singer. Her stage presence is charming; unaffected and graceful, she wins her audience even before she begins to sing. For years her church choir positions have been the most lucrative of any soprano in the West. She is at present singing at the Kenwood Evangelical Church. Her time has been so fully occupied with her concert, choir and other public work that her teaching has been of necessity limited.

She is, however, a rarely sucessful teacher, enthusiastic, conscientious, painstaking and inspiring. She is greatly interested in pupils who are ambitious to make a reputation for themselves, and, in addition to the usual routine work of a teacher, gladly gives them the benefit of her experience. As a result many prominent young musicians have been and are among her pupils.

Mrs. Carrie Jacobs-Bond.

MRS. CARRIE JACOBS-BOND.

Mrs. Carrie Jacobs=Bond.

Athough a native of Janesville, Wis., the musical achieve-
nts of Mrs. Carrie Jacobs-Bond have been so a part of her
in Illinois that the music and poetry-loving public of Illi-
s and Chicago claim her as their very own.

From earliest childhood Carrie Bond was devoted to
sic, always writing and singing the little tunes that rang
her baby-heart. When only four years old, with one tiny
'er she played many airs, and when seven, played any-
ng she heard, omitting the octaves which her little hand
ld not grasp. When nine years of age she gave a re-
rkable exhibition of her phenomenal musical ear. Blind
n was playing in Janesville, and giving his customary ex-
itions of his ready ear for music by playing after other
mpositions he had never heard before. An old man rose in
audience and said: "A little girl here can do that." Blind
n smiled and said: " Send her here; she has never heard
, for I composed it," and played the march which has since
ome famous.

The child listened, and then, to the astonishment of the
lience, played it accurately, except the octaves, and has
'er forgotten it. In her characteristic way, Mrs. Bond
s: " This is, I believe, the only remarkable thing I ever

did," a statement which will hardly receive endorsement from those who know best what she has accomplished. In 1888 she was married to Dr. Frank Bond, and went to Northern Michigan, where they had their home in the midst of a forest, Dr. Bond being physician to the miners of that district. Their life was ideal in its happiness, and out of her glad heart, to please her lover-husband, she began to write songs. Impressed with their merit, Dr. Bond urged her to come to Chicago, bring her two best songs with her and submit them to the judgment of competent critics.

She came and met "Amber," beloved and lamented by so many thousands, and through her obtained entrance into the most coveted circles. Of her "Amber" wrote, "A dear tramp who came in one day to leave a song, and stole my heart away." Greatly encouraged by this gifted woman, she offered her songs to Brainerd Sons, who at once accepted them. After three months in Chicago she returned home, and began in earnest the work of composition. In about a year, 1895, Dr. Bond, as the result of an accident, died suddenly. Dazed with grief, the desolate wife turned to "Amber," and they planned a home together; but five weeks after Dr. Bond passed away "Amber's" brave, sweet soul entered into rest. Doubly bereft, Mrs. Bond tried to see through tears what might be left for her in life. Feeling it would best please the husband whose memory she idolizes, she gathered her slender resources together and went to hear the music of the old world. While there she received great encouragement from Frances Allitson and others, and after six months returned to Chicago, where seven years of constant endeavor have brought reward.

She has been her own promoter, giving recitals, and thus

introducing her songs and verses to the public, and for the past two years her own publisher, carrying on this work in her home. This business is conducted successfully, but in a very feminine way; but Mrs. Bond is a very feminine woman, from whom success has stolen none of the charm of a sweet, magnetic personality. She has published one hundred and twenty-five musical compositions, most of them songs, and a booklet, " Little Stories in Verse," of which the first edition— one thousand copies—is exhausted. Her verses remind one of James Whitcomb Riley, being pictures of heart-life told in dainty dialect. Three books of ballads, one of seven, one of eleven, the last of twelve songs, have been published by her, and are being sung everywhere, receiving endorsement from the finest musical critics and used by the best teachers in the country.

Mrs. Bond has put *herself* into all she has done. Someone has said: " No one can sing well till the heart is broken;" the sorrow of her life has been her inspiration, and from her own heart she has sung to the heart of humanity and won it.

From Berlin David Ffrangeon Davies wrote: " I am fond of violets * * * that's way I like your little songs. * * * There's work in the world for such as you. Many thousands are awaiting your message." From Nordica, David Bispham, Genevra Johnstone Bishop, Amy Fay, Bogea Oumiroff, and many others, she has received the most flattering letters and the heartiest endorsement possible—their use of her songs. Among many distinguished patrons she counts none dearer than Mrs. Gov. Yates, who has been her friend and helper in the struggle of the years, for the road to fame is not flower-strewn. While now she is laurel-wreathed, with the sunshine

on the cover an artistic wreath of wild roses, enclo
words " Unpretentious as a wild rose," and this has
be the emblem of her work.   Rejoicing in her success
it a tribute to the one so dearly loved, so early gone be
life is full of ministries to those in sorrow, and throu
and ballad she is a daily inspiration to thousands who
earnest words or voice her sweet songs.

Dr. George F. Root.

DR. *GEORGE F. ROOT.*

Gift
men hav
of this c
He
there fo
near Bo
Al
every i
from ch
In
study o
cleanin
instruc
Hi
of his
in tea
to stud
estima
A
for th

Dr. George F. Root.

Gifted composer, successful teacher, sweet singer, few men have so interwoven themselves with the musical history of this country as did the late Dr. George F. Root.

He was born in Sheffield, Mass., Aug. 20, 1820, and lived there for the first six years of his life, when North Reading, near Boston, became his home.

Always passionately fond of music, he learned to play every instrument within his reach, and the dream of his life, from childhood, was to be a musician.

In 1838, through the influence of friends, he began the study of the piano at Harmony Hall, Boston, sweeping and cleaning rooms, doing part janitor service to gain the coveted instruction.

His teacher, Mr. Johnson, recognized very soon the talent of his pupil, and also the fact that his best success would lie in teaching and in his vocal work. Six weeks after he began to study he had his first pupil, a fact which showed plainly the estimate his teacher placed on his ability and progress.

About this time Lowell Mason advertised for new singers for the Boston Academy Chorus, and Mr. Root joined that organization. Soon after, he became a member of the famous Bowdoin St. Choir, and also a pupil of George James Webb, at that time the best vocal teacher in Boston. From 1840 to

1844, he was associated with Mr. Johnson in musical work, dividing with him service as organist, teacher, and beginning the teaching of music in public schools. In 1844, he was invited to New York to sing at a musicale with a view to becoming associated with Mr. Abbott, the well-known educator, and also to the obtaining of a position in the Mercer St. Church, of that city. His appearance was a great success, and he at once moved to New York.

From this time every hour was crowded with work. As a result, in 1850, his health failed him, and his physician prescribed change and rest as imperative. He went to Paris and, later, to London, but during his absence of more than a year he was not idle. He heard many celebrities, investigated various methods, and returned in 1851, improved in health and with new enthusiasm for his work. About this time he published his first book for schools, entitled "Academy Vocalist," and soon after, for choir use, " The Shawm," which had a large circulation, and the cantata of " Daniel." The firm of Root & Cady was established during this year in Chicago, Mr. E. T. Root, brother of George F., being a member of the firm. In 1852 he published his first successful song, " Hazel Dell," and soon after " The Shining Shore " (which has been sung in almost every known language), " Rosalie, the Prairie Flower," and other sweet ballads. In 1858, he became one of the firm of Root & Cady, of Chicago, and thus first identified himself with the musical work of that city.

In 1859, he became associated with the Normal Institute at North Reading, Mass., and from that time labored indefatigably and successfully in Normal work all over the country. He delighted in this line of work, and seemed to have a special genius for it. His genial presence and sweet voice became most widely known, and his methods and ambitions obtained cordial recognition from the best music teachers of the land. From 1861 to 1870 he made Chicago his home, and wrote the war songs which, alone, would have made him famous. Who has not felt the thrill of patriotism when " Tramp, Tramp, Tramp " has been sung or played ? " Just Before the Battle, Mother,"" The Battle-cry of Freedom,"" The Vacant Chair " are a few of the very many songs he wrote which have stirred the very hearts of the people. Always busy with Normal work, or at his desk composing, he again overtaxed his strength, and his health failed. He was urged to go abroad, but did not feel equal to the ocean trip. He began (his own idea) a series of exercises on the principle of the " Healthlift," and thus effected his own cure, and really started what has since become a widely practiced treatment.

In 1876, he sailed for Glasgow, Scotland, and after a delightful vacation returned to prosecute his beloved work with renewed vigor. He and his daughter, Mrs. Clara Louise Burnham, enjoyed working together, and wrote a well-known Christmas cantata, " The Flower-Queen," etc.

Dr. Root was a very prolific writer, and much of his music has gained a prominent place among the favorite songs, cantatas and hymns of this country. His was a generous nature, and his delight was to help others. In 1859, a musical society was greatly in debt. Dr. Root gave his cantata, " The Haymakers," twice and cleared off the debt. This society became, in 1875, the Apollo Club, of Chicago, with Mr. Tomlins as leader.

Mr. Moody felt that Dr. Root's hymns were of great value

his pleasure in the music of his home circle was one of t
greatest and most sacred delights of his life.

He died in the midst of his usefulness, enshrined, as f
have ever been, in the hearts of music-lovers all over the cou
try.

So long as patriotism, love of home and love of God sh
endure, so long will the hymns and the songs of Dr. Geor
F. Root have a place among the best musical publications
America.

James Gill.

JAMES *GILL*.

James Gill.

Among Chicago musicians who have been identified for many years with the advancement of musical interests, perhaps no one is more widely known than James Gill.

He was born in Glasgow, Scotland, and derived his musical talent from his father, who was devoted to the violin. When five years old, he lost his parents, and the rest of his youth was a continuous struggle with relatives, who discouraged his idea of making music his profession. He was Scotch, however, and that means he persisted till he triumphed over obstacles. Sent to Paisley, at the death of his parents, to live with an aunt, he earned enough money playing the organ for the Swedenborgian Church and drawing designs for Paisley shawls to pay his first year in the Leipsic Conservatory, which he entered in 1867. He made such rapid progress there that friends came to his aid. In the third year his name, with that of Charles Dodge, another musician who has taught in Chicago, was put on the list of competitors for the first prize. Both names were, however, excluded, in accordance with a decision that only Germans were eligible. His first public appearance was in 1870, in the Gewand Haus, the celebrated concert hall in Leipsic. He came to Chicago the year after the fire, with Dr. Ziegfeld, who went to Germany after him. Since that time Mr. Gill has been identified

tone roles. He has been the teacher of singing at the Northwestern University and chorister of the Grace M. E. Church, Chicago.

Mr. Gill had the honor. in 1870, of singing at Weimar, under the direction of Liszt.

For three years he conducted most successfully a large chorus choir at the First Baptist Church, in Elgin, Ill. In connection with this work he gave several concerts in Elgin and one in Rockford. After hearing him sing in one of these concerts, a local paper wrote—" Mr. Gill is built for a singer of humorous songs, so jolly is his appearance. When he laughs the audience cannot help doing the same."

The past year he has met with a great loss in the death of his wife. Mrs. Gill was a charming woman, and played accompaniments with rare tact and taste.

Mr. Gill is an enthusiast in his profession, loyal in his friendships, personally interested in the success of his pupils —not only those under his present instruction but those who were students with him in the past.

No one rejoices more than he in the advance which music has made in the years since he first became identified with the musical life of Chicago; no one can be more sanguine for the future.

Mrs. Clara H. Scott.

MRS. CLARA *H*. SCOTT.

Mrs. Clara H. Scott.

The history of music in Illinois would be incomplete without mention of Mrs. Clara H. Scott, who enjoyed the distinction of being the first woman to prepare and publish an anthem book. She was born, December 3, 1841, in Elk Grove, Cook County, Ill., her father, Abel Fiske Jones, being an excellent teacher of rudimentary music, and her mother, Sarah Rockwell, being also musical. From her maternal grandfather, a clergyman, she inherited the clear faith which underlies her religious compositions. Her childhood was lived close to nature. With a dear brother, she sought the fields and woods, and well they knew the lore of birds and flowers, a fit curriculum from which to lay the foundation of a true education.

At the age of eleven, she was placed in one of the preparatory schools in Chicago, under the tuition of the founder of the then only Normal School in this country. In this rare atmosphere was greatly developed the deep determination of character which has surmounted many obstacles, not only in bringing her genius to the front, but in giving to the world the vibrations of a true soul.

Her first introduction to the study of harmony and composition was in 1856, under the auspices of the first musical institute ever organized in Chicago, conducted by C. M. Cady.

225

A few years later, her first piano composition appeared. At the age of eighteen she was called to the charge of the music department of the Ladies' Seminary, at Lyons, Iowa. For years she was before the public in concert work, and as the conductor of cantatas, conventions and minor work.

In 1861, she married Henry Clay Scott, son of the late Judge Scott, of Arkansas, who seconded his wife's efforts in giving her musical gifts full sway. Soon after, she met Dr. Palmer, now of New York, to whose books she became a frequent contributor. A close student, the next few years she had the best instruction within her reach, East and West. The result was a large collection of songs and piano composition in sheet form. In 1882, her " Royal Anthem Book," already mentioned, appeared, and was a great musical success. Her pen was never idle, and, although hampered by ill health, she composed continuously. Her subjects were almost wholly sacred, and she often wrote the most beautiful words to her own compositions. Possibly her best known anthem is " Oh, When Shall I be Free ?" Her late song, " God is Love," and her verses, " A Wanderer," will always prove her ability to sing and write to the hearts of the people.

In the midst of the best work of her life, she was suddenly called to the great Divine school of harmony, but her works do follow her.

William H. Sherwood.

William H. Sherwood.

William H. Sherwood.

One of the world's greatest musicians, admittedly the greatest of American piano virtuosos, the history of William H. Sherwood's life and work is so familiar as hardly to need recapitulation to American readers.

He was born at Lyons, N. Y., and began the study of music with his father, Rev. L. H. Sherwood, M. A., who founded the Lyons Musical Academy. His father was his principal instructor until, at the age of seventeen, he went abroad. His European teachers were Theodore Kullak and Deppe, in Berlin; Liszt, in Weimar, (piano); Scatson Clark, in Stuttgart, (organ); Dr. Weitzmann, Carl Doppler, R. Wuerst and E. V. Richter, (theory, counterpoint and composition).

He played at the Singakademie in Berlin, when eighteen years old, and the *Spenersche Zeitung* said of him—"The greatest interest of all was awakened by a young man named Sherwood, who played Chopin's F Minor Fantaisie with such fine feeling, both in touch and conception, that even in one satiated with music, as ourselves, it produced the deepest emotions." He also played Beethoven's Emperor Concerto with full orchestra, under the direction of Royal Capellmeister Wuerst, before an audience of four thousand people, and produced so great an impression that he repeated the performance five times in Berlin. He was the first pianist to play Grieg's Concerto in America, having studied it with the composer and played it for its second production in Germany. With the great Philharmonic Orchestra in Hamburg he received an ovation, being encored many times and receiving a fanfare from the orchestra.

He had various offers to play with the great orchestras of Germany, but Mr. Sherwood is a true American, and returned to his native land. He has played with unvarying success in the large cities of the United States and Canada, and has received unstinted praise from the public and press critics.

Mr. Sherwood is an untiring student, as is evinced by the fact that during the past four or five years he has evolved more and better results than during any corresponding period of his career.

His book on " Music Study and Interpretative Technique " will unfold his best thought, and is different from anything of the kind ever before attempted in print. Some of America's most distinguished artists have been Mr. Sherwood's pupils. That he believes in the just recognition and remuneration of American talent is evidenced by articles from his pen which have appeared in Chicago's daily papers.

Of a genial nature, Mr. Sherwood is never happier than in the encouragement of real talent, and takes greatest pride in the successes of young aspirants to musical fame.

His compositions and works revised by him occupy a place among the best musical compositions of the day. As artist, teacher, composer, he easily merits the prominence given him not only as one of the best living pianists but as " the shining light in the history of music in this country."

W. C. E. Seeboeck.

A repro
ability a:
eational
selects. p
that anno
Marshe
from her.
ment. I
ing had th
he had the
nities.
Settelu-Ir
the same
character
after sp
complete
among t
has ma
Mr. Sec
his own
in its n
most su
throug

W. C. E. Seeboeck.

A representative musician, a man who, by his strong individuality and thoroughly artistic nature, has done much in an educational way for musical attainment in Chicago, W. C. E. Seeboeck, pianist and composer, occupies a most important position among the musicians of that city. His mother, a pupil of Marchesi, while in Vienna, was a most charming singer, and from her, no doubt, Mr. Seeboeck inherits much of his musical talent. He is a man of scholarly tastes and attainments, having had the advantages of a college education. In every way he had the best possible instruction, and improved his opportunities. Among his teachers were Hermann Gresendener, Nettebolm and Leo Hill. To the study of music he brought the same honesty of purpose and untiring perseverance which characterized his college life. He came to Chicago in 1880, after spending some eighteen months in St. Petersburg to complete certain studies, and at once commanded a place among the best musicians of the city. The Chicago of 1880 has made great strides to become the Chicago of 1903, but Mr. Seeboeck has kept pace with its growth and ambitions in his own work, has made himself a part of the advancement in its musical standards. As a pianist, Mr. Seeboeck has been most successful, giving many concerts not only in Chicago, but throughout the country. His playing is remarkable for the

into his interpretation of musical thought. In his compositions he has displayed great versatility of talent, and his piano solos and songs are widely known, and have been well received through the country. A quintette, written by him, was given by the Bendix Quartette and himself, and another of his compositions by the same Quartette and Mrs. Lapham, at concerts given by the Amateur Club.

A concerto No. 2, D Minor, composed by him, he has played with the Thomas' Orchestra, achieving unusual success. As a teacher, Mr. Seeboeck is most thorough, presenting the intellectual side of music to his pupils in an attractive way, inspiring true scholarly ambition in every student. In this work he has excelled, with gratifying results, and the large classes constantly under his direction have been instructed not only in technique but in the very soul of musical inspiration.

Mr. Seeboeck has given many recitals, always with the educational feature in view, and has thus impressed his pupils with the necessity of thoroughness in the veriest detail of their work. That his pupils have caught something of his enthusiastic spirit of research is evidenced by the progress made by many of them. No one can doubt but that Mr. Seeboeck's unquestioned influence on the musical life of Chicago has been always for its best achievement and the maintenance of the highest ideals.

Annice E. Bradford Butts, M.A.

Annie E Beresford Butts

Annice E. Bradford Butts, M.A.

It is interesting to note how often a Puritan ancestry is given in a review of the lives of the leading men and women in the American literary world. Possibly no historic name appears more frequently in such connection than does the name of William Bradford, Governor of Plymouth Colony, and re-elected Governor of that colony frequently. Annice E. Bradford Butts, the subject of this sketch, was named after her grandmother, Annice Bradford, who was the wife of Daniel Butts, of Canterbury, Conn., and the ninth direct descendant of the distinguished Governor Wm. Bradford. Miss Butts was born, September 22, 1844, in Rome, N. Y., and was the daughter of David K. Butts and Emily Wilcox Butts. She was educated at the Rome Academy, and was graduated from Stanwix Seminary, Rome, a branch school of the Clinton Liberal Institute.

Her whole life has been devoted to education and the advancement of educational interests, and she has achieved a success in this direction accorded to but few women.

She early began her work as a teacher, and was, from 1867 to 1871, Principal of the West Division High School, Joliet, Ill.; from 1871 to 1877, a teacher in Dearborn Seminary, Chicago; from 1881 to 1886, Principal of the Fifty-fourth St. School, Chicago. Since that time, she has been the

Principal of Kenwood Institute, which became an affiliated academy of the University of Chicago, in 1893. She has been exceedingly ambitious that the highest standard of scholarship should be the aim of her pupils, and her school has an enviable reputation not only in this country but abroad. During the past few years she has spent some months in Europe, but she has gone not merely as a tourist but as a student. She has spent much time in the art galleries of the old world, familiarizing herself with their treasures, and has been much interested in the investigation of the methods of education employed in other lands.

Art history is the subject which has deeply fascinated and appealed to her, and to it she has devoted years of study and research.

Her second trip to Paris was made in 1901, and at that time a branch of the Kenwood Institute was opened as a school for American girls. While there she succeeded in establishing a co-operation with the Franco-English Guild, which has been in existence in Paris for ten years. During the time she has spent abroad, studying and storing her memory with much which escapes the ordinary traveler, she has collected many most valuable and interesting works of art.

She is to-day just as indefatigable and earnest a student as ever, and is an inspiration to those fortunate enough to come in touch with her busy life.

Dr. Frank S. Whitman.

Frank S. Whitman

Dr. Frank S. Whitman.

In reviewing the lives of the prominent men and women of Illinois, one is impressed by the fact that very few of them are natives of that State. A notable exception is Dr. Frank S. Whitman, Superintendent of the Illinois Northern Hospital for the Insane.

Dr. Whitman was born in Belvidere, Boone County, Ill., and has lived there most of his life. His father was Hiram Whitman, of Fairfield, Vermont, and his mother Clarinda Whitman, of Chatauqua, N. Y.

His early education was received in Belvidere and at Chicago University, and preparation for his professional career was made in Chicago. He may, therefore, be called, without reservation, an Illinois man, and the record of his life and its work may be reviewed with pride by his native State.

He was graduated from Hahnemann Medical College, in Chicago, in 1872, and from the Chicago Homœopathic College with the honorary degree ad eundem, in 1876. June 21, 1877, he was married in Belvidere.

His fellow-townsmen have accorded to him every honor within their power to bestow. He served as Coroner for Boone County, and in the city of Belvidere has been elected Alderman, President of the Board of Education, and twice its Mayor. For twenty years he has been a member from Boone

241

County of the Congressional Committee, was once a delegate to the National Republican Convention, and repeatedly to the State Convention. Recognition of his business ability is evinced by the fact that he is the Vice-President of the People's Bank, of Belvidere.

While a busy man, Dr. Whitman keeps in touch with whatever means advancement in his profession. He is a member of the American Institute of Homœopathy, of the Illinois Homœopathic Medical Association and of the American Medico-Psychological Association. June 12, 1899, Dr. Whitman was appointed Superintendent of the Illinois Northern Hospital for the Insane, a position of trust and honor which he still holds, and in which he has shown himself a wise leader and competent advisor, not only professionally, but in the many matters presented to him for decision.

It is by the daily performance of life's tasks, thoroughly, conscientiously and persistently, year after year, that greatness is achieved. Such has been the history of Dr. Whitman's life. His integrity has been absolute, his devotion to duty unfailing, and those who knew him felt their interests safe in his hands.

Dr. Whitman is a man who thinks along broad lines, and who is interested in all the vital questions of the day. With strong convictions and decided principles, he has also the kindest heart and tenderest sympathies. Although his life has been eminently practical, he is a man of culture and is literary in his tastes. Music and art appeal to him strongly, and he is keenly interested in all the higher educational questions of the day.

J. S. Watson, M.D.

J. S. Watson.

is hardly
ingh with ev
e opportuni
physician.
here the so
He is open
incentive fo:
of Aurora.
ped use o
cined, not
arable rej
er, Octobe
late (Trac
Ill. in 185:

He we
ill 1878, t
age. He i
on, from
ean of th
ence to p
post-grad
Edinburg

J. S. Watson, M. D.

In hardly any walk of life does a man come so closely in touch with every possible human experience, or have as great an opportunity to achieve so many-sided an influence, as does a physician. The practice of his profession places him where the social, moral, intellectual, as well as the physical, life is open to his inspection, a tuition which should be an incentive for the best self-development. Dr. J. S. Watson, of Aurora, Ill., is one of those physicians who has made good use of such wide and varied observation, and has gained, not only in his profession but outside of it, a most enviable reputation. He was born in Bealytown, New Jersey, October 10, 1851, the son of Charles Watson and Charlotte (Trace) Watson. His parents moved to Kane County, Ill., in 1852, a county in which he has resided ever since.

He worked on his father's farm, near Kaneville, Ill., till 1878, teaching school winters, till he was twenty years of age. He received his education at the University of Michigan, from which he was graduated as a surgeon and physician of the regular school of medicine in 1881, and began at once to practice in his profession. In 1881-82 he took a post-graduate course at the Royal College of Surgeons in Edinburgh, Scotland, and on his return practiced for seven years in Elburn, Ill. In 1889 he moved to Aurora. Ill., his present home. In 1900 he traveled through Europe, a trip of professional profit as well as pleasure.

Dr. Watson is an earnest student, desirous of being in the foremost ranks of a profession whose progress each year is almost incredible. He is a great reader, a keen observer, and embraces every opportunity for intelligent scientific investigation within his grasp. Dr. Watson is fond of rare and beautiful books, and in his library may be found some of the most desirable and costly books of the day, embracing works on music, art, and various branches of literature and science.

In 1893-94 he went to New York and took another post-graduate course at the College of Physicians and Surgeons of that city. He is a man of wide literary tastes, fond of music and interested in the development of the best in art, as well as in literature and science. He is known most favorably, not only in Aurora but throughout that part of the State, as a successful physician and skilful surgeon. He is one of the attending physicians and surgeons at the St. Charles Hospital, Aurora, an institution which is recognized by the best hospitals, and has a good standing among them. Dr. Watson was married, May 8, 1884, to Miss Eliza Stewart, and their pleasant home is the center of much that is attractive in the best social life of Aurora.

Dr. Watson is just starting, October, 1903, on a tour around the world, which he hopes to accomplish in six months.

Eliza Stewart Watson

Mrs. J. S. Watson.

Some time since, an eminent physician wrote a most taking little story, which he called " The Doctor's Wife." In it he portrayed the many ways not usually recognized in which a doctor's wife is helpful to her husband, the days when she shares in loving sympathy his responsibilities, rejoices in his successes, and sorrows when skill and science are baffled. He spoke of the lonely hours of which every physician's wife knows, and the daily tax upon her time, of which few ever dream who have never thought of the peculiar duties which enter into the life of the doctor's wife. It is a glance into such a life which is here given. Eliza Stewart was born in Campton, Keene Co., Illinois. Her father was John Stewart, of New Brunswick; her mother Martha (Thomas) Stewart, of Pennsylvania. She was first graduated from the High School of Geneva, Ill.; later attended Ferry Hall, which is a part of the Lake Forest University *régime.*

She was married May 8, 1884, to Dr. J. S. Watson, a widely known physician of Aurora, where they now reside. Dr. and Mrs. Watson have four children, two daughters, Helen and Margaret, and two sons, Stewart and Dean. The home is always full of pleasure for these four children and their companions, and its atmosphere is not only that of sun-

cisions, and is most valuable as one of the senior members of the Aurora Board of Charities. With her husband she is inspired by high literary ideals, and is conversant with the best in literature and art. Their fine library is a source of mutual pleasure to Dr. and Mrs. Watson, and their children are being educated to read and to think for themselves, a condition only possible as the result of access to the best the world of literature can offer.

Mrs. Watson is ambitious for her husband's success, interested in his scientific researches, anxious to aid in all that will promote his influence. She is a member of the Aurora Woman's Club, a literary association which is doing excellent work. No one can be more interested than is Mrs. Watson in all that is beautiful in art, charming in music, instructive and entertaining in the realm of literature. She is greatly beloved by those who are perhaps the less favored, so far as wealth is concerned, in the community, for no worthy object ever appeals to her in vain, and her kind alleviation of need is well known and appreciated.

Mrs. John Vance Cheney.

MRS. JOHN VANCE CHENEY.

When, eig
Mrs. John Vai
acient and p
ually receiv
Society, i
usical, liter:
For by h
with extraor:
graces most
Mrs. Ch
te in this d
Continent al
ciety of the
been her hoi
In fact
ter of the U
in study in
mode; for v
indissolubl
higher thin
osophy of

Mrs. John Vance Cheney.

When, eight years ago, time and tide wafted to Chicago Mrs. John Vance Cheney, had she been a princess of the most ancient and proudest lineage she could not have been more royally received.

Society, in the most restricted form of the word—society musical, literary and artistic—did her homage.

For by her inherent qualities of mind and heart, coupled with extraordinary outward charms of person, Mrs. Cheney graces most royally any society.

Mrs. Cheney's fame had preceded her to her new home, for in this day of the telegraph and rapid transit across the Continent all knew of the high position held by her in the society of the western metropolis (San Francisco), which had been her home many years prior to her removal to Chicago.

In fact, Mrs. Cheney's name is not unknown in any quarter of the Union, nor in Europe, where many years were spent in study in her youth, and many sojourns have since been made; for wherever Mrs. Cheney spends any time her name is indissolubly connected with every movement tending to the higher things in life, particularly where music and the philosophy of *right living* are factors.

Pleasant as society is to one so eminently fitted to shine in it as is Mrs. Cheney, she has been gradually drawn from it into the work now absorbing her, and her whole joy in life is teaching mankind to solve the secrets of health, success and a contented mind, and teaching students of the art of piano-playing that *all technique is in the mind.*

The press and public have extended to Mrs. Cheney the most cordial support in her efforts to help humanity, and she is now a leader in the large field of public work on the lecture platform.

Her investigations in psychology, in its relation to music and health, have received the most respectful attention of educators throughout the country. The results of her work are but little short of miraculous.

" Music," she says, " should be studied as a means of service to humanity. To give joy must be the student's aim, not selfish pleasure. One who sings, works or plays with no thought of self is never ' nervous.' Touch is never dilated upon, as that comes naturally, the result of perception. The pupil is taught to observe, to think, to reason, recognizing the soul as master and the body as purely the instrument of ' expression.'

" Physical, mental and spiritual development," says Mrs. Cheney, " are three equal factors of a perfect whole; the three natures must be cultivated equally and harmoniously, with a keen appreciation of each to all. The mind is the creative power, the body the instrument of expression, and it can express only what the mind directs, be it health or disease, beauty or ugliness."

And Mrs. Cheney is beautiful!

Bernard Ziehn.

Bernhard Ziehn

Bernard Ziehn.

The world has no more scholarly musician, no greater theorist, no more profound musical writer than Bernard Ziehn. The works of the old masters, of more modern composers, such as Liszt, Brahms, Bruckner and Wagner, are as familiar to him as the most simple chord, and he has mastered some of the greatest mysteries of the musical world. This is abundantly evidenced by the fact that to him the world owes the solution of two most baffling musical problems. One was the query concerning the unfinished fugue in Bach's " Kunst der Fuge," a problem which had remained unsolved for almost one hundred and fifty years. Another was the answering of the question, " Who is the composer of Luther's ' Ein Feste Burg?' " a problem which had defied solution for almost three hundred and fifty years.

He is a deep thinker, logical in his decisions and positive in the expression of his theories.

Bernard Ziehn, whose father was a shoemaker, was born in Erfurt, Germany, January 20, 1845. He received a common school education, and later took the course of study at a Normal School. For three years he taught school at Mühlhausen, in Thuringia. He came to Chicago, November, 1868, and has remained here since that time, the first two years as a teacher, since then devoting himself to the musical profession.

257

During these years he has written several books and articles of very great importance, which have appeared in the *Allgemeine Musikzeitung*, Berlin. His article on " The Ecclesiastical Modes " is published in *Die Musik,* Berlin. His " System of Exercises for the Piano-forte " and " A New Method of Instruction for Beginners," founded upon the Contrarium reversum and the Symmetrical inversion, were published in Hamburg, 1880. "Alte Klavierstücke " (Joh. Chr. Bach, Krebs, Graun), containing also explanations on the correct execution of the ornaments in classical works, was published in Hamburg, 1883. " Harmonie and Modulations Chre," founded upon a new principle, the works of the masters in music, published in 1887, in Berlin. A Berlin critic recommends this book in the warmest expressions " for every teacher or pupil, every master or disciple." A Leipzig critic says— " This work is unique in the musical didactic." Hans von Bülon, in 1891 and 1893, declared—" Bernard Ziehn is the greatest theorist in the world." As a musician Bernard Ziehn is in advance of his time. The years will prove the truth of his prophecies, the wisdom of his ideas.

Free from affectation, with the simplicity of bearing which always characterizes true greatness, he has the respect of the musical world. He is idolized by his pupils, some of them artists of world-wide fame, to whom his commendation is their brightest laurel.

Among his " advanced " pupils are Mrs. Bloomfield-Zeisler, Mrs. W. S. Crosby, Mrs. Eleanor Everest Freer, Mrs. Regina Watson, Mrs. Grace Wassall, Miss Helen Louise Birch, Miss Helen Rudolph, Messrs. Frederic Lillebridge, Wilhelm Middelschulte, Otto Wolf, Gustav and Albert Grube.

Marie Von Elsner.

MARIE VON ELSNER.

Marie Von Elsner.

Litta, Marie Von Elsner was born, June 1, 1856, in Bloomington, Ill., inheriting from her father, Hugo Von Elsner, rare musical talent.

When only six years old, she sang in concerts, and four years later, under her father's management, gave concerts in Chicago, Cleveland, New York and other cities.

In 1869, she sang in the German Theatre, Cleveland, Ohio. Prof. John Undermer, at this time, heard her wonderful voice and offered to teach her, and, later, Mr. A. B. Huff, of Cleveland, claimed the privilege of sending her abroad for further study. October 24, 1874, she sailed for Paris. Her first teacher, in that city, was Mme. Viardot, and, later, Mme. La Grange, who was so delighted with her voice that she gave her tuition without charge. Under these teachers, she mastered the operas "Aida," "Mignon," "Somnambula," "Hamlet," "Figaro" and "Barber of Seville."

May 20, 1876, she made her début at the Drury Lane Theatre, under Mr. Mapleson, as Isabella in "Robert le Diable," with Nilsson as Alice.

She next filled an engagement, as Marie Litta, at the Grand Opera House, in Paris, in the title role of Lucia di Lammermoor. Her fame spread rapidly over Europe. In April and May, 1878, she filled a successful engagement at

Vienna, where Dr. Hauslich, the most critical of critics, showered her with praise.

Returning to Paris, she accepted an offer from Max Strakosch for an American tour, and, after four years' absence, returned to her native land. Her first appearance in opera was made November 16, 1878, in Chicago, at McVicker's Theatre, in Lucia di Lammermoor, and created an almost unparalleled furore. In 1880, Marie Litta signed a contract with Henry L. Slayton, and gave three hundred and fifteen concerts in the principal cities of the United States and Canada. Her last appearance in Chicago was September 28, 1882, when she sang in Central Music Hall to a most enthusiastic audience.

Before Litta could complete her last season with Mr. Slayton she was taken ill with spinal meningitis, and, after terrible suffering, passed to the other life, July 7, 1883, at her home in Bloomington, Ill. Her death was one of earth's sad mysteries. Young, one of the most gifted singers the century had known, she left the world of music and art to mourn her loss. The people of her native city erected a magnificent monument to her memory.

Marie was a blonde, of statuesque form, strongly-marked countenance, and agreeable stage presence. Her voice was remarkably pure in all registers and of extraordinary compass. Its peculiar quality was its phenomenal flexibility, coupled with purity of tone and dramatic power. She always impressed her audiences with the thought that her ideals and ambitions were the highest, and had not the sweet voice been thus early silenced, without doubt her fondest dreams would have found realization.

Emil Liebling.

EMIL LIEBLING.

Emil Liebling.

No one has been more closely in touch with the musical life of Chicago for the past thirty years than has Emil Liebling. A man of varied talents, he has been able to promote along many lines the progress of the profession to which he has devoted his life. Perhaps he is most widely known as a teacher of the piano, for in this capacity he stands among the foremost in America. He is a recognized authority as to the best methods in teaching, and has been consulted by those who have come long distances to talk with him. But, aside from his important work as a teacher, Mr. Liebling has established a most enviable reputation as composer, pianist and lecturer. As concert pianist, he represents the best modern type. His repertoire is very extensive, embracing some five hundred compositions, any of which he can play at will, an example of memorizing alone, which is almost phenomenal. He has made of his recitals not only a delightful musical treat in his brilliant rendition of the most difficult music, but has excelled in the giving of musical lectures in connection with his playing, making the entertainment thoroughly educational. He is a fluent speaker, familiar with the details of every branch of his subject, with the history of composition, with the lives of the great masters, and he delights in this line of work, not usually attempted by eminent pianists. As a the " Concert Romances," Opus 20 and 21, and a special edition, edited by him, of the Heller and Loeschorn études. In 1900, in connection with the concert of the Mendelssohn Club, he played, for the first time then in this country, Moszkowski's new concerto, and gained from both his audience and the press the most unqualified endorsement of his masterly work. Mr. Liebling has been so long identified with the best musical life of Chicago that he has become part of the musical history of that city. Genial, enthusiastic, ready to impart his knowledge to others, always a student, his influence has been, and is, far-reaching and uplifting. He has been heard in many places throughout the country in his concert tours, and has always delighted his audiences. From his studio have gone out some of the most promising of the pianists of to-day, and he is always ready to inspire them with renewed ambitions; but the results of his influence as lecturer, writer and composeser will never be known.

Chicago counts itself fortunate in being the home of this courteous, scholarly and gifted artist, and recognizes the fact that the musical ambitions of the city have been greatly stimulated by his influence.

W. S. B. Mathews.

W. S. B. MATHEWS.

W. S. B. Mathews.

Probably no man is more widely known throughout this country by his publications, which are most extensively used by teachers everywhere, than is W. S. B. Mathews. Mr. Mathews was born in London, New Hampshire, May 8, 1837. From a very early childhood his fondness for music made itself apparent, and when but a boy he decided that his life-work should be teaching music. It was not, however, till he was twelve years old that he began his musical studies. His unusual progress may be inferred from the fact that the following year, when but thirteen years of age, he began to play the organ in church. Before he was eighteen years old he was a teacher in an academy at Mt. Vernon, N. H. At the same time, he was pursuing his studies along both musical and literary lines, and was able to gratify his ambitions by studying with Southard in Boston and, some time later, with Thalberg, then in the very midst of his famous career. Mr. Mathews was always interested in literary research, particularly as connected with his musical life. From 1859, as long as the paper had existence, he was a frequent contributor to *Dwight's Journal,* and, in 1868, became the editor of the *Musical Independent,* a position he held for four years. For many years he was the musical critic on various Chicago papers, and is to-day recognized as unquestioned authority on musical

269

matters. His musical text-books are widely known. Among them are "Mathews' Graded Materials for the Piano," "Mathews' Beginners in Phrasing," "A Primer in Music," in which Dr. Wm. Mason was interested, and " The Pronouncing Dictionary of Musical Terms." He also published in two volumes " Graded Pieces," in which work he was assisted by Emil Liebling, and has written other books of value to musicians. While Mr. Mathews is a critic, and sometimes severe in criticism, he is always deeply interested in the success of those who have real talent. Among his pupils are many who have made for themselves most enviable reputations as solo pianists. They find pleasure in attributing much of their success to the thorough drill and encouragement they received from Mr. Mathews while studying with him. Mr. Mathews has been greatly interested in the musical advancement of Chicago, and has done much to further it. Through his books, which have a place among standard musical literature, he has come in touch with thousands, and thus his influence in the musical world has been widespread. More than this, his strong personal influence has made itself felt in Chicago, so long his home, for the maintenance of the highest possible musical ideals. Whenever the history of the musical life of Illinois and Chicago shall be written, the name of W. S. B. Mathews will be found in a conspicuous place, and his efforts for the creation of the best thought in music will end only with his life.

Mrs. Jessie Bartlett Davis.

MRS. JESSIE BARTLETT DAVIS.

Mrs. Jessie Bartlett Davis.

Perhaps no singer of to-day is more enshrined in the hearts of her audiences than is Mrs. Jessie Bartlett Davis.

From her parents she inherited a passionate love for music and a voice which obtained recognition as one of the finest contraltos in America. She was born near Chicago, and, at the age of fourteen, moved to that city, where her musical education began.

Mr. Davis was organizing the Chicago Church Choir Company to give " Pinafore," then the craze of the day. She was assigned the part of Buttercup, and at once captivated all who heard her. At the close of the year's engagement she married Mr. Davis. They went to New York, where she devoted herself to study, and, through the influence of Col. Mapleson, sung many times with Patti. After a year's study in Paris, she returned to New York and joined the American Opera Company, but it proved an unsuccessful venture. Later she joined the Bostonians, with whom she won many laurels, becoming a great favorite with the public all over the country. She has sung in more than forty operas, among them " Il Trovatore," " Carmen," " Faust," " Bohemian Girl," " Pygmalion and Galatea," " Fatinitza," " Merry Wives of Windsor," and afterwards in " Maid of Plymouth " and " Robin Hood."　　　　273

Jessie Bartlett Davis seems one of nature's favorites. Added to her wonderful voice are rare beauty and great personal magnetism, which have made her a power wherever she has sung. Her devotion to " the sweetest boy on earth " has dominated her life to a great extent, and into her home life she has carried the same winsomeness and enthusiasm which have marked her professional career. During her vacations she has been devoted to outdoor exercise, such as boating and walking, which have given her the superb health so essential to her work.

Wonderfully free from petty jealousy, she knows no greater pleasure than to aid some deserving aspirant to recognition in the musical world. As a ballad singer she is peerless. Who that has heard her sing of " Baby and I in Our Rocking-Chair " would willingly lose that sweet picture from memory's gallery?

" Five O'Clock in the Morning " and " Nothing Else to Do " recall the lamented Parepa of years gone by, but lose nothing of their witchery when sung by Mrs. Davis. As she has sung so exquisitely " O Promise Me," it has been an inspiration to every heart, and so on through a long repertoire of songs she has made her own.

The truest artist is the one who most deeply stirs the heart, whether it be singer or poet or painter, and this has been Mrs. Davis' power in song all the years. Long may she be spared to delight audiences with the sweetness of her wonderful voice and to be an inspiration to the best musical impulses of the day.

Frederick Grant Gleason.

FREDERICK GRANT GLEASON.

Frederick Grant ·Gleason.

A Chicago musician who has climbed to the top round of the ladder of success is Frederick Grant Gleason, well known as critic, instructor and composer. Dudley Buck was his first instructor, at Hartford, Conn. Subsequently he pursued his education at Leipzig, under Moscheles, Richter, J. C. Lobe and Plaidy, and in Berlin under Carl Frederick Weitzmann, Albert Loeschhorn and Oscar Reif. Other eminent teachers in Berlin and London aided the ambitious young American in his work. In Berlin he prepared his work on Gleason's Motet Collection. On his return to Hartford he became organist in one of the city churches, but his zeal for composition was unabated, and he did some excellent work. In 1878, he came to Chicago, and, for a time, was musical critic on one of the daily papers; but such work had little charm for him, and he soon abandoned it. Mr. Gleason has composed a three-act opera, " Otto Viconti," another opera, " Montezuma " (selections from which have been played by Theodore Thomas' Orchestra), an Overture Triumphale, for the organ, two cantatas, the Auditorium Festival Ode, and a Praise Song to Harmony. His compositions show the real melodious instinct, and merit high praise for their beauty of harmony. He is indisputably one of the most scholarly and accomplished musicians in the country. Unlike many composers, he has a practical side to his character, as well as an artistic. In 1884, he was elected a member of the Board of Directors and an examiner of the American College of Musicians, an office he held for many years, and then resigned. He was chosen to represent the American Music Teachers' National Association at the meeting of the English Society of Professional Musicians, at Cambridge, England, but could not accept the honor. He feels great pride in a gold medal given to him by the Associazione dei Benemeriti Italiana, of Palermo, Sicily, " for distinguished services in the cause of art."

The public of New York, Washington, San Francisco, and other cities, have heard portions of his two operas, which have been performed for them by the Thomas and other orchestras. An organ transcription of the " Otho Visconti " is much played, and was even heard in the Cathedral at Honolulu at an organ recital. His symphonic poem, " Edris," has added laurels to those already won by Mr. Gleason.

In this poem he has risen to great heights, and while this symphony is rich in that sort of melody which pleases, it also wins more favor with each hearing. His latest symphonic poem, " The Song of Life," is a scholarly work, suggesting religious feeling, the " ever present sorrow " and " the remembrance of the love-episode," and many of the themes are of great beauty.

December 6, 1903, Mr. Gleason entered into rest, leaving to his colleagues and friends the memory of a courteous, scholarly man and a most thorough musician.

Carl Wolfsohn.

BEET*H*OVEN.

Carl Wolfsohn.

One of the best-known and most widely recognized musicians of Chicago is Carl Wolfsohn. This celebrated musical scholar and artist was born at Alzey, Reinhessen, Germany, December 14, 1834. At an early age he began the study of music, and for two years was a pupil of Aloys Schmidt, of Frankfort, till interrupted by the revolution of 1848. That year he made his début, at Frankfort, in Beethoven's pianoforte quartette. After studying with Vincent Lachner and Mme. Heinfeiter, he made a very successful concert tour through Bavaria, and, later, went to London, where he spent two years. He came to America in 1854, and settled in Philadelphia, where he remained many years. While there he established an enviable reputation as a pianist and a true musician. He played frequently in public, introducing many of the pianoforte concertos with orchestra, and giving every year, for nearly twenty years, series of concerts of chamber music. To this he added the work of an orchestral conductor, and for two years gave symphony concerts. He first attracted national attention as a singularly broad musical scholar of the piano by his series of recitals of Beethoven's Sonatas, in 1863.

These he gave two successive seasons in Philadelphia, and repeated two seasons in New York Steinway Hall. Still later,

Mr. Wolfsohn played all the pianoforte compositions of Schumann in recitals, and followed by the works of Chopin.

As an interpreter of Schumann, Mr. Wolfsohn excels, his musical intelligence making clear what the ordinary virtuoso passes over unconsciously. Mr. Wolfsohn came to Chicago in 1873, and became conductor of the Beethoven Society. This society produced Bruch's " Odysseus," Beethoven's " Mass in C," Gade's " Crusaders " and Hofman's " Legend of the Fair Melasina " for the first time. He repeated here the Beethoven's Sonatas, as given in Philadelphia and New York, affording some of the most advanced teachers their first opportunity of hearing these beautiful compositions. Later he projected a series of historical recitals covering the whole range of musical literature, one hundred in number, but circumstances compelled him to abandon the project when he was just reaching the most interesting part. He gave trio concerts in Chicago for more than ten years, attended by the best music-lovers of the city. As a teacher, he has accomplished most honorable work. Many artists, among them Mrs. Fannie Bloomfield-Leissler and Miss Augusta Cottlon, are indebted to him for making them so thoroughly musicians that other teachers developed virtuosos. He visits his relatives, near Frankford-on-the-Main, often, and attends the Baireuth festivals. He was one of the earliest workers in Wagner societies in this country, and gave Wagner selections in Philadelphia years ago. He is a musician of highest possible honor, and his name deserves to be perpetuated among those of the musical apostles and saints of America.

Carl Wolfsohn

ad. Fannie Bloomfield Zeisler.

MAD. FANNIE BLOOMFIELD ZEISLER.

Mad. Fannie Bloomfield Zeisler.

Few women have ever achieved such a recognized position among the artists of the world as has Fannie Bloomfield Zeisler, one of the world's greatest pianists. She was born at Bielitz, in Austrian Silesia, but when less than two years of age came to America with her parents. They settled in Chicago, which is still her home. When but a little child, her musical talent showed itself, for when only about six years old, without instruction, she picked out the tune of "Annie Laurie" on the piano. She first received instruction from Bernard Ziehn, and, later, from Carl Wolfsohn, both of whom are still living in Chicago, and have witnessed the triumphs of their famous pupil. When the great pianist, Mad. Essipoff, came to this country, in 1877, she heard the gifted child play, and, recognizing her talent, insisted that her parents send her to Leschetizky, then, as since, known as one of the best piano teachers in the world. In 1878, Fannie Bloomfield went to Vienna, and for the next five years was the conscientious pupil of this celebrated teacher. Before leaving Vienna, in 1883, she played several times with great success, and as soon as she reached America, the autumn of that year, began her career as a concert pianist in this country. For the next ten years she played during every winter, and, as soloist, appeared with the best orchestras of this country, such as the Chi-

cago

Orchestra, the Boston Symphony Orchestra, the New York Symphony and Philadelphia Harmonic Societies. In 1893, she went abroad and played in Berlin, Leipsic, Vienna, Dresden and other cities. Everywhere she gained recognition as one of the greatest pianists of the world, the greatest woman pianist ever known. As a result she made a concert tour of Europe in 1894-95, during which she played in the leading cities of the Continent, the whole season being a succession of the most wonderful triumphs.

In 1895, she returned to America, and since that time has appeared every season with all the best orchestral organizations in the largest musical centers. In 1896, she made a tour of the Pacific coast, where her reception was of the most gratifying sort. While in San Francisco she gave eight concerts, in every one of which her audiences seemed always more and more enthusiastic. England was the scene of her triumphs in 1898, when in London the musical public were most demonstrative in their delight at her playing. She received, while there, the honor of an invitation to be the piano soloist at the annual Lower Rhine Music Festival, which occurred, May 29-31, 1898, at Cologne. Her audience there consisted of the most renowned musicians and critics of the world, and her success was absolutely complete. Quite recently she has become identified with the Bush Temple Conservatory of Music, where she receives advanced pupils between her concert seasons.

Hans Balatka.

HANS BALATKA.

Hans Balatka.

It is scarcely necessary to tell the people of America about the world-renowned Hans Balatka. Like many another artist, he never fully enjoyed the fruits of his labors, but the acknowledgment of his greatness by press and people, at his death, enshrined him forever in the memory of the music-loving American public. Hans Balatka was born in Hoffmengsthal, Austria. His fine voice secured for him the position of alto soloist in the boy choir of the grand Cathedral of Olmütz, and he there received an excellent musical education. At the University of Olmütz and Vienna he was appointed conductor of the academical singing societies, studied singing under Gentiluomo, and harmony and composition under Proch and Sechter. The political revolution of 1848 influenced Mr. Balatka to come to America. Locating in Milwaukee, he founded the famous Milwaukee Musical Society, introducing most of the standard symphonies, oratorios and many operas with full vocal and orchestral forces. His fame spread rapidly, and he was appointed conductor of a number of musical festivals at Cleveland, Cincinnati, Detroit, Pittsburg, Milwaukee, Chicago and other places. In 1860, Mr. Balatka was urged by prominent musical people to make Chicago his home, and conduct the then new Philharmonic Society. He came to Chicago, and also became conductor of the Germania Mannerchor, the Musical Union and other musical organizations of high standing.

289

The concerts, operas and oratorios, in which he introduced Mad. Parepa-Rosa, Neilsson, Pappenheim, Carey, Whitney, Remmertz and others, are among the prominent musical events of Chicago.   But his principal occupation was vocal teaching. Many talented singers owe their introduction to the lyric stage to his efforts, and a number of the first musicians and teachers in Chicago have been his pupils.   In 1868, he gave the first orchestral concert in Library Hall, which, from a musical standpoint, was a success.

In 1879, Mr. Balatka laid the foundation for the Balatka Musical College by establishing the Balatka Academy of Musical Art.   As a director, he was the head of the institution for twenty years, and his cultured mind was the controlling influence in all its departments.

In 1895, Mr. Balatka celebrated his fiftieth anniversary as a musical conductor.   On this occasion the musical world —not only of America but of Europe as well—gave enthusiastic acknowledgement of his genius.   He received most flattering recognition from European musical authorities, and was favorably mentioned in the great Encyclopædia of Dr. Riemann, an honor bestowed only on unquestioned merit.

He was not only great as a musician, but excelled in literary work.   His pen, while sharp and witty, was just, and his musical criticisms valuable.

Hans Balatka died in April, 1899, aged seventy-four years, after more than fifty years of service in the field of music.

His busy life and invaluable work will always occupy an important place in the musical history of Chicago.

Christian Balatka.

CHRISTIAN BALATKA.

Christian Balatka.

Remembering always with loving pride the achievements
of his illustrious father, Hans Balatka, Christian Balatka,
inspired by this memory, is rapidly making for himself a
widespread reputation as a true musician, a successful teacher
and fine conductor. Chicago was his birthplace, and, at a very
early age, he began studying music under his father. So remarkable was his talent that at the age of thirteen he was able
to play Clementis Gradus ad Parnassum, and to accompany
such difficult compositions as Beethoven's " Ninth Symphony," Bruch's " Odysseus," etc. After studying a number
of years under local teachers, he went abroad and completed
his studies under the best instructors of the Royal Academy
of Music, at Berlin. So great was his success as a pianist in
Europe that he was honored by a command to appear before
royalty. His success as a concert pianist in this country is
well known wherever he has appeared, and has been such as
to warrant his making this his lifework. But his ambition
has been to finish the work which his father began, and on his
return to this country he assumed the directorship of the piano
department of the Balatka Musical College, and devotes his
time to teaching the piano.

Among the large number of brilliant students graduating
from this department many have won more than ordinary dis-

of twelve he played with ease the " Hungarian Fantasie," by Liszt, and Dr. Balatka feels that a wonderful career is open before him.

Christian Balatka has received marked recognition from the highest musical authorities in this country. In 1901-02 he was made Doctor of Music by the New York State University, and, in 1903, was elected Dean and Examiner for the State of Illinois, for the same university. This is the only music school in America empowered by Act of Legislature to confer the regular university degrees. Under the skilful management of Dr. Christian Balatka, the college which his father founded has made great advance in numbers, in the excellence of its corps of teachers and in the grade of work accomplished. At the time of Hans Balatka's death, the college numbered possibly two hundred and fifty pupils, now it enrolls about a thousand. Dr. Balatka has exercised great care in the selection of his faculty; many of them are well-known soloists, ranking high in their profession.

He is devoted to his work, ambitious for his school, interested in the success of his pupils and constantly planning for the achievement of the high ideals of which he never loses sight.

Charles W. Clark.

Charles W. Clark

Charles W. Clark.

One of Chicago's best-known singers, greatly beloved for his personal characteristics and admired by all musicians everywhere for his splendid musical achievements, is Charles W. Clark. A native of Northwestern Ohio, it was not till 1888 that he came to Chicago and began to really devote himself to the study of music. So thoroughly has he identified himself with musical life here that he seems as much Chicago's very own as if a native of this city. So great a result has followed his devotion to musical study that he has won a most enviable reputation in concert and oratorio work throughout the country.

Mr. Clark's first engagement in Chicago was as one of the Quartette Choir of the Centennial Baptist Church. Afterwards he sang in the choir of the First Presbyterian Church, Evanston, of which church Dr. Hillis was then the pastor. When Dr. Hillis succeeded the late Dr. Swing at the Central Church, so greatly was he attached to Mr. Clark that he persuaded him to come with him, and for years he was soloist at that church, except when absent from the city studying, or engaged in concert work in London and other places. Mr. Clark made his début in London, with Mr. George Henschel conducting, February 18, 1897, in a Wagner concert, and ten days later made his second appearance in Bach's Passion music,

"St. Matthew." Mr. Henschel was most enthusiastic in regard to Mr. Clark's voice and the possibilities before him, and offered him the finest concert engagements if he would only consent to make the English metropolis his home. While in England, he sang in the best concerts in London, Manchester, Liverpool and other cities, with the most prominent societies, as soloist in cantatas and oratorios, also taking part in many miscellaneous programs. Mr. Clark is, however, an American at heart, and returned to this country about 1898, where his services were at once in demand by the finest organizations East and West. Mr. Edward de Reske used his influence to have Mr. Clark engage in the work of the grand opera, and Mr. Grau, of the Metropolitan Opera House, made him flattering offers to sing in leading roles in his company. His long list of engagements, however, prevented such a possibility, although both the great artist and the experienced manager felt assured that success would be his. He has sung with the best clubs and societies in the country, and has become, everywhere, distinguished as a favorite in musical circles. He has appeared with the Handel and Haydn Society, of Boston, and other oratorio societies; in a Wagner concert and Brahm's "Requiem;" with the Chicago Orchestra, under Theodore Thomas, at the Auditorium, Chicago; with Chicago's Apollo Club, and other organizations. His wonderful voice, genial personality and scholarly work readily accord him a leading place among the best singers of America.

Sara K. Connor.

It is difficult to specify the influences which make the successful musician. Lessons with the best masters and years of persevering practice are absolute essentials, but to this must be added the invaluable tuition of experience and environment.

Possibly few have had this sort of tutelage in greater degree than has Miss Sara K. Connor. She was born in Indianapolis, Ind., in 1868, the daughter of the late Alexander H. Connor, well known as an editor and a criminal lawyer.

In the seventies, the family moved to Nebraska, and the ever changing conditions of the Middle-West had a marked influence in the formation of the young daughter's ideals and ambitions.

Books and music were her companions, and the years spent in school, college and music study were years of character-building, of preparation for the duties of life. These unstrained, quiet years of preparation and observation have been widely instrumental in establishing that poise and broad mental attitude which are her strongest characteristics. As a teacher, Miss Connor was most successful in Nebraska, becoming widely and favorably known, and numbering among her clientele pupils from all parts of the State.

She is by nature a teacher, having, in addition to a sensitive and discriminating mentality, a rare faculty of imparting her knowledge to others, and of stimulating in them a desire for the acquisition of knowledge. She has thought intelligently on the facts relative to the results of musical study. While not pessimistic, she is convinced that the too general disappointment in this direction indicates a vital weakness in educational methods. Too often she feels that the teacher fails to be imbued with the spirit of sympathetic helpfulness, and that without this great element the student nature remains unknown and its powers undeveloped.

While she recognizes that there are common platforms on which all artist effort must meet, she feels the supreme importance of developing the individuality of her pupils, and her success in her work along this line has been so great as to be almost phenomenal. That supreme desire for achievement is the only foundation for successful effort she fully believes, and she gladly welcomes all methods of education which are in harmony with this truth. She deems them the most efficient, the most enjoyable and the most permanent in result.

The success which has attended the venture in which, with Miss Patten, Miss Connor is interested, is a most significant commentary upon the fact that a receptive mind registers with great sensitiveness the impressions gained from early environment. It is a proof, too, of the truth that all growth is the result of contact with the stern realities of life.

Marden School of Music and Elocution.

The Marden School of Music and Elocution, organized in 1899, and incorporated in 1900, has achieved a most enviable reputation, and has taken its place among the most prominent art schools of Chicago.

Last year over two hundred scholars were enrolled. In 1902, seven pupils were graduated, representing five States, and in 1903, five were graduated. At the commencement exercises each of the graduates gave a solo program, the selections being tests of their skill in interpretation as well as in technique. The manner in which the pupils acquitted themselves was certainly the most flattering commendation both of the methods employed and the skill of their teachers. The history of this school is sufficiently exceptional to awaken interest in its founders, Cora Mel Patten and Sara Katherine Connor. After years of professional experience, Miss Patten and Miss Connor united their efforts, in 1899, in the organization of this school.

A modest catalogue was issued, and every effort was made to enlist interest in their enterprise. Four months later, after the school had safely passed the experimental stage, it was named in honor of Orrin Swett Marden, known as a philanthropist and the editor of *Success*. It seemed as though these two young artists were intended to work together, so aptly do the characteristics of one supplement those of the other. Miss Patten, gifted, of magnetic presence, fearless and ambitious, came to Chicago seven years ago, a stranger, with no one to aid her. She soon, however, made a brilliant record as a student and a reader, and became a well-known teacher of literary interpretation. At the same time, Miss Connor was conducting a large class in Nebraska and becoming widely and favorably known. While she was accomplishing much in the line of musical culture, she was also gaining a practical knowledge of the varied conditions of life, and thus developing the strong individuality which marks her teaching. A fine personality, unusual repose of manner and rare discrimination, have united to make Miss Connor invaluable in the work to which she is devoting her energies. Through their united labors Miss Patten and Miss Connor have accomplished much.

The school has given a large number of recitals, thus affording pupils the advantage of frequent appearance before the public.

A series of readings by the greatest exponents of elocutionary art have been successfully given, and these are only indications of the spirit of activity which is a marked characteristic of this school. Success has crowned their efforts from the beginning, and it is safe to predict a brilliant future for the school, whose beginning was so unobtrusive yet, after all, the result of indomitable perseverance and unfaltering ambition.

The school has now a well-selected faculty, and the efforts of the principals are untiring to increase the usefulness of the institution.

Cora Mel Patten.

Cora Mel Patten.

The first glimpse we have of Miss Patten is of an eager, pale-faced child, listening to stories from her mother's lips, inventing marvelous tales of her own, while she resented, in her childish heart, the suffering which debarred her from the happy freedom of the playground.

She gained strength with the years, and was graduated, in 1887, from the Newton, Iowa, High School, and later from the Normal School of the same county. Miss Patten was born in 1869, in Jasper County, Iowa. Her nature is emotional, her imagination vivid, her ambitions high, her enthusiasm most contagious, yet withal she is of a rarely sensitive nature. She inherited a voice of unusual sympathy and power. As a girl, she attained quite a reputation as an elocutionist, and was foremost in all literary entertainments. She began her professional career at the age of twenty, and has achieved unusual success. For three years she taught in the public schools of her native town, but, dissatisfied with that work, she went to Chicago, and took a short course in elocution. She then became the teacher of this branch in the Iowa Wesleyan University, and, as the result of her influence and the interest thus stimulated, a chair of oratory was established. After a year devoted to travel, she returned to Chicago and completed her course in elocution. In 1895, she graduated with the honors

after which she accepted a position with her Alma Mater for two years. After resigning this position, she devoted a year to study and teaching private classes. By this time she had gathered about her so many and such devoted friends and pupils that she was able to carry out what had been a cherished hope, and established a school of her own. She is, we believe, the youngest woman at the head of a professional school in Chicago, and has now a reputation as one of the really strong teachers in her line. She is energetic and untiring in her effort, broad in her thought, independent in her plans, fearless in their execution. Believing that vocal interpretation should be inspiring as well as entertaining, only such literature as she feels embodies the spirit of truth finds recognition in her school. Her chief ambition is to become a great teacher, and with this career in mind she has steadily refused all platform work which would take her away from Chicago. With so single an aim, with such devotion to her chosen work, Miss Patten will make for herself a place of rare achievement.

George Hamlin.

George Hamlin

George Hamlin.

The foremost tenor of Illinois—by many regarded as having no superior in this country—George Hamlin is constantly adding to his laurels and making himself a place in the hearts of his audiences. He is a native of Illinois, and is a most notable example of what can be achieved by an American in America, for his entire musical education has been received in this country and from American teachers. For about fifteen years he has sung in many of the leading churches in Chicago, but it is only some seven or eight years since he made his début on the concert platform.

During the musical season of 1898-99, he gave, for the first time in America, the most delightful Lieder of Richard Strauss, and won highest praise from both the press and musical critics. Mr. Hamlin's voice is sweet and clear, with great carrying power, and he sings with an ease of manner which puts him at once *en rapport* with his audience, and gives a rare charm to whatever he does. He has appeared at various times with all the best oratorio and other societies of the country. Among them may be named the Apollo Clubs of Chicago, Cincinnati, Des Moines and Toledo, the Mozart Club of Pittsburg, musical clubs of St. Paul and Louisville, Handel and Haydn Society, of Boston, the Chicago Orchestra concerts under the direction of Theodore Thomas, the New York

said of him—" Mr. Hamlin has a voice of fine, manly timbre, which he uses with great taste, and his musical instincts are evidently of the best. One of the most delightful features of his singing is the unvarying purity of his intonation." Wherever he has sung, all over the country the press has been unstinted in its praises both of his voice and his method. We can quote but from a few—" Mr. Hamlin has a tenor voice of sweet and sympathetic quality, and is evidently a conscientious student," said the *Boston Herald*. The *Louisville Commercial* wrote—" At the head of American tenors;" the *Minneapolis Times*—" The most satisfactory tenor ever heard here." At a recent concert given by the Mendelssohn Club, of Chicago, in the season 1903-04, Mr. Hamlin was the soloist. He gave four groups of songs—French, German, Italian and English; his perfect pronunciation and enunciation in whatever language he sung were a most remarkable proof of his achievements as a linguist, and his rendition of each number showed the exquisite finish only attained by persistent study and unceasing practice.

Mr. Hamlin, unlike many public singers, is most generous in his response to encores, a genial courtesy greatly appreciated by those who hear him.

Anne Shaw Faulkner.

Anna Shaw Faulkner

Anne Shaw Faulkner.

Miss Anne Shaw Faulkner, a native of Chicago, is a young lady whose progress in her chosen line of musical work is a source of congratulation and pleasure to all who know her. She was born September 26, 1877, and her entire education has been obtained in Chicago. She has worked mostly with Miss Julia Lois Carruthers (now the Director of the Carruthers' Normal School), also with Mr. Calvin Cady. It was in the fall of 1897 that she began the Orchestra Concert Study Classes which have become such an important factor in the musical work of Chicago. Her object was to simplify and explain the programs to young girls just beginning to attend the orchestra concerts. She was so instructive that it was suggested that she open classes for older pupils, and the second season Miss Faulkner started six classes in private houses. These proved so satisfactory that the third year she started a small public class, and the next season she not only had a large class, which held its meetings in Assembly Hall, but also opened a studio in the Fine Arts Building. In 1902-03, in addition to the regular twenty-four morning talks on the Chicago Orchestra programs, she gave three evening concerts for the purpose of greater familiarity with the instruments of the orchestra. The first was a lecture on " The Orchestra, its Instruments and their Music," illustrated by seventeen members of the Chicago Orchestra, and the other two were programs of wood-wind music.

These concerts attracted much favorable comment, and Miss Faulkner is arranging four similar programs for next season. Miss Faulkner also has charge of the History of Music in the Columbia Conservatory, and has supplemented her regular work there with a program study class for music pupils.

A course of six studies on " Music and its Relation to the History of Art " has also been given by her for Carruthers' Normal School, this season. " This comprises," Miss Faulkner says, " my regular work." In additon to this, much outside work has been done in lecturing for clubs, arranging private musicales and benefit concerts.

Miss Faulkner spent last summer abroad, as assistant musical director, on a musical pilgrimage with a party under the direction of the Bureau of University Travel, of Boston.

This is only a glance at this gifted girl's busy life. The " Loves of Beethoven," which she has given with Miss Stevens; " The Bayreuth and the Wagner Festival;" a stereopticon lecture with music behind the scenes, and many another musical novelty, attest the genius of this wonderful artist.

Miss Faulkner will supplement her history course this season with six lectures on " History of Music as an Art," which will be illustrated with stereopticon views, showing the development of notation, instruments and composition by contrasting pictures. She is very sanguine as to the success of this, her newest, musical venture.

Mary Florence Stevens.

Mary Florence Stevens

Mary Florence Stevens.

One of Chicago's rising young vocalists is Miss Mary Florence Stevens.

Possessing a rich, highly cultivated soprano voice and a most pleasing personality, she becomes at once a favorite wherever she is heard. She was born in Baltimore, Md., but has spent most of her life in the West, and has identified herself with the best music of Chicago and Evanston, where she lives. She has been the soloist for the Evanston Musical Club—a club doing as artistic work as any in the West—a recognition of her talent rarely accorded to a local singer. For four years she studied under Mrs. Sarah Robinson Duff, and later under the instruction of Mr. Sydney Lloyd Wrightson, the noted teacher from London, one of Mr. Wm. Shakespeare's representatives in this country.

More recently still she has studied with William L. Tomlins, who is unsurpassed in interpretation of oratorio, and represents the most notable advances in modern musical education. She expects to study with him this winter (1903-04).

Exceptionally well fitted for oratorio and song recital work, she is also happy in her interpretations of smaller songs, and whatever she sings it is done with the utmost ease and a delightful absence of effort. It is the sentiment in what she sings which appeals to her, not its technical difficulty, and so

319

she sings not to display her voice, but that she may reach the hearts of her hearers and express to them the beauty of the song and the poetic idea which was in the mind of the composer.

Young, attractive, with an easy, graceful presence, an artistic temperament, and wonderful voice, she is destined to become one of the leading artists of the country. She has made a novel specialty of giving musical illustrations for music lectures. In this work she has been associated with Miss Anna Shaw Faulkner, who has made so great a success of her Thomas' Orchestra classes. Her delightfully clear enunciation and her voice, combining brilliancy and sweetness with warmth of color and breadth, make her particularly adapted to this work, in which she is winning many laurels.

One of this series is the " Loves of Beethoven " lecture, which is illustrated with Beethoven songs. She has been equally successful in her rendition of the music of the North American Indians and primitive peoples, and has devoted some time to research in the field of such music.

Miss Stevens is also a teacher of voice culture, and has her studio in the Fine Arts Building, where, in spite of the many demands upon her time, she is attaining success with her rapidly increasing class of pupils.

A favorite among clubs in Chicago and other cities, popular as a concert singer, she is none the less conscientious and devoted to her work as an instructor, and is an enthusiast in whatever she undertakes.

Carrie Woods Bush.

Carrie Woods Bush

Carrie Woods Bush.

This accomplished musician and able critic, now of Chicago, received her early education in Erie, Pa., where her father, James R. Wood, was a prosperous wholesale merchant, and her mother a successful physician. From them, no doubt, she inherited the energy, the industrious habits and the enthusiasm which have had very much to do with the success which has followed everything she has attempted to accomplish. At an early age Mrs. Bush played the piano well, and all her life she has been a most devoted student of music, having received instruction from some of the best teachers in Chicago. Every possible advantage which could best fit her for the position she now occupies has been given her, and she has made good use of them all. Not only has she had a most thorough course in instrumental music, but she has devoted years to the study of the theory of music, and the various methods employed by the foremost musical educators of the day. The duties devolving upon her as a critic and correspondent are, of necessity, somewhat exacting, requiring a vast deal not only of musical knowledge but of native tact as well. Until recently she has devoted much of her time to the teaching of the piano, pipe organ and the theory of music. As a pianist and teacher she acquired a most excellent reputation. She has given to whatever she attempted a dauntless energy, which meant suc-

323

cess. Some years since, she became identified with several
well-known musical publications, and this brought her prominently before those engaged in a like line of work.

or the three years the *Boston Musical Record* was represented in Chicago, Mrs. Bush held the position of critic here,
a position she filled most acceptably. Her experience as a
teacher has given her a great advantage as a musical critic,
and her knowledge of the theory of music has been helpful in
the same direction. Through this experience she is often able
to look back of result, and recognize effort, and hence an appreciative and intelligent criticism. The task of a critic is
often a thankless one, but Mrs. Bush brings to her work such
unusual preparation, such experience, such tact, that the success she has achieved seems the only result possible. She is
now on the staff of the *Chicago Musical Leader,* and is thoroughly interesting herself in its aim and work. The publication has awakened an interest in the music of the West, and
is receiving more and more the consideration of those observ-
ing new lines of musical work.

Mrs. Bush is identifying herself with this magazine with
her characteristic energy, and in so doing is making herself
part of the musical history of the West.

Helen Buckley.

HELEN BUCKLEY.

Gifte
an artisti
tionally t
Helen Bu
world. 1
musical e
she went
most bri
was wid
letters f
land, Es
Jacques
land.
ses, th
Ronald
and vei
uicali

Helen Buckley.

Gifted with a beautiful soprano voice, rare intelligence, an artistic temperament, a magnetic personality and exceptionally fine stage presence, it is not surprising that Miss Helen Buckley holds a distinguished position in the musical world. Being an American, Miss Buckley received her first musical education in this country under Frank Baird. Later she went to England, where she became one of Randegger's most brilliant and successful pupils. In London her ability was widely recognized, and she received many congratulatory letters from eminent musical critics, such as J. A. Fuller-Maitland, Esq. (music critic of the *Times,* London, England), and Jacques Blumenthal, the well-known composer, London, England. While in London, she sang for many prominent persons, the Duke of Wellington, Duchess of Manchester, Mrs. Ronalds, of the "American Colony," Jacques Blumenthal, and very many others. She was honored by being the only vocalist selected to appear before the Duke of Genoa and his Italian fleet at Portsmouth.

She and Mark Hambourg made their London début at St. James Hall with the Joachim Quartette, and were received with great enthusiasm. Returning to America, she sang first in Chicago with the Chicago Apollo Club, in the " Messiah." Since then her engagements have been many and successful, embracing New York, Chicago, Cincinnati, Minneapolis, St. Louis, Milwaukee, in fact nearly all musical centers in the United States.

In Chicago she took Gadski's place with the Apollo Club in a performance of Massanet's " Mary Magdalen," learning the difficult music and singing it most effectively on ten days' notice.   She filled an engagement at Mendelssohn Hall, New York, after courageously singing for the manager's approval over a long-distance telephone.   She made a tour of a hundred and two concerts, her associates being Mary Louise Clary, William Rieger and Arthur Beresford.   Miss Buckley occupies the responsible and lucrative position of leading soloist at the Fourth Presbyterian Church, Chicago.   Her interpretation of all sacred music has in it a most admirable inspiration, which is a special characteristic of her oratorio work.

She made her fifth appearance with the Chicago Apollo Club in the " Damnation of Faust," and soon after sang at a festival at Hutchinson, Kansas, which extended over a week. She has sung with the Mendelssohn Club, of Chicago, and with the Milwaukee Musical Society.

Newspapers in England and all over the United States have teemed with the most enthusiastic notices of this distinguished and captivating singer.   Whether she has sung in oratorio, or rendered the most difficult songs by Grieg, Goring-Thomas, Massanet and Salvator Rosa, or appeared in opera, she has merited the same applause.   It is difficult to discriminate when a singer is so successful in everything she undertakes.   Miss Buckley has won her place among the best artists, and is daily adding to the laurels so honestly hers.

Leopold Godowsky.

LEOPOLD GODOWSKY.

Leopold Godowsky.

There is to-day no artist, in the realm of tone, whose career is followed with more attention and interest than that of Leopold Godowsky, who was born at Wilna, Russian Poland, February 13, 1870. Showing a remarkable talent at a very early age, he was taken upon the road as a child-wonder, and concertized all over Russia and parts of Germany until he was twelve years old. He then entered the Hoch Schule at Berlin, where he remained for two years. At this time he determined to come to America, and he toured this country in connection with Ovide Musin, the violinist, and his company. But the young artist soon tired of the monotony of travel, and made strong efforts to return to Europe for further study. He realized that Saint Saëns, the great French composer and pianist, would best preserve his individuality, and he set about to procure an audience with him. His first meeting with this distinguished musician forms one of the most interesting chapters in Godowsky's life; suffice it to say that, after hearing one of Godowsky's own compositions, entitled " Das Maerchen," he at once accepted him as his pupil. The protection and favor which Godowsky thus enjoyed were soon known in Paris, and served to introduce him to the most exclusive social and musical circles of the French capital.

From the salons of Paris to those of London was but a

step, and in a short time Godowsky had become favorably
known in London.   Ere long his matchless art was recognized
in the most aristocratic homes of that city, in the palaces of
the Duke of Westminster (recently deceased), the Duke of
Norfolk, at Grosvenor and Marlborough House.   It was during the many festivities in connection with the Queen's golden jubilee, in 1887, that Godowsky was ordered to play at the
Marlborough House, where a most august assemblage formed
his audience.   On that occasion the Princess of Wales, now
Queen Alexandra, was so much pleased with Godowsky's
" Valse Scherzo " that she accepted the dedication of it by a
special court order.

In 1890, at twenty years of age, Godowsky returned to
America.   On April 30, 1890, he married Miss Frieda Saxe,
of New York.   He made his home in New York until 1895'
when a brilliant offer was made him to take charge of the
piano department of the Chicago Conservatory, which offer he
accepted.   His success there is too well known and too recent
to call for comment.   Godowsky has been heard repeatedly
with every important musical organization of the United
States and Canada, and is known as a concert pianist from the
Atlantic to the Pacific, from Canada to the Gulf of Mexico,
receiving everywhere the most flattering encomiums.

Godowsky has already made a strong impression upon
contemporary art.   A work which will make his name a house-
hold word with every aspiring pianist is just receiving its finishing touches.

The extremely conservative firm of Schlesinger, of Berlin, Germany, has just contracted for the publication of fifty
of his newly written studies on the études of Chopin.   They

have caused a stir in musical circles, such as has not been known since Liszt and Brahms have ceased to write for the piano.

Many critics stand in amazement before them, declaring them absolutely impossible to perform, yet Godowsky plays every one of them from memory. They have earned for Godowsky the title " The Apostle of the Left Hand." Technically they are likely to revolutionize the art of piano-playing, while harmonically they are as interesting and modern as the tendencies of our time will permit, and doubtlessly much in advance of our time.

Of Godowsky's original compositions quite a number have recently been published. They disclose the author's remarkable melodic and polyphonic gift. It is the predominating polyphonic treatment which makes the execution of most of Godowsky's compositions quite difficult, even after solving every technical problem successfully. Yet they are original in melodic invention, and contain interesting harmonic progressions as well as refined workmanship. As a concert pianist Godowsky stands in the very front rank of contemporary artists.

As a technician, he is in advance of all, yet Godowsky has little pride in this distinction, and takes special care not to be identified with the mere mastery of technique.

The latter, it is true, is of the most astounding order, and thus impresses the listener, but to Godowsky technique is only a means and not an end, and he makes it subservient to the intellectual and practical requirements of the work in hand. There is no ostentation or frivolity in his playing, but rather largeness and broadness of style, brilliancy, grace, fluency and poetic feeling. It is piano-playing at its very best, well-balanced, noble work. His repertoire embraces practically the entire piano literature. His special favorites are the larger works of Schumann and Chopin. He has a warm admiration for the more important Bach fugues, the last sonatas of Beethoven, for Tschaikowsky, Brahms and Wagner. Though a brilliant performer of Liszt's compositions, he admires the original works, such as the concert studies, the gigantic B minor sonata, more than the rhapsodies or operatic fantasies and paraphrases. Of larger works, he commands the entire literature of the concerts of Beethoven, Schumann, Chopin, Liszt, Rubinstein, Brahms, Grieg, Tschaikowsky, Saint-Saëns, etc., as well as almost the entire chamber music literature.

The last two years have witnessed Godowsky's appearance as composer and concert pianist in the capitals and principal cities of France, England, Germany, Austria and Russia, and the sensational successes he achieved in Berlin, the musical metropolis of the world, are of such recent date as not to require special mention.

In February, 1903, he was decorated by the King and Queen of Roumania with the order of the crown. His salons in Berlin, where he resides at present, have become the rendezvous of the most renowned artists of the day, not musicians alone, but poets, painters, sculptors and scientists are all made equally welcome at his hospitable board.

If Godowsky, as composer and concert pianist, has created admirers wherever he has been heard, Godowsky, the man, makes everyone his friend with whom he comes in contact.

Mr. Maurice Aronson.

Maurice Aronson

Among the
s succeeded i
tion of suc
rson, the
each a total
ed for hi
to season t
The Maur
adquarters
reckoned
equipped priv
Maurice
the Baltic co
his music. I
received a
nasium, fro
ten years.
Then t
prompted M
eral years h
other conti
the most u

Mr. Maurice Aronson.

Among the younger artists of Chicago there is none that has succeeded in creating for himself, within the last decade, a position of such prominence in his profession as has Maurice Aronson, the well-known pianist, instructor and critic. Though a total stranger in Chicago seven years ago, he has created for himself a following that taxes his time from season to season to the utmost limit.

The Maurice Aronson studios in the Auditorium are the headquarters of a large number of talented pianists, and they are reckoned among the most exclusive and most elegantly equipped private studios in the entire West.

Maurice Aronson was born June 24, 1869, in Mitau, near the Baltic coast. He showed, in early youth, a decided talent for music. In connection with thorough musical instruction, he received a comprehensive academical education at the Gymnasium, from which he graduated at the unusual age of sixteen years.

Then the inborn love for music asserted itself, and prompted Mr. Aronson to adopt it as a profession. For several years he pursued his studies in St. Petersburg, Berlin and other continental cities, appearing frequently in public with the most unqualified success. In 1888, he came to America, settling in the South, as pianist and organist. Within a short time he gathered large classes about him and became one of the best-known and most successful musicians in the South.

The desire to continue his studies and search for a large field of activity prompted Mr. Aronson to come to Chicago, in the fall of 1896. He studied for some time with Leopold Godowsky, the eminent pianist and composer, whose chief assistant he became in the Chicago Conservatory. In that institution Mr. Aronson's services proved so valuable that he became one of the most prominent members of its famous faculty.

Mr. Godowsky's departure for Europe brought Mr. Aronson the most flattering testimonials from the pen of the distinguished Russian. After refusing some very tempting offers from prominent colleges and conservatories of music, Mr. Aronson established his own studios. In January, 1903, Mr. Godowsky invited Mr. Aronson to come to Berlin, Germany, to become associated with him again in professional work. This invitation was a great compliment to Mr. Aronson's ability, and was accepted by him. He has been located in Berlin since July of this year. As a pianist, Mr. Aronson possesses most artistic qualities and has a large repertoire. He has been heard repeatedly in individual recitals and with other artists in Chicago and other cities.

Outside of his piano and theoretic studies, Mr. Aronson has made extensive researches in musical history and literature, and has evinced ability as a writer.

The results of these studies frequently appear in musical journals here and abroad.

A Christmas Reminiscence.

By Maurice Aronson.

One of the most precious reminiscences of my boyhood is a piano recital by Anton Rubinstein, the great Russian composer and pianist. The recital took place in Riga, and was announced for the day preceding Christmas. The silent consciousness that Santa Claus had generously remembered me, that a prohibitive price of admission had been set, etc., caused me to desist from persuasion and resign myself to the inevitable. But fate willed it otherwise. On the morning of December 23d, the mail brought me a handsomely written note, the contents of which I translate freely from the French—

"My dear young friend:—Your playing of the Mozart Rondo and the Mendelssohn Songs without Words on the occasion of the 'soirée musicale,' at the Baroness C.'s, gave me much pleasure. If you learn to play Beethoven, Chopin and Schumann as well as you played Mozart and Mendelssohn we shall be proud of you in years to come. The enclosed cards will enable you to hear Meister Rubinstein play Beethoven, Chopin and Schumann to-night. Our carriage will call for you at noon. A very merry Christmas!

"Your friend,
"Princess W."

339

The children of the Princess were my friends. The Princess, a beautiful and cultured woman, an enthusiastic musical amateur, had befriended me frequently ere this. At the appointed hour I joined the party, consisting of the Princess, her children, two handsome lads, and their tutor. We arrived at the brilliant concert hall, which was taxed beyond its capacity with a most cultured audience, only a few moments before the great master of the keyboard would make his appearance. The moment came. Anton Rubinstein was on the stage! Slowly, his head bent forward, he approached the exquisite grand piano, and in bowing his thanks to the expectant audience his long, raven black hair fell over his face.

Throwing it backward, without preluding at all, he attacked with full force the first number of the program, his own arrangement of Beethoven's overture to Egmont. Suddenly the master's vehement left hand landed upon a crashing E, instead of the famous F of that overture. A pianist inferior to Anton Rubinstein would have withdrawn after such a mishap, but in Rubinstein the audience recognized a Titan who played with boulder rocks. A stone might, perchance, fall to the side, but his playing remained incomparable. The heroic Beethoven was followed by the highly romantic Schubert, whose works no pianist has interpreted more beautifully than Rubinstein. What charming change of humorous joking, of mystic laughing, of sorrow, anger and innocent joy he offered in the Impromptu in F Minor, in the B Minor Minuet, and in the "Moment Musical." The master must have felt, by this time, that his audience was under the full control of his magic power, and he led his hypnotized listeners into the fairyland which the wonderful Chopin has disclosed to the

world. After all the fantastic poetry of the F Minor Bal-
lade and the soulful, wistful yearnings of the A Flat Nocturne, he turned, in charming realism, to the joys of the world.
To the exciting rhythm of a mazurka and the caressing A Flat
valse, the dreamy Chopin steps into the ballroom and the
clumsy, Titanic Rubinstein becomes the most graceful dancer.

Rubinstein's interpretation of Schumann's " Études
Symphoniques " is my most cherished reminiscence of that
occasion. Whether it be due to the susceptibility of my enthusiastic nature or the impressibility of my youthful mind,
I remember the playing of those wonderful tone pictures as
if I heard them now, and I confess that, despite the beautiful
readings which, in after years, Sophie Menter, Timanoff, Essipoff, D'Albert, Godowsky, Paderewski, Zeisler and many
other pianists have given them, I can never dissociate Rubinstein's reading from them. With Liszt's second " Hungarian
Rhapsodie" he proved his virtuosity. What we now hear from
time to time of those whimsical, rhapsodic improvisations is
but the echo of such glorious playing as characterized Rubinstein's treatment of them. As he executed the most intricate
cadenzas of his own creation in the closing number, his own
" Valse Caprice," the enthusiasm of his audience increased.
In the middle part, at those famous skips of the right hand, it
seemed as if he would tear the piano apart, and many a note
was struck near by. At the close there was the most overwhelming ovation for the great, the only Rubinstein. The
audience was beyond control. Ladies tore the flowers from
their corsages and threw them to the artist, who seemed deeply moved. Rubinstein had to appear again and again. Finally the door was barricaded, and he found himself compelled to

He did not play it, he sang it, and as the melody was glid-
ing swan-like away the pearly water-drops could be heard falling from its wings.

With a shrill dissonance he began his program, with as
pure a harmony as the human hand ever struck he dismissed
his audience.

Such was Rubinstein's magnificent art. The occasion re-
ferred to was but one of the many triumphs of his genius

We returned home the next day. My Christmas gifts
were many, but, of all the gifts, I prized most highly the consciousness that I had heard Anton Rubinstein, one of the
world's greatest masters. Five years later I heard the master's entire series of seven historical recitals, which terminated his career as a concert pianist. It was a gigantic undertaking, worthy of its illustrious promoter.

Milward Adams.

Milward Adams.

In a lecture on "Amusements," long ago, Henry Ward Beecher presented that subject to his audience, following a line of thought peculiarly his own, not usually recognized. The fact that one man's amusement might be to another a burden, and that the ability to devise avenues of amusement worthy the name was a sort of genius, were among the ideas suggested. Perhaps no man in Chicago has devoted more thought to the place which amusement occupies in the daily life than Milward Adams. His father was a surgeon in the U. S. Army, living in Lexington, Ky., but about the early sixties moved to Ohio, where Milward was born. He inherited the impulsiveness and enthusiasm characteristic of those from the Sunny South, and everything he has undertaken has been prosecuted in this whole-hearted way. In 1870, he came to Chicago, and a year and a half later, impressed with the dearth of proper amusement for the people, entered upon his lifework. In those days concerts and lectures appealed most strongly to the best class of people, and Mr. Adams, in his work, was brought in touch with artists such as Charlotte Cushman, Ole Bull, Rubinstein, Henry Ward Beecher, and many others.

While thus engaged for others, he was constantly enlarging his own thought and developing within himself artistic impulses and ambitions which have, no doubt, influenced his subsequent life. His aim for the choicest, particularly in lines of musical endeavor, never wavered, and for the consummation of his hopes he worked. When Central Music Hall was built (a place dear to memory as the home, for years, of Chicago's best music), and its projector, George Benedict Carpenter, passed away, Mr. Adams, who had been the assistant manager, had full control. This position he retained from Jan., 1881, to December, 1887, when work connected with the projected Auditorium, of which he was offered the management, occupied his entire time. To his efforts, his never flagging attention to detail, probably more than to those of any other, that magnificent structure owed its complete and satisfactory realization. Few understand how tremendous are his responsibilities to-day in his position as manager of the Auditorium Theatre. In 1882 and 1884 Mr. Adams had charge of the May Musical Festivals in the old Exposition Building, which were a delight to all who attended, and among the best events in Chicago's musical history. He also arranged for the Theodore Thomas summer night concerts to come to Chicago, from which experiment the Chicago Orchestra resulted. For twenty-five years Mr. Adams has been connected with almost every large musical achievement in Chicago, and has so endeared himself to both artists and the amusement-loving public that his friends are legion.

Frank T. Baird.

Franks T. Baird

Frank T. Baird.

The career of this well-known artist and teacher of vocal culture is deserving of particular attention in any review of Chicago's past popular musicians. His proficiency in this branch of musical art is so widely recognized that his time is completely absorbed with pupils, many of whom come from a long distance to Chicago for the express purpose of pursuing their studies under his guidance.

Mr. Baird was born in Worcester, Mass., a town which has had the honor of being the birthplace of quite a number of well-known musicians. He began his musical career by studying the organ with D. B. Allen. While yet a boy he came to Chicago and continued the study of the organ, taking up also composition with Dudley Buck. Later he revived his organ studies with Clarence Eddy. He also devoted much time to piano study, his most noted piano teachers being Alfred Pease and Emil Liebling. For twenty-three years Mr. Baird was organist at the Third Presbyterian Church, during which time he found opportunity to do not a little concert work. He has appeared both as soloist and accompanist with many artists, among them being Annie Louise Cary, Clara Louise Kellogg, Muer Scalchi and Myron W. Whitney.

It was as the result of advice from Miss Cary that he decided to take up the study of vocal music. For this purpose he went to Europe, and in Paris studied with Sbriglea, in Dresden with Lamperti and in London with Shakespeare and Henschel.   Returning to America, he resumed the work of teaching, in which he has been wonderfully successful.   His wide experience as an accompanist and the opportunity he has had of studying the methods of celebrated artists have been of very great value to him in his teaching.

During his career as a vocal teacher he has developed some very popular and talented singers.

George J. Hamlin, one of America's greatest tenors, studied with Mr. Baird for four years.   Miss Helen Buckley considers that she was very fortunate in having, at the beginning of her career, an instructor who knew so thoroughly the essentials of voice production and how to teach them.   S. Fisher Miller, the popular New York tenor, who is one of the highest salaried choir singers in that city, also studied with Mr. Baird.   Besides these and other well-known artists, Mr. Baird has a large number of pupils who occupy some of the very best choir positions in and near Chicago, and sing most acceptably in concerts and oratorios where strictly professional service is not required.   Mr. Baird at one time organized and successfully directed choral societies, but the demands upon his time by pupils became so great that he has been compelled to abandon all work except teaching.

For the past fourteen years Mr. Baird has spent his summers abroad.

John Robert Gray.

JOHN ROBERT GRAY.

John Robert Gray.

There are few duties more important than that which honors and perpetuates, as far as possible, the memory of an eminent citizen; one who, by his blameless and honorable life and distinguished career, reflects credit upon his city and State. His example, in whatever field his work may have been done, thus remains an object-lesson to those who come after him, and, though dead, he still speaks. Long after his personality shall have faded from the minds of men, the less perishable record may tell the story of his life and commend his example for imitation. A man worthy of such perpetuity was John R. Gray, who was born in Belle Plain, Marshall County, Illinois, February 13, 1860. His parents were William Henry and Wilhelmina Augusta Gray. He lived in Lacon and Eureka, Ill., and for six years prior to his death in Bloomington, Ill. He spent two years at the Illinois Wesleyan University, taking the collegiate course and studying piano with Mrs. Flora Hunter, of Bloomington.

In 1881 he went abroad, and for five years studied music in Leipzig, Germany, where he and his wife were both graduated from the Leipzig Conservatory. While there he improved to the utmost his opportunities under such masters as Eibenschutz, Wiedenbach, Richter and Jadassohn. After his return to this country he spent one year, 1886, as musical

came musical instructor in the Wesleyan College of Music, Bloomington, Ill. He was a member of the Bloomington Choral Society, and had held the position of Director of the Eureka Choral Society.

With his gifted wife, he spent some time in concert work, meeting with great success. As a musician Mr. Gray was enthusiastic, and devoted his life and energies to his profession, being a most thorough and conscientious instructor. A work on harmony, published a short time before his death, is an exhaustive treatise, presenting the matter in a condensed and concise manner, and may be considered one of the best textbooks on the subject ever written by an American musician.

Mr. Gray was a man who not only made himself felt in his chosen profession, but was beloved and respected in the community where he lived for his genial disposition, his integrity of character and his high moral standards. Free from the petty jealousy too often found in a professional career, recognizing talent and success wherever found, he was never happier than when aiding some aspirant to fame in his struggle for position and recognition.

He was one of nature's noblemen, respected and loved by all who became intimately acquainted with him. His character was above reproach, his ideals were high and noble, and the world is certainly better for his having lived.

Mrs. Mary Emeline Iliff Gray.

MRS. MARY EMELINE ILIFF GRAY.

Mrs. Mary Emeline Iliff Gray.

There are few musicians and teachers who have a more enviable reputation throughout the Middle-West than has Mrs. Mary Emeline Iliff Gray, possibly better known in musical circles as Mrs. John R. Gray. She was born November 25, 1860, in Marshall County, Ill., the daughter of John M. and Caroline E. Iliff.

Except when absent to pursue her studies, her life has been passed in Illinois. She received her common school education in the High School of Washburn, Ill., and has lived in Lacon and Eureka, and for the past sixteen years in Bloomington, in Illinois.

With her husband, she spent five years in study in Leipzig, Germany, under the instruction of Eibenschuets, Wiedenbach, Richter and Jadassohn. She has not, however, confined her musical tuition to that received abroad. Although, with her husband, she was graduated from the Leipzig Conservatory of Music, she has also studied with Mr. E. D. Hale, Mr. Capen and Miss Haney, all of Boston, and with Mr. Frederic Grant Gleason, of Chicago.

With her husband, she spent some time in concert work, meeting with most gratifying success.

They were, however, united in their decision to devote themselves to the work of teaching, and Mrs. Gray has entered with enthusiasm into the endeavor to prosecute this work

357

along the best possible lines for the attainment of the most
satisfactory results. She has been identified in the pursu-
ance of her work with the Eureka Conservatory of Music,
and for the past fourteen years has been a Director of Music
in the Wesleyan College of Music, in Bloomington, Ill. She
is an honored and valuable member of the Amaturian Musical
Society, of that city. As both a musician and a teacher, she
has been eminently successful. She unites a brilliant technique with a sympathetic interpretation, and possesses a remarkable power to inspire her pupils with intense enthusiasm.
The brilliant concert success of so many of her pupils and
their established reputation as teachers are a tribute to her
ability.

Her method is one of directness and thoroughness, insur-
ing speedy and permanent improvement. Her success in
transforming a hard, defective touch and in developing the
technique is not only the result of knowledge and experience but of judgment, rare tact and inexhaustible patience.

Under her supervision, in Illinois, Kansas, Nebraska,
Missouri and Minnesota, are large classes under the instruction of her pupils. By following a specific course and under-
going the test of yearly concerts the pupils are enabled to accomplish the preparatory work for Mrs. Gray's classes, and
on passing a successful examination receive a signet creden-
tial from Mrs. Gray. The normal class for teachers has been
largely attended, all classes under Mrs. Gray's direction being
larger than any previous year.

Mrs. Gray's widespread influence is a great musical uplift, so recognized and appreciated by those who thus come in
touch with her.

Edna B. Dunshee.

Edna B. Dinushee

Edna B. Dunshee.

The story of the life of Edna B. Dunshee is the story of a busy life filled with effort to make opportunity for self-culture and to improve to its utmost every opportunity thus won. She was born Oct. 3, 1871, and was educated at the Mount Carroll Seminary and Conservatory of Music, at Mount Carroll, Ill. June, 1891, she graduated, having taken a course in voice culture, harmony, musical history, and a special literary course.

The following spring she became an assistant teacher in voice culture in the same school. September, 1892, found her teaching in the music department of Cotley College, Nevada, Mo., having charge of the classes in vocal music, harmony and the history of music.

This position she resigned in 1894, and, in spite of offers of advanced salary, returned to her home for a year of rest. In the spring of 1896, she was called to Wayland Academy, Beaver Dam, Wis., to take charge of the department for voice culture. Ambitious for further self-improvement, she resigned this position in 1897, and returned to her Alma Mater to complete the college course. From Wm. P. McKee, Dean of the Frances Shimer Academy of the University of Chicago, located at Mount Carroll, Ill., she has the highest endorsement. He classes her as an exceptional teacher, and predicts that " whatever she undertakes she will do

possesses a fine voice, and is an excellent concert and choir artist. * * * She is universally popular with her pupils. She is painstaking and forceful in her voice-teaching, hence her success." In September, 1898, she opened a private studio in Clinton, Iowa, where she has taught ever since, and where she still resides. She has had more pupils come to her than she could accept, and wherever she has taught she has held the best choir positions most successfully. She has become much interested in, and very enthusiastic over, public school vocal work. She is now studying the Modern Music Series for use along this line, with the thought of adding this to her other teaching.

That she may keep in touch with the newest and the best in her profession, for the past five summers she has studied with Prof. J. Harry Wheeler, of New York City. In addition to this, last summer she coached with Mrs. Genevieve Clark Wilson. Devoting her summers thus to earnest study with the best instructors, she is able to come to her pupils in the autumn with a new inspiration and fresh equipment for her work.

Miss Dunshee will surely be enrolled among the best and most successful teachers in this part of the country.

Vernon d'Arnalle.

VERNON D'ARNALLE.

Vernon d'Arnalle.

Although educated in Germany, Vernon d'Arnalle is an American by birth, a Virginian, of an old colonial Huguenot family. He was born in Richmond, Va., in 1873, and has resided at various times in Raleigh, North Carolina; Leipzig, Paris and Berlin.

His remarkable musical talent was shown at an early age, and even as a child he was organist for a church and well known as a concert player. His early efforts were devoted to the piano, and his playing won enthusiastic praise from European press and public. It was not till he was a full-fledged piano virtuoso, with the standard piano literature at his command, that he began to turn his attention to the art of singing. But his really wonderful voice soon became his chief study, and he was fortunate enough to be able to secure for his master the celebrated Leopold Demuth, of the Imperial Opera, in Vienna. In addition to Leopold Demuth, Mr. d'Arnalle has studied with Mrs. T. J. Simmons and Prof. Martin Krause, of Leipzig. After finishing his studies with Demuth, Mr. d'Arnalle made his first appearance in Leipzig at the Kaufhaus, once the old Gewandhaus. Here he achieved a brilliant success in the very cradle of German traditions and classicism. Following this success came others in the principal cities of Germany, as well as in the salons of the nobility.

His appearance in New York, Chicago and other cities has always been welcomed by critics and audiences with enthusiasm and applause. Mr. d'Arnalle's beautiful voice, perfect control and, above all, his splendid temperament, guided by deep musicianly instincts, have all been the points which have delighted audiences and critics. Especially happy is this artist in German "Lieder," and his immense repertoire and musicianly interpretations of this wonderful song-literature place him in the front rank of singers to-day.

For the past three years he has made his home in Chicago, where his studio is a coveted resort for musicians and music lovers.

Perhaps few young singers have won more unqualified commendation from the press, not only in America but abroad as well, than has Mr. d'Arnalle, who has received the honors showered upon him with a modesty which bespeaks the true artist.

His voice is a wonderful baritone—as one has not inaptly expressed it, " he is a really God-given singer." His method is above criticism, his interpretation broad and poetic, his phrasing and shading beautiful, his enunciation and diction of the most finished order.

The repertoire at the command of this gifted singer is practically limitless, and interpretations of the classic German Lieder are accepted as rare examples of excellence, although he sings with equal ease in English, French, Italian and German.

Mrs. Luella Clark Emery.

Luella Clark Emery

Mrs. Luella Clark Emery.

Mrs. Luella Clark Emery was born in Cincinnati, Ohio, and has a musical and cultured ancestry. When only two years old, she sang many songs accurately, and when eight years old, she played her first solo at a public concert. Still her unyielding determination to master every difficulty and her improvement of every opportunity for musical advancement have, doubtless, been greater factors in her success than her inherited talent. At the age of twelve, she was church organist, and when sixteen, at Lock Haven, Pa., she had a large class of pupils, and was church organist and pianist for the Handel and Haydn Society. Soon after her marriage to Col. J. M. Emery, they moved to Lemars, Iowa, where they resided many years. During these years Mrs. Emery spent much time in the East, pursuing her studies in piano, pipe-organ and voice, with the best teachers in the country. At Lemars she had a class of over fifty pupils; was church organist and director of music until her removal to Chicago, in 1895; was President of the Mendelssohn Club, and arranged programs for public and private rehearsals. The study of the different composers and their works, as planned by Mrs. Emery and consummated under her directions, did much to elevate the standard of music in that city. She was teacher of piano, pipe-organ and voice in the Northwestern Normal

School, and also in the Lemars School of Art. She has the rare gift of being a fine accompanist, and for nine years was accompanist at the Spirit Lake (Iowa) Chautauqua, six years at the Marinette (Wis.) Assembly, and at other Chautauquas. In assembly and convention work she is simply invaluable, not only for the artistic excellence of her work but for her attention to every detail, her zeal and her enthusiasm. Few appreciate what it really means to be a fine accompanist; it is a gift born with one, rather than acquired, and this gift Mrs. Emery has in a rare degree. Since living in Chicago Mrs. Emery's success has been gratifying and deserved. Her concert engagements have been numerous, and her work commended by both city and out-of-town critics. As an accompanist, she has been in frequent demand by visiting artists. For seven consecutive years she has been the accompanist for the May Festival concerts in the Auditorium, and has always given the most complete satisfaction. She was also accompanist at the Auditorium meeting of the Thanksgiving services of the National Peace Jubilee, and on other important occasions. Mrs. Emery's organ work in Chicago has shown the same high grade of artistic excellence which has characterized her other lines of work. She is pianist for the Mendelssohn Trio, which has received flattering mention on all occasions. Her classes in piano and organ pupils have increased rapidly in numbers and in interest. Her tact, pleasing personality and gift for imparting knowledge, with an absorbing love for her work, have placed her among the most successful instructors in Chicago.

Max Heinrich.

Max Heinrich.

Max Heinrich.

Of the distinguished artists who have made Chicago their home no one has wielded a more elevating influence upon the musical life of the city than has Max Heinrich—an accomplished singer, a successful teacher and enthusiastic lecturer.

He was born in 1853, and from an early age showed a decided taste for music. His first musical education was received in the city of Zwickau, Saxony, where he studied the piano with the famous composer of church music, Emanuel Kronoch (Dr. Klitsch). Later he studied piano, composition and singing in the conservatory of music in Dresden. In 1870 he made his first professional engagement, accepting the position of " corepetitor " of an opera company in the Grand Duchy of Neustrelitz. In 1873, Mr. Heinrich came to America, and for several years devoted himself largely to teaching, principally in Philadelphia, at the same time conscientiously preparing for the work which made his reputation. He made his début in New York, in the oratorio of " Elijah," under the leadership of Dr. Leopold Damrosch. His singing on this occasion aroused the greatest enthusiasm, and he received many honors and attentions. His interpretation of this great oratorio has been adopted by many of our most celebrated oratorio singers. From this time he became widely and favorably known both in this country and in Europe as one of the

most distinguished interpreters of oratorio, German Lieder
and English ballad singing.

To quote from a recent musical journal, he is celebrated
for " the rare beauty of his voice, his magnificent dramatic
ability, and the correctness of his interpretation."

In 1888, Mr. Heinrich went to London, where he accepted
a professorship in the Royal Academy of Music, in London,
and remained four years. Each year, during this time, he
made a trip to America for a brief season of public work.

From 1892 till he came to Chicago he resided in Boston,
devoting himself very largely to oratorio work and classical
song recitals. Someone has said of him, "As an interpreter
of classical songs Mr. Heinrich is without a peer, and his recitals are masterpieces of scholarly, artistic singing." His
recitals given in Chicago have been notable musical events
to lovers of high-class vocal music. For a time he held a position as professor of vocal culture with the Chicago Conservatory.

His clientelle became so large that he established himself
in a studio in the Fine Arts Building, where he is at present.

Every hour of the day is occupied in the work of teaching, and yet he finds time to keep in touch with the best musical life of the city he has made his home. He is exceedingly
modest in regard to his achievements, and ambitious for the
best results.

His songs are widely sung, and his two melodramas,
" Magdalen " and " The Raven," have met with distinguished
success.

Mary Elizabeth Linck.

Mary Limet

Mary Elizabeth Linck.

One of America's greatest dramatic artists, Mary Elizabeth Linck, was born in Evansville, Ind. Her ancestry were Scottish nobility, English, German and Virginian Quaker ministers. The best qualities of these various peoples seem to have been concentrated in this wonderful singer, with her dramatic instincts and her beautiful mezzo-soprano-contralto voice.

At an early age she showed the independence, perseverance and energy of the Scotch, the elegance and refinement of the English, the sincerity and gentleness of the Quaker, and the artistic and musical temperament of the German. Her father, Charles E. Linck, died six months before her birth, leaving her mother widowed for the second time, with three children, Mary making the fourth. Horatio C. Cooper and Laura V. Cooper are her half brother and sister, and Maria Louise Linck was her own sister.

She began at the age of ten years the study of the piano. It was not, however, until her seventeenth year that either she or her friends discovered that she had a wonderful voice. A local amateur production of the " Grand Duchess " was given, in which she was assigned a short solo. Her rendition of it was a surprise to her audience and a revelation to herself. She at once began voice study, and spent two years at the College

377

free scholarship on account of her unusual talent and wonderful voice. After another year's study in Milan, Italy, and in London, she made her operatic début in Liverpool, England, at the Royal Court Theatre, in February, 1893, with the Royal Carl Rosa Company, the opera being " Faust." She remained the prima donna of this company till 1895, when she came to America. She made her début at Daly's Theatre, New York, with Sir Augustus Harris' London Opera Company, in Humperdinck's great German opera " Hansel and Gretel." She at once became a favorite, and since that time she has sung in every city of importance from New York to San Francisco, and her career has been a succession of triumphs such as few singers have known. Among her repertoire of thirty-five operas, her greatest successes have been the characters of Fidelis, Azucena, Santuzza, Amneris, Carmen, Mignon and Ortrud.

The experiences of stage life have not spoiled her sweet nature, for she has had the companionship of her beloved mother and sister Laura.

Her voice is remarkable for its great range, power and sympathetic quality. She is also a great actress, completely merging her own individuality into that of the character portrayed. She stands in the first rank of American Grand English opera prima donnas.

Victor Heinze.

Victor Heinze

Victor Heinze.

Victor Heinze, the head and founder of the Heinze School of Artistic Piano-Playing, in Chicago, is known here and in the old country as one of the first pianists, while as instructor he ranks with the best in the world.

The attainments of his class have created surprise in this country and in the musical centers of Europe, from which flattering offers have been extended to him.

From his father, Leopold Heinze, the author of theoretical and didactical works in use in Germany, England, France, Austria, Italy and Russia, he has inherited a powerful mentality, a tireless perseverance, thoroughness and acute perception, which characterize the real student.

In early manhood, the German Government appointed him director of the Musical Department of the Royal School at Schweidnitz, in recognition of his eminent capabilities as a musician and his rare faculty as an instructor.

His collegiate and musical education was acquired in Breslau, Berlin and Vienna, where he placed himself under the tuition of Leschetizky, and became an enthusiastic admirer of his principles of piano-playing. Having thoroughly mastered this simple, but definite, method of instruction, he now makes teaching his principal work.

The training of finished pianists and capable teachers is

his chief ambition, and for this work his undeniable efficiency as an eminently competent educator peculiarly fits him. As a pianist, his versatile style demonstrates a rare brilliancy and breadth, evincing warmth and passion without undue sentimentality, being the scholarly work of a thinker as well as an artist.

Mr. Heinze is probably the most successful exponent of Prof. Leschetizky's incomparable system of piano-playing in America. The annual recitals (from eight to ten in number), given by students of his class, both young and adult, have attracted large musical audiences, and the artistic performances of the most exacting programs have seldom been equaled here. As one of America's best-known musical critics and writers, Mr. Mathews, says: " They are the most remarkable series of piano-recitals ever given in Chicago. The most difficult and largest piano works were performed, and the rendition was marked by the high degree of finish which alone will gratify and satisfy the artist." As a consequence, Mr. Heinze has gathered about him appreciative and ambitious artists and students, from near and far, who avail themselves of his instructions, many of them holding high positions in musical schools and educational institutions.

He has, in addition to his arduous work as a teacher, published a most valuable booklet, "An interesting, instructive and honest word to parents, students of music and especially piano pupils and teachers and all friends of musical art," which should be read carefully by all who take an interest in music and its advancement.

Mrs. Marie White Longman.

Marie White Longman

Mrs. Marie White Longman.

Although now so closely identified with the musical life of Illinois, and particularly of Chicago, Mrs. Marie White Longman is a native of Michigan, in which State she began her career as a musician. She came from a musical family, and very early developed not only a love but a decided talent for that highest of arts. She began her musical studies when only eight years of age, first on the piano and soon after on the pipe-organ. At fourteen she was appointed organist of a prominent church, and for three years played a large three-manual organ. In her seventeenth year, while pursuing literary studies in a Michigan college, she was repeatedly urged by the vocal instructor of the institution to devote herself to the cultivation of her voice. From the beginning she made rapid progress, and was soon sought for as a soloist by churches and musical societies throughout Michigan and other States. In the year 1897, she was graduated from both the instrumental and vocal departments of the Conservatory.

Desiring to place herself under the tuition of the best teachers, and wishing for opportunity to enter more extensively into the professional field as soloist and teacher, Mrs. Longman came to Chicago, where she has since lived.

The excellence of her work was soon recognized by leading musicians, and by such organizations as the Apollo Club,

has always acquitted herself most admirably to the satisfaction of the club and her audiences. For six years she has been the contralto soloist of the St. James Methodist Church. While Mrs. Longman is, perhaps, best known on the concert platform, she is no less successful as a teacher, and devotes much of her time to a large class of pupils.

Earnest application and careful attention to details—requisites of musical success—have been marked characteristics of her work, from the first simple exercises to the later finer and more elaborate work which make the finished artist. She is ambitious for her pupils, and is faithful in her effort to exact from them work as conscientious and as painstaking as was that of her own student life. Her voice is of the true contralto quality, rare as sweet, and seems especially adapted for oratorio work. At the same time she has great versatility of talent, and gives the most delicate vocalization necessary for concert or recital with a charm peculiarly her own. Her presence before an audience is most dignified and pleasing. At ease herself, she brings to her audience a sense of delight, even before it is thrilled with the beauty of her voice. She has won for herself the just praise and respect both of critics and the general public.

Max Kramm.

Max Kramer

Max Kramm.

Few musicians have attained so marked a recognition of their abilities at so early an age as has Max Kramm, the pianist. He was born in Soldin, Germany, in 1872, and when but seven years old was placed in the Kullak's Academy, in Berlin, where he remained fourteen years. His conscientious endeavor and marked talent attracted the attention of the director, and he had the great advantage of receiving tuition for four years from Kullak himself.

In 1892, he came to New York with letters of introduction from Philip Scharwenka, the composer, to a number of prominent musicians and managers, among whom was the pianist, Max Liebling, brother of the Chicago pianist. After remaining a short time in that city as the guest of Mr. Liebling, he accepted an engagement with a concert company as solo pianist, and made an extended tour through the South and West. While on this trip he came to Chicago, and was so attracted to the city that he decided to remain there and establish himself as a teacher.

It was at first a venture fraught with disappointment and, to a degree, with hardship. His absolute lack of familiarity with American methods, and his feeling that it was unprofessional for him to introduce himself by advertising, prevented his receiving the immediate recognition which his genius as an artist and his ability as a teacher deserved.

389

came known the public began to realize the fact that in Mr. Kramm Chicago had an artist of unusual talent. He remained in the college for a year, and then opened a studio of his own. It is now about ten years since he came to Chicago, and he has established himself in the foremost ranks of musicians here.

With each year his possibilities as a teacher and pianist have revealed themselves to a greater degree, for his diligence in study is unceasing, and his devotion to his chosen art is absolute.

In 1897, Mr. Henry Meeker wrote of Mr. Kramm—" Of a modest and retiring disposition in general life, at the piano he grows to gigantic height. The most complicated technical difficulties are to him but child's play; his tone-building displays an active perception, his expression is full of animation, and betrays a deep, sunny spirit. From a musician so gifted by God's grace great things may be expected. We hope and believe Mr. Kramm will soon receive the recognition which he deserves."

Mr. Kramm's studio, in Kimball Hall, is a favorite place with true music-lovers, and every hour of his time is taxed to the utmost to accommodate those who desire to place themselves under his instruction, and he feels that his success is all he could possibly desire.

Mme. Francesca Guthrie Moyer.

Frances Guthrie Moyer

Mme. Francesca Guthrie Moyer.

To Mme. Francesca Guthrie Moyer belongs the honor of being one of the principal dramatic sopranos produced by this country. She occupied a prominent place on the lyric stage of America from 1880 to 1892, after which she devoted herself to oratorio and concert work. She was born in San Francisco, Cal., where her father occupied important public positions, having come to California from the Empire State. Mme. Guthrie Moyer inherited rare musical gifts from her mother, nee Emma Gosson, of Dublin, Ireland, an artist of prominence and a friend of Delsarte, Garcia, Panofka, and others. To her talented mother she is much indebted for her careful early vocal training and for the inspiration of that enthusiasm which led her to pursue her studies in Paris, Berlin and Milan. She speaks fluently French, German and Italian. Her repertoire is most extensive, including sixty grand operas, many oratorios and an unlimited number of concert arias from great composers. Her fine soprano voice ranges from lower G to high E, and has remarkable volume and power, yet is flexible, smooth and deeply sympathetic. She sings equally well the florid music of the French and Italian masters and that of Wagner's music-drama, Valentine in "Les Huguenots," Violetta in "Traviata," Norma, Marguerite in "Faust," Elizabeth in "Tannehauser," Santa in

393

" Flying Dutchman,'' and others. Her versatility is demonstrated by the success which attended her appearance as Zerlina in " Fra Diavolo '' and other works. In oratorio and concert work in the Worcester Music Festival, in 1894, and the Wagnerian Festival, in Indianapolis, the same year; at Madison Square Garden concerts, under Seidl, Damrosch, Sousa, and others, Mme. Guthrie achieved great success. In oratorio she reminded one of the lamented Parepa Rosa, in opera one was inclined to class her with Albani. In opera she sang with Theodor Reichmann, Sig. Ravelli, Anton Schatt, and other eminent artists. As a church singer she occupied the most prominent position in Chicago for some years in connection with concerts, oratorios and Catholic church music. The newspapers, from Maine to California, have vied with each other in highest praise of her singing. Personally she is a handsome, graceful woman, possessed of a magnetic presence. Those who have enjoyed hearing her will ever bear her in pleasant memory, and those who know her best as the great, true artist, the loving wife and mother, realize that her beautiful voice mirrors a grand nature and a true woman.

In 1890 Francesca Guthrie married Charles Daniel Moyer, and as the presiding genius of an elegant home in Chicago, the mother of two lovely children and the center of a truly musical circle, she still finds much pleasure in devotion to her much-loved and beautiful art. Mme. Guthrie-Moyer is the sister of William D. Guthrie, the eminent lawyer of New York City.

Luman A. Phelps.

Luman A. Phelps.

Luman A. Phelps is a native of Burlington, Vermont, where he was born, January 12, 1854. From his childhood there was something in the tones of his voice which betokened a musical destiny, for his gift of song attracted attention while he was passing through the grades of a common school education.

In 1870, he came to Chicago, and took his first course of instruction in the Chicago Musical College. The first prize ever awarded to any pupil in that institution was won by him, in 1873. The year following he went to Europe, and for six years studied in Leipsic under Dr. Powell for the piano, and with Adolph Ichimin for the voice. From Leipsic he went to Italy, where, under the tutorship of Lamperti and Vannuccini, he made progress, winning recognition from these " grand old masters " for his brilliant and elaborate playing. In spite of his prospects as a pianist, he decided to make voice culture his permanent aim. After completing his course with these masters, he sang and acted the role of Faust at Savigliano, Italy, with such success that he received a flattering offer from Carlotta Patti, then in the zenith of her fame, to accompany her as tenor in an American tour. Under these then brilliant auspices he returned to his native land and made an extensive tour through the East and West. Coming

397

to Chicago in 1880, he decided to abandon the operatic and concert stage and devote his energies to his cherished ideas of vocal culture.

Mr. Phelps' specialty is " the placing of the voice properly," and his wonderful success may be seen in the brilliant line of pupils who have studied with him. He is a firm believer in the Italian method, and since success is measured by results, the popular acceptance of singers trained under this regime would seem to mean public endorsement. Mr. Phelps may well feel pride in naming among his pupils August Liverman, who has been acclaimed as the best basso profundo America has ever produced, at present at the Royal Opera House, in Munich; George Iott, who has found responsive listeners through the West; Clarence E. Whitehill, a young singer of rare promise; Frank Ormsby, a tenor of great ability, and others already known to fame. His passion for complete musical expression through the human voice has become a kind of religion.

Entering Mr. Phelps' studio one feels at once enveloped in the atmosphere of art. The choicest rugs, rare bits of claisonnè, portraits of masters, gems of art which invite attention, make a room characteristic of the man.

From all parts of America Mr. Phelps has constantly applicants anxious to place themselves under his valuable tutelage.

me. Ooliato Zimmerman.

Obliata Zimmerman

Mme. Ooliato Zimmerman.

In the very foremost rank among America's great singers and successful teachers is Mme. Ooliato Zimmerman. She possesses a contralto voice which is magnificent in quality, sympathetic to a rare degree and perfectly cultivated. Her singing at once reveals her complete mastery of her chosen art. Few artists are endowed with such an exquisitely musical nature, and this, added to the intellectual interpretation she gives to the songs of the great masters, places her high in her profession. Mme. Zimmerman was for several years associated with the leading singers of Europe, and, after a most successful tour through its leading cities, has returned to her own country. Wherever she appeared in those cities she achieved the most pronounced success, both in song recitals and the most exacting oratorio work.

She has received the most flattering encomiums, both on her excellence as a teacher and her skill as an artist, from the best professional critics of the day. We quote from a few of them. Of her singing Edouard De Reske said—" You are an artist; some are musicians, so few are artists." George Henschel, after hearing her sing, said—" You have great conception." Mme. Mathilde Marchesi said to her—" I meet very few Americans who are as good a teacher as you." M. Delle Sadie, in enthusiastic way, exclaimed—" You sing good;

mony—" It is a pleasure to meet so great a teacher." These are only a few of the many flattering comments which artists have made upon the work of this great singer and teacher.

Many have wondered that, with her magical voice, her charming personality which wins her friends wherever she goes, she has not devoted her life entirely to the career for which she seems so well fitted on the concert or operatic stage. But the work of teaching, for which she is peculiarly well endowed, appeals to her most strongly, and her success has been so great in this direction that she feels she must not give it up. Her studio is perhaps one of the brightest spots in all Chicago. One recognizes there her rare charm of manner and fascinating way of presenting even the work which must be done. The devotion shown her by her pupils is really a beautiful tribute to this teacher. They seem to look forward with pleasure to their lessons, instead of regarding them, as is too often the case, as a dreaded task. And yet Mme. Zimmerman is an energetic teacher, impressing upon her pupils the thought that there is no royal road to success, that only by *work,* systematic and untiring, achievement is obtained.

For the past two years Mme. Zimmerman has been associated with the Chicago Auditorium Conservatory.

Wilhelm Middleschulte.

WILHELM MIDDLESCHULTE.

Wilhelm Middleschulte.

There is no question but· that Wilhelm Middleschulte
stands in the very foremost rank of the organists of to-day.
His early education was the best, and he has been, all his life,
an indefatigable student.   When little more than a child he
entered the Royal Academy of Church Music, in Berlin, and
for three years was a student of August Haupt in organ and
theory, of Albert Loeschorn in piano study and of Dr. Julius
Alsleben for conducting.   His progress so enlisted the inter-
eśt of these great masters that Haupt made him his assistant
organist at the Royal Academy.

In 1868, he accepted a position as organist and choir-
leader in one of the largest churches in Berlin.   In 1891, Mr.
Middleschulte came to Chicago to enter upon the duties of
musical director and organist of the Holy Name Cathedral.
In America he was at once accorded a place among leading
musicians, and as the years have passed he has added to his
laurels, and in the modest, unassuming way which is one of
his characteristics, has steadily advanced in his profession.
He was invited, before he left Berlin, to play at the memorial
service for Emperor Frederick III., at the church in Born-
stedt, near Potsdam, a church which the Emperor frequently
attended.   The day before he left for America the funeral of
his beloved teacher, August Haupt, took place.   In compli-

ance with the request of the family, he played on Haupt's own organ Bach's " C Minor Fantasie," which was a great favorite with the deceased organist. At this funeral Joachim and many distinguished musicians were present.

At the time of the Columbian Exposition, Mr. Middle-schulte, by special invitation, gave three recitals before those wonderful audiences of artists from all parts of the world.

A year later, he played at the Auditorium with the Chicago Orchestra the solo of Alexander Guilmant's first concerto. His success was such that he immediately received the appointment as organist for that organization, a position he has filled to the great delight of the orchestra and its audiences. Those who are best fitted to judge prophesy his success as a composer, for what he has already written shows most unusual merit. He has studied both the classic and modern schools of music, and plays all his programs from memory, which is very exceptional with organists. Bernard Ziehn, the highest authority in the realm of musical composition, said of Wilhelm Middleschulte's " Passacoglia "—" Since the ' Passacoglia ' of Bach, no work of that kind has come to light which deserved comparison with Middleschulte's ' Passacoglia.' " Clarence Eddy showed his estimate of his ability as a teacher by leaving his pupils in Mr. Middleschulte's charge while on a trip abroad.

· For the past seven years he has been at the head of the organ department of the American Conservatory, Chicago, and is putting the impress of his own scholarly musical interpretation upon some of the best organ pupils in that city.

Lucile Stevenson Tewksbury.

Lucille Stevenson Tewksbury

Lucile Stevenson Tewksbury.

Miss Lucile Stevenson Tewksbury was born October 1, 1873, in Evans, Colorado. In 1878, the family moved to St. Louis, and there she began the study of the piano, while a little child, and continued it till she was nineteen years of age.

In 1882, she moved to Des Moines, Iowa, where she still pursued her piano study with Della Winders Bonbright. In 1893, she began the work of voice culture with Prof. Lieb, of Kansas City. The following year she came to Chicago and studied for a short time with Clement Tetedoux and A. D. Dunvier.

It is, however, to Charles W. Clark, now residing in Paris, whose pupil she was for five years, that she gives highest praise, and whom she credits largely with her success. Recognizing her ability, he gave her special work and taught her to know and to use her musical resources. She has held some of the most coveted church choir positions in Chicago. Among them are the New England Congregational Church, Forty-first St. Presbyterian, Hyde Park Presbyterian, Plymouth Congregational and, for the past four years, with the Second Presbyterian Church. She has a very large class of pupils, which she teaches in her home, many of whom fill prominent church positions in Chicago and neighboring cities. Her voice is a true soprano, whose tone production is excellent, and she sings with much taste and expression. Her interpretation of themes is intelligent, her tones pure and sympathetic, while her vocalization shows the splendid musical education she has had. She has also a dramatic quality of voice which is most effective, and wherever she has sung she has at once become a favorite with her audiences. She is peculiarly fitted for oratorio work, and this she regards as her greatest accomplishment.

The facility with which she interprets even difficult themes, her dramatic rendering of many passages and the sweet, sympathetic tone which is never lacking, make a *tout ensemble* which should win for her a place among the very best singers of oratorio.

Her class work and her church work have been so absorbing as to leave little time for the concert work in which she delights and for which she is so pre-eminently fitted. She is, however, exceedingly ambitious, and past successes will not allow her to rest on her laurels, but will stimulate her to still greater achievement. Those who know Miss Tewksbury best recognize her versatility of talent, and predict for her a brilliant future, not only as a concert singer but in the more difficult and, to her, most fascinating work in oratorio. With her pupils she lays special stress on the right interpretation of every theme, recognizing the truth, so often ignored, that without intelligent interpretation the most brilliant vocalization fails to charm.

Joseph Vilim.

JOSEPH VILIM.

Joseph Vilim.

Joseph Vilim was born in Chicago, January 18, 1861, of Bohemian parentage. His father was a musician, and the child, whose youth was spent in Chicago, early imbibed the love for the music which was his home environment. He began the study of the violin with his older brother, Frank, but made such rapid progress that he continued his studies, first with Prof. Prosinger, afterward with Wm. Fehl. He evinced very soon a rare ability as a musician and a peculiar deftness and delicacy of touch on his chosen instrument. His first appearance of any note was in the old Matteson House, now the Wellington Hotel. At this time he won many laurels, and in musical circles a brilliant career was predicted for him. In 1880 he went to Prague, where he passed the examination and entered the fifth year of the famous Conservatory of Music.

He graduated from this Conservatory in 1882, and the following year he returned to Chicago. Very soon after his return he became a teacher of the violin in the Chicago Musical College, and remained in this position for three years. He then accepted the directorship of the violin department of the American Conservatory of Music, which position he held for more than twelve years. An ardent lover of music, devoted to the violin, and with the faculty of imparting his knowledge to others so as to be a real inspiration to the best effort, his

413

success as a teacher has been most pronounced.   During this time he made a visit of nine months to Euorpe, in 1886-7.   Returning to Chicago, he became identified with the Theodore Thomas Orchestra, and for two years, the seasons of 1894-5 and 1895-6, he held the position of first violinist in that organization.   He also founded the Vilim Trio.   In 1899, his ambition was realized in the founding of his own school, a hope he had cherished for some years.   This school was incorporated as the American Violin School, and immediately obtained recognition as an important factor in musical circles in Chicago.   From this school have gone out violinists who have been in demand for the first and most important places in leading orchestras, and also some who are known as fine soloists.   Mr. Vilim is now at the head of the Vilim Trio and Vilim Orchestral Club.   The programs given by Mr. Vilim have received flattering comment both in Chicago and in Europe.   Among his friends abroad are numbered many known to fame, as the entire family of Bedrich Smetana, of Bohemia; Dr. Antoine Dvorak, of Prague; Frant. Ondrieek, now abroad; Prof. Hlavac, of St. Petersburg; Jan Kubelik, Jaroslav Kocian, Bogea Umiroff, and others; while in Chicago he has the friendship and heartiest good will of all his colleagues, who recognize in him not only a rare teacher but an artist as well.

rs. Delilah Patty Wesener.

Delilah Patty-Wiener

Mrs. Delilah Patty Wesener.

Mrs. Delilah Patty Wesener is a native of the State of Indiana. She is the great-granddaughter of a Huguenot and the second daughter of Nathan Patty, who served in the Mexican War. From such ancestry one looks for talent, enthusiastic devotion to whatever is undertaken and for early maturity of thought. Expectation was not disappointed in Delilah Patty. She was endowed with a wonderful contralto voice, dramatic, yet sympathetic in quality, and of extraordinary range and power. Realizing, at least to some extent, the possibilities before her, she very early decided to devote herself to grand opera. To this end she labored conscientiously and successfully. Before she was twenty years of age she had devoted two years to mastering a dramatic reputation, and her achievements awakened the most flattering hopes in the hearts of her friends and stimulated her own ambitions. At this time she came to Chicago to continue her musical studies, and at the same time educate herself along general lines. Here she met and subsequently married Dr. J. A. Wesener. Many a time has matrimony taken one of brilliant promise from an expectant public to be the center of a home, and such was the case with Mrs. Wesener. She abandoned all thought of the operatic career which till then had meant so much to her. The talented nature could not, however, lie dormant, and her time since her marriage has been devoted to the study of the languages, philosophy, and the literature of song.

In this way her artistic impulses have been gratified, and from her pen has come much of interest and value. We are glad to give place to some of her thoughts on the oft-recurring question, " Why many singers fail to become artists." Mrs. Wesener has no repining over the giving up of public life, for which she was so eminently fitted, and to which she had dedicated herself. She is happy in the quiet of her home life, and her music, pictures and books are her delight. She is deeply in sympathy with every student, with every art-loving soul, and her experience, wide reading and intelligent observation make her a wise counsellor for those who are perhaps beginning with trembling steps to tread the path which may lead to fame. The article from her pen is stamped with the individuality of thought which is a characteristic of this gifted woman.

Music and musical archievements are as dear to her as in the olden time. The literary treasures of many lands have been made possible to her by her mastery of languages, and she delights to delve beneath the surface with a spirit of true philosophy in her quest after the real inspiration of result.

"What Becomes of the Many Students in Singing?"

If it is not generally known that our large cities yearly receive and contain many hundreds of students, who cherish the hope of becoming great artists, at least almost every person has had, or still has, a relative, friend or acquaintance for whom the ambition was cherished that they might prove to be the " coming singer." Possibly few questions with musical life suggest themselves with greater frequency than this, " What becomes of the many students of singing; why do they not rise to prove themselves real artists?"

Commencement day came, applause was rapturous, a gold medal was awarded, and hope beat high in the hearts of the ambitious pupil and admiring friends, while even those indifferent remarked, " What a beautiful voice! That pupil should have a great future." But what has been the result? For a time—perhaps two years, possibly a little longer—this " coming singer " is much spoken of, and then a long silence follows; for the " coming singer " seldom, or never, materializes, and those of comparatively ordinary merit must still hold the positions in our churches, our concert-rooms and our theatres.

A rich, beautiful voice is a most glorious thing, a divine gift, but were a voice never so grand the possessor of it who does not conceive and clearly portray the text of his song, and make it the central feature is, and must ever be, rated an " ordinary singer."

From a clear, true conception of the text evolves the right distribution of voice power, the right quality of tone, refinement of feeling, and everything belonging to artistic singing. Now there are many students who know well enough a voice alone, however beautiful, will not make a great singer, but, with this knowledge, they usually swing to the other extreme.

They indulge in extravagant emotional outbursts and exhaust their energies in vain attempts toward instantaneous achievement.

A right attitude of mind is as necessary to artistic singing as a beautiful voice; there are many who even give it precedence.

All thoughts of self, " genius " and " fame " should be avoided by the young student. Unfortunately, however, his studies properly begin after that unconscious state of mind belonging to childhood has passed away and before the development of that indifferent state which is the result of experience. As a result, he is overconcerned about himself, and the outcome of his work and self-consciousness ruins the most conscientious effort. Knowing that the life of the voice is short, he forgets that " He who would build surely *must* build slowly." A gentle, reposeful, meditative state of mind, which patiently examines everything submitted to it, a disposition to compromise with circumstances if necessary, and a cheerful courage to accept failure, is a better conductor to artistic excellence than ambitious striving, laborious effort and lasting vows to become " great or nothing."

MRS. DELILAH PATTY-WESENER.

Bicknell Young.

Bicknell Young

Bicknell Young.

A profound student himself and able to effect wonderful results in the way of voice culture, Bicknell Young is that rare exception, a professional singer who really enjoys the work of teaching. Mr. Young is an American, and believes most thoroughly in American teachers, feeling not only that they are the most conscientious teachers, but that they have, somehow, a peculiar aptitude for imparting knowledge, which gives them advantage over other teachers. Mr. Young received his musical education in London, his instructor being Visetti, a widely known Italian teacher. His tuition, however, embraced French and German songs quite as much as Italian and English, an experience of great value to him in his career as a teacher. In all of these languages he sings with perfect accent and a most delightful clearness of pronunciation. Oratorios and their interpretation especially attracted Mr. Young, and to this line of study he has devoted much time. For several years before his return to America he sang in oratorio concerts as well as in miscellaneous programs in London and vicinity. He has, for some years, however, become so wholly absorbed in the work of teaching that he has practically abandoned the concert platform, for which he was so admirably fitted. He has made a special study of the human voice from viewpoints not usually particularly recognized by those engaged in voice culture, and has thus been enabled to ascertain defects in a voice, and remedy them, with marked success.

He has so widely established a reputation for skill in this branch of his work that he is often consulted not only by singers but by teachers as well.

Mr. Young's ambition for his pupils is very high, and in this he has found an able coadjutor in his gifted wife. Mrs. Young was born in Italy, and is a very highly-educated woman and well known as a composer, though her compositions are rarely published. She excels as a teacher of harmony and composition, and in the beautiful studio where she and her husband work for a common end she teaches sight reading and harmony. Here Mr. and Mrs. Young give recitals, with programs selected from their extensive repertoire. Thus their pupils have not only the advantage of the best instruction, but are enabled to hear what they are studying rendered in the most artistic way. The pupils graduated under these teachers are most completely fitted for any line of musical work they may desire to undertake as singers or as teachers, and among them are some well known artists. Mr. and Mrs. Young are becoming more and more recognized factors in the musical advancement of Chicago.

Annie McFarland Sharpe.

MRS. ANNIE McFARLAND SHARPE.

Mrs. Annie McFarland Sharpe.

There are few women who have been educated along so many lines as has Mrs. Annie McFarland Sharpe, of Jacksonville, Ill.

She was born, October 10, 1867, in Lexington, Ky., her father being Dr. George McFarland, her grandfather Dr. Andrew McFarland and her mother Mary E. (Bush) McFarland. At the age of twelve she went with her parents to live with her grandfather, at Oak Lawn, Jacksonville, Ill. After a four years' course she was graduated from the Jacksonville Academy, in 1887, with the degree of B. A.; and followed this by a business course at the Kentucky University, where she became a skilled bookkeeper and stenographer. Dr. McFarland felt that his granddaughter possessed the characteristics from which his theory of the fitness of women for the care of the female insane could be tested, and, in 1888, she entered the Woman's Medical College, Northwestern University, Chicago, from which she was graduated with honors March 30, 1891, receiving the degree of M. D. Since receiving this degree, Mrs. Sharpe has become Medical Superintendent of Oak Lawn Sanitarium. She is a member of the Morgan County Medical Society and Illinois State Medical Society, and was for some years associate editor of the *Woman's Medical Journal,* the only woman's medical journal in the world.

427

In 1896, she was married to Vincent C. Cromwell, by whom she has a daughter six years of age. Mr. Cromwell died in 1899. In 1901, she was married to J. Thompson Sharpe, who has become the efficient business manager of Oak Lawn.

Mrs. Sharpe's success in her responsible position has been such as to furnish the most emphatic endorsement possible of her grandfather's theories, and has surpassed his expectations. It is a position requiring rare tact, quick decision and a vast deal of determination, since the constant appeal to the sympathies has the tendency to unsettle judgment, however positive. While she is really devoting her life to this great work, the magnitude and difficulies of which it is impossible for an outsider to grasp, Mrs. Sharpe has found time to educate herself along other lines and enlist in other enterprises. Fond of music, she studied the piano with Mrs. Kate Murdock-Smith, and voice culture with Mrs. Burdon Tiffany at the Illinois Conservatory of Music. She is a member of the Wednesday Musical Club, of Janesville, of the Janesville Woman's Club and the Janesville Country Club, and is President of the Woman's Guild of Trinity Episcopal Church. Mrs. Sharpe is a member of the Society of Daughters of the American Revolution, and is also a Colonial Dame. Nothing in the line of humanitarian work, in the literary world, or in the realms of music and art, fails to enlist Mrs. Sharpe's interest and patronage. Her life, devoted to the care of those most sadly afflicted, is a daily example of life's possibilites most helpful to those about her.

Madame Ragna Linne.

Ragna Linné

Madame Ragna Linne.

Mme. Ragna Linnè, who, on her father's side, is a descendant of Carl von Linnè (Charles Linnæus), the eminent scientist, was born in Christiania, Norway.

Besides a voice which attracted the attention of musical connoisseurs, she possessed, even in her earliest childhood, a tenacity of purpose and a devotion to whatever she undertook to do that, during her musical career, have been important factors in her success as one of the most captivating singers of the day.

Mme. Linnè loves her art, and she has loved it with the devotion and the passion which outwit all difficulties and surmount all obstacles to reach the pinnacle of true greatness. She began her musical career by appearing as soloist, when twelve years old, in the Catholic Cathedral of her native city. When sixteen years of age she had an offer to sing in "Faust" the part of Margareta in Swedish opera.

She soon became restless, and sighed for greater opportunities to improve herself in her beloved art, longed for scenes beyond the snowy mountain tips of her native land.

Her ambitions were gratified; she went to Paris and became a favorite pupil of the famous Mme. Marchesi. This master teacher of Apollonic art predicted a great future for her gifted pupil from the "land of the midnight sun," and her prophecy found fulfilment. In all the numerous operas and concerts in which Mme. Linnè has appeared in the principal cities of Europe and America, she has at once become a favorite with all lovers of true music. Her last concert tour to the Pacific coast was a series of ovations from her many friends and admirers.

Among the many organizations with which she has sung a few may be mentioned: The Metropolitan Grand Opera Co.; Chicago Orchestra, (Theodore Thomas); Chicago Symphony Orchestra, (Adolph Rosenbecker); Schubert Club, St. Paul; Ladies' Thursday Musicale, Minneapolis; Beethoven Club, Memphis; Apollo Club, Kansas City; United Scandinavian Singers' Festival, Omaha; United Swedish Singers, Rockford, Ill.; A. Capella Club, Milwaukee; Castle Square Opera Company. Besides singing with these and other organizations, she has sung in numerous miscellaneous concerts all over the country.

Nature has been lavish in the gifts she has bestowed upon Mme. Linnè, for, in addition to her wonderful voice, she possesses beauty of a high order, an effective stage presence and most charming personality. She has that sympathy and pathos of voice which are nature's own gift, which cannot be acquired and which win the hearts of an audience. Her faultless technique shows the faithful, untiring artist, and into all her singing she carries a daintiness of finish and inspiration which are entirely her own.

Thus endowed, and having added to natural gifts the result of earnest study with eminent artists, it is not too much to say that Mme. Ragna Linnè stands in the very foremost ranks of her profession.

Frederick W. Root.

Frederic W. Root

Frederick W. Root.

Frederick W. Root is descended from a musical ancestry. His grandfather, Captain Frederick Ferdinand Root, was a singer, and his grandmother, Sarah Flint, was a solo singer who could accompany herself on the instruments of the day. Her oldest child was George W., the father of Frederick W. In his family were eight children, all of whom were musical, being singers and teachers of piano and voice.

Frederick W. began the study of music with his father when six years of age, and for the next ten years studied with different relatives, who were music teachers. He lived always in an atmosphere of music. He was, later, put under the instruction of B. C. Blodgett, then just graduated from Leipsic Conservatory, now in charge of the Musical Department of Smith College. From him the boy acquired early familiarity with Bach's fugues and Beethoven's sonatas. At the age of sixteen he became a pupil of Dr. William Mason, in New York. While in that city he received organ lessons from J. Flint, organist of Madison Square Church.

The winter of 1864-65 he lived in St. Paul, Minn. There he spent hours every day in piano practice, endeavoring to lessen the gap between his quick conception and his slow execution of music. Coming to Chicago, he took a position in the store of Root & Cady.

435

At this time William Lewis, then the popular violinist of Chicago, used frequently to take Mr. Root with him as a solo pianist. In 1869, he went to Europe for a year and a half of study and travel, doing some piano work in Berlin, and taking voice lessons, in Florence, of the celebrated Vannuccini. He never lived long in one place, so he never had opportunity to complete any regular course of study. He made up for this lack, however, by persistent reading of the best essayists and philosophers. He has been prominently connected with the Music Teachers' National Association, declining the nomination for President in 1892, as he was again going abroad.

In 1873, he published works for use in vocal and instrumental instruction, and later made occasional additions to them. It was not, however, until 1896 that he produced a work which proved widely influential. This was a volume entitled " The Polychrome Lessons " in voice culture, followed since by "Analytical Studies Op. 20," and a series of works issued under the general title of " Technic and Art of Singing." Among prominent singers who have been Mr. Root's pupils are Hope Glenn, Jessie Bartlett Davis, W. H. Clark, McKenzie Gordon, Chas. W. Clark, and many others.

Mr. Root has also taught some of the best gospel singers, among them Messrs. McGranahan, Case, Excell, Towner and Billhorn.

Mr. Root has been identified with summer classes and normal institutes, most successfully.

He has also achieved enviable reputation as adjudicator of musical contests both in and out of Chicago.

This is but a glimpse into the successful life of one of the best known and most beloved musicians of Chicago.

Mrs. Lillian French Read.

MRS. *LILLIAN* FRENCH *READ.*

Mrs. Lillian French Read.

Mrs. Lillian French Read was born in Wakeman, Ohio, October 6, 1875. At the age of seventeen she was sent to Oberlin, Ohio, where she remained for three years studying singing and piano in the Conservatory and languages in the College. During her last year there she held the position of soprano soloist in the First Congregational Church choir, with a chorus of one hundred and twenty students. After leaving school she came to Illinois, and at the age of twenty was given charge of the vocal department of the college at Lincoln, Ill. She remained there for one year, and the following year held a similar position at Onarga, Ill. While teaching there she secured the position at the Englewood Baptist Church, which she filled to the delight of her audiences till she resigned, January 1, 1903, and accepted the position as soprano soloist in the double quartette of Sinai Temple (Dr. Hirsh's church). This position is indicative of the success she has achieved, for Chicago offers nothing finer in this line of musical work.

Since coming to Chicago she has been teaching and studying most of the time. She obtained leave of absence from her church engagement and spent one summer abroad. She devoted the time to hard work with Henschel, in London. Since then she has filled many good engagements through all this part of the country, both in song recitals and oratorio work.

439

five years ago, and won, at that time, many laurels for the excellence of her work. Her charming personality wins for her friends wherever she goes, and since her appearance with the Apollo Club she has sung with many good oratorio clubs, all the way from Ohio to South Dakota, and from Michigan to Missouri.

In this way she has become widely known, and has more opportunities than she can improve to do work with the best musical societies. She has done some work at various Chautauqua assemblies, and went this year for the second time to Bay View, Mich., for two weeks' work.

Her wonderfully strong, yet sweet and sympathetic, voice, her quick interpretation of a theme and her enthusiasm, make her invaluable in the work of assembly, convention and club. She is particularly adapted for oratorio work, and we predict for her a bright future along this line of musical achievement, a line she enjoys. In June, 1900, she married John Threlkeld Read, also a professional singer. They have a new home on West Sixty-second street, where they have a large music room. In this room their pupils give recitals, and here also they entertain their many friends in most delightful, hospitable fashion.

Gertrude M. Radle.

GERTRUDE M. RADLE.

Gertrude M. Radle.

With a sensitive nature, keen intuition and graceful ease
f manner, inherited from her mother, and marked musical
bility, inherited from her father, Gertrude M. Radle, from
he earliest childhood, had the highest musical aims and a
efinite ambition to make a reputation as a teacher of music.
ntil eleven years of age, her only piano was the windowsill,
nd as the childish fingers thrummed the song that filled the
hildish heart, dreams of possibilites to be fulfilled flitted
hrough the busy little brain. So, beginning life's work with
erious thought and earnest longing, the work of life has been
rosecuted with a sweet seriousness which has wrought suc-
ess. When thirteen years old she became a pupil of Edward
'. Holt, who had studied with Albert Ross Parsons. Im-
ressed with the remarkable ability of his young pupil, he
rged her to go to New York and see Parsons. He said of
er—" Even now she is far in advance of me in many points,
arther than I myself can ever hope to get." Through his
nselfish, enthusiastic effort he arranged for her going, and
ngaged an hour for her to play before the great teacher.
fter submitting her to a severe test, Dr. Parsons expressed
is suprise at her achievements at her age, fifteen years, and
or the next three years she was his pupil. At that time she
vent to Warren, Pa., and soon gathered a large class, but re-

turned to New York, and studied a year with Dr. Parsons, a year with Dudley Buck, two years with Harry Rowe Shelley. While still a student in New York, her parents moved to Chicago, believing it would afford to their daughter better opportunities to teach. She opened her studio in Englewood with one pupil, but rapidly became favorably known, and in her more recent studio, in the Fine Arts Building, has had many pupils whose success is her proudest laurel. Gertrude Radle was born Sept. 23, 1871, at Kane City, Pa., the only child of John Nelson Radle and Julia Guy Radle. Her method of teaching is in harmony with the laws of life, and evolves most wonderful results in developing not only the musical nature but the entire personality. Instead of urging a pupil on with the idea that musical excellence can only be attained by stretching every nerve to its utmost tension, the student is encouraged to relax every nerve and let the real self dominate mind and body. With less of self-consciousness comes a delight in effort which before seemed unattainable. Miss Radle says—" For a sensitive child to practice with the thought ever present that a critical teacher is to be met is self-destructive, for fear of displeasure makes success impossible."

Miss Radle has a charming personality and a sympathetic presence which win the confidence of her pupils and inspire each one to the best effort.

Theodore Spiering.

Theodor B. Ofiriing

Theodore Spiering.

Surrounded with the atmosphere of music and culture, Theodore Spiering (well known throughout the country as leader of the celebrated Spiering Quartet) spent his childhood and youth. He was born in St. Louis, Mo., September 5, 1871, of a distinctly musical and literary family, who came to America in the middle of the nineteenth century.

Chas. L. Bernays, his grandfather, living in the same house, was one of the first American proclaimers of Schafenhauer and Richard Wagner, and was widely known as a writer and musical critic for the St. Louis and foreign German press. His father was the well-schooled violinist, Ernest Spiering, leader of the Philharmonic Quintet Club, of St. Louis, which for several seasons had a prosperous existence. After careful instruction from his father, Theodore Spiering made his first public appearance in connection with the work of this organization in the early eighties.

In his home he met not only the musicians of St. Louis but the visiting celebrities of the musical world.

In 1886, his father took him to Cincinnati and placed him under the instruction of the eminent violinist and teacher, Henry Schrodieck. The father died in 1887, but the son remained under the instruction of Schrodieck another year, and then went to Berlin. Here he entered the Hoch Schule, where he remained four years as a pupil of Andreas Moser and Dr. Joseph Joachim, training as a violin virtuoso, but practicing diligently ensemble playing. During the last years at school, he was concertmeister of the school orchestra. He also had the honor of assisting Barth, Hausmover and others, while such musicians as Brahms, Max Busch and George Vierling von Herzogenberg gave the young artist many proofs of their friendliness. In 1892, Spiering returned to Chicago, bringing a highly eulogistic letter from Joachim to Theodore Thomas. For four years he was one of the leading violinists in the Chicago Orchestra, appearing with great success, February, 1893, as soloist in the most difficult Schumann Phantasia.

In the summer of 1893, the Spiering Quartet was organized, and has given over four hundred concerts throughout the United States, often playing where chamber music was entirely unknown. It has reached a perfection of ensemble of finish and true musical interpretation which are the marvel of public and critic alike.

Theodore Spiering has devoted some attention to composition. He has written a group of piano pieces, some songs, and three concert studies for the violin, all of which are still in manuscript. The songs have obtained public hearing and recognition. As an orchestral conductor, he has won many laurels, and has shown that he is greatly gifted in that branch of his profession.

There is no question but that he is now one of the most promising of the younger generation of conductors in the world.

Sybil Sammis.

Sibyl Sammis.

Sybil Sammis.

Sybil Sammis was born in Foreston, Ill., and when little more than a baby evinced a marvelous ear for music, humming any tune she heard. She is a descendant of John Quincy Adams, and inherits marked musical and literary ability. When four years old, her parents moved to Deadwood, South Dakota, later to Pierre.

After coming to Chicago, Miss Sammis first studied under Mad. Ragna Linnè, who, recognizing her unusual ability and ambition, became interested in her. After a few lessons, she secured for her a position in the Sinai Temple choir. Later she became the leading soprano of the Grand Boulevard Presbyterian Church choir, and afterwards soloist in the Fifth Presbyterian Church. Giving up her church work, she became the soloist with the Chicago Marine Band, a position successful artistically and financially, and renewed for several seasons. Before she had entered her 'teens, Miss Sammis cherished the highest ambitions. For their achievement she hoarded her resources and went abroad, where she studied in Paris with Mme. Lurig, who rendered her valuable assistance.

Returning to New York, Miss Sammis accepted engagements in concert and oratorio work, and at the Maine festival appeared with Schumann-Heink and Campanari in concerts, and sang " Elijah " with Ffrangeon-Davies. At the Ver-

451

mont festivals she sang " Elijah " with Gwlynn Miles. She possesses a wonderful dramatic soprano voice, of three full octaves, ranging from E below middle C to E above high C. She has the low tones of a contralto, the full medium of a mezzo, and the pure, clear, upper tones of a lyric soprano. Born with a genius for interpretation, the themes of difficult arias are easily mastered by her. Following her Festival work, she appeared with the " Three great star combination," the trio being Evan Williams, Gwylm Miles and Miss Sammis.

This summer (1903) Miss Sammis sang with the Metropolitan Opera House Orchestra, at Madison Square Garden, New York. During the season she gave a phenomenal example of her ability and the repertoire at her command. It was Wagner night, and the soloist of the week who, until six o'clock, expected to sing, found herself unable to do so. Speaking of it the *New York Herald* wrote: " The bandmaster was at his wits' end till about seven o'clock, when he learned that Miss Sammis was in New York. He found her, and, without rehearsal, she took Miss Cumming's place, and sang with marked success the selections already chosen." The first was " Dich Theure Halle," from Tannhauser. She was called back twice, and sang "After the Ball," by Gillet. For the second number she sang Wagner's " Traüme," and received much applause, her encore being " My Old Kentucky Home." This wonderful success has greatly encouraged her, has stimulated ambition and quickened hope.

Miss Sammis has a bright, sunny disposition, a very sweet and winning face; her enunciation is distinct, and of her audiences she makes friends.

Charles Henry Aldrich.

Charles Henry Aldrich.

The legal profession has made great strides in America during the last decade. Many things have combined to bring about this result. Meetings of national bar associations, at which some of the most distinguished lawyers of this country and England have spoken on questions of international interest, and engaged in discussions on matters of grave import, have quickened thought and stimulated a generous rivalry among the eminent legal lights of the country.

Comparatively few realize the opportunities for advancement offered by the legal profession, from the time of graduation from the Law School till possibly a seat is gained on the Supreme Bench of the United States. Chicago is not second to any city in the Union in the ability, sound judgment and brilliant successes of the representatives of the various courts of the city. Some of the most important cases known in this country have had their trial here.

Among the representative men of Chicago, in this profession, no one has achieved a more enviable reputation than Charles Henry Aldrich. Mr. Aldrich was born, August 26, 1850, and was educated first in the public schools of his native city, and later in the Northeastern Indiana Academy. In 1871, he was graduated from the High School at Ann Arbor, Mich., and in 1875 from the classical course of the Michigan

University with the degree of Bachelor of Arts.   For distinguished services the University' conferred upon him the degree of Master of Arts in 1893.   He practiced law at Fort
Wayne, Indiana, until 1886, when he moved to Chicago.   He
was appointed Solicitor General of the United States in 1891,
in which capacity he served until 1893.

He has been prominently identified with much important
litigation in the various courts, particularly the Federal
Courts.   Among some of the most important cases may be
mentioned the one involving the constitutionality of the Chi-
nese Exclusion Act (Geary Act), and the " Fourteen Diamond
Ring " case, involving constitutional questions growing out of
the late Spanish War.

Mr. Aldrich, while a close student along his own line of
work, has read extensively in other directions, and is a man
of decided literary tastes.   He has a large library, in which
he takes much pride, and is very fond of fine engravings.   In
this way he has been, and is, a patron of the best in the world
of literature and art, and in his home there is the atmosphere
of culture.   He was married, Oct. 13, 1875, and has three children, one son and two daughters.   Mr. Aldrich is of a retiring nature, and has devoted his life almost exclusively to professional achievement.   That he has won the success at which
he aimed, those who know him best will most readily attest.
He cares little for social functions, and is rarely seen except in the courts, at his office or in his home.

ignor Pasquale Capone.

Signor Pasquale Capone

Signor Pasquale Capone.

The word Italy seems to surround us at once with an atmosphere of music and of art. We think of the long line of illustrious Italian composers who have given us some of the most beautiful music the world has ever known, and of the artists whose pictures and statues are immortal. And so a name which reminds us of that land of beauty seems to bring us in touch with an artist life. Signor Pasquale Capone was born in Salerno, Italy, and from childhood evinced a love for music. At an early age he began the study of the violin, harmony and countersign with well-known masters of that city. He soon proved that he had exceptional talent and indefatigable perseverance. After studying for some years in his native city, he made such remarkable progress that his parents were advised to send him to Milan to continue his study in that rarely musical atmosphere, and avail himself of the many unexcelled advantages offered there. He entered the Regio Conservatory, of Milan, and at once received special attention on account of his exceptional talent.

After the most thorough course possible, he was at length graduated from that institution with the highest honors, being presented with a gold medal, the first award for musical progress and exceptional ability. While in Milan, Signor Capone became well known in the musical world, and filled

marked success. He was also patronized by the most distinguished families of that cultured center. One result of his life in Milan was to create the highest ideals in the mind of this young artist, and he has never been satisfied with anything less than the best in the music-world. He has gained a very excellent reputation as a soloist, his playing being marked by smoothness and ease of execution, yet great distinctness and purity of tone, and his interpretation of the most difficult themes being intelligent and delightful. He was engaged to play at the famous theatre " La Scala " as first violin, under the conductor Com. Bassi, and subsequently was secured as concertmaster at the opening of the theatre " Caccia," of Piemonte, where Verdi's " Otello " was given under the direction of Tascanini.

On coming to America, Signor Capone received immediate recognition among musicians, and has appeared as violin soloist and conductor in this country as well as in Italy.

He has been engaged for five years as the head of the violin department of the Chicago Conservatory, and has under his direction the symphony orchestra and chamber music of the conservatory. Among his pupils are some who are making themselves well known in the best musical world.

rs. John Harrison Francis.

Mary C Francis

Mrs. John Harrison Francis.

The history of music, not only in Illinois but in America, reveals the fact that, as a country, we have as yet produced no really great music.

Possibly the many reasons for this suggest themselves readily to the observer of American life. We are still a young nation, and the best music is the outgrowth of years of national history. We are a busy nation, living a strenuous life, and have not cultivated the arts as have the European countries. Yet that America will gain recognition in the foremost ranks of the musical compositions of the world one cannot doubt.

There are everywhere musical men and women, ambitious, conscientious in endeavor, and a musical atmosphere is being created from which, in time, will be evolved great composers and great artists, worthy of place with the most honored masters of other countries.

Among those who are thus a musical inspiration may be named Mrs. John Harrison Francis, who has long been one of the most progressive, intelligent and enthusiastic of Peoria's musical patrons. While her own gifts in that direction—which were of no mean order—have never been given especial cultivation, she possesses a fine natural taste which a long residence in Paris and Dresden (during which she directed the studies of her daughter, Miss Maude Francis) has generously ripened. Since her return from Europe, some years ago, Mrs. Francis' handsome home has been the center of much of the musical life of Peoria. No worthy enterprise has been denied her substantial assistance and support. No youthful aspirant for the meager and uncertain rewards of a musical career has failed to receive from her the encouragement, sympathy and advice her wide experience so amply fitted her to give.

No one with real ability and talent has come to her without obtaining not only recognition, but introduction to the best musical people, hints as to the best musical methods and helpful suggestion, which have been an inspiration to many now achieving excellent reputation for themselves.

Such a woman, who uses her exceptional opportunities rather for others than herself, aids far more in the development of a true musical taste in the community than does the professional artist, whose ambitions and interests are necessarily self-centered. There is an absolute freedom from the jealousy which is too often apparent where there is the least possible opportunity for rivalry, and to such generous large-heartedness the most timid feel a certain assurance in approach. The community blest with such a spirit should count itself most fortunate, for it is the greatest incentive to public-spirited musical effort.

The influence of Mrs. Francis on the musical history of Peoria can scarcely be estimated, but it has been such that no record of the progress made in that art in the last few years would be complete without the mention of her name.

ss **Maud Engle Francis.**

MISS MAUDE *INGLE* FRANCIS.

Miss Maude Ingle Francis.

Early in the nineties, a young girl sang for the first time before a select gathering of Peoria's musicians. She was very young—her age, indeed, scarcely reaching sixteen years —yet there was about her performance a strange lack of crudeness common to " first efforts." She sang as the birds sing, naturally and easily, with all of the birds' roundness, freshness and sweetness of tone. The musicians listening were greatly surprised. Really expecting nothing at all, they had asked the young girl to sing with the good-natured tolerance often felt by musicians towards young people who are cherishing musical ambitions. In the few moments of her song, the relative positions of the company had undergone a curious change.

A new star had risen in that little circle, a star that promised to eclipse them all, and the congratulations that followed were not of the perfunctory sort which commonly reward beginners.

A few months later the young singer, Maude Ingle Francis, daughter of Mr. and Mrs. John H. Francis, went to Europe. Three years of study followed—study under the best masters in the world. Lamperti, Marchesi (names forever interwoven with the history of the greatest triumphs in the realm of song) were her teachers, and they found in her
467

an apt and gifted pupil. Then came her return to this coun-
try, and two years' study under the late Charles Adams, of
Boston, followed by a year's coaching with Victor Harris, in
New York.

When next Miss Francis appeared before an audience in
Peoria, it was as a finished artist in a higher sense than the
usual hackneyed acceptation of the term. Musicians and the
general public alike surrendered themselves delightedly to the
charm of her singing.

It was this young singer's fortune to be placed beyond
the necessity of earning a livelihood by her voice. Her inherent love of singing was never made secondary to hopes of a
" career." The exquisite quality of her tones was never sacri-
ficed to the ordinary greed for quantity. Their pure roundness never was lost and drowned in the volume of sound
requisite to the filling of a vast auditorium. Her voice has
always retained, therefore, to a remarkable degree, its first
girlish freshness and charm.

In addition to her wonderful voice, she was endowed with
a handsome face, beautiful figure and rare grace of manner
and bearing.

As a singer of French chansons, Miss Francis has had
scarcely an equal in this country. Her success in this field at
private musicales, both in New York and Chicago, was instantaneous and complete.

In 1902, however, Miss Francis was married to Mr.
Thomas Colston Kinney, of New York, an event which ab-
ruptly terminated her semi-public career. Since her marriage Mrs. Kinney has lived abroad, where she expects to reside permanently.

Lorado Taft.

Lorado Taft

Lorado Taft.

Although still a comparatively young man, Lorado Taft stands in the foremost ranks in his profession, not only in Chicago and Illinois but in this country. An unceasing student, with genius of touch and vivid imagination, the results he has achieved have been such as to win for him a reputation which the years will enhance.

He is a native of Illinois, having been born in Elmwood, Peoria County, in 1860. His father, Don Carlos Taft, was a professor in the State University at Champaign, Ill., and here Mr. Taft was graduated in 1879. The following year he went abroad, and for three years was a student in l'Ecole des Beaux Arts. At the expiration of this time he came back to America for a visit, but returned to Paris for two years more of study.

In 1886, he established himself in Chicago, and very soon took charge of the classes in modeling at the Art Institute. This position he has held ever since, and has made the standard of scholarship in this department very high, requiring from his pupils the same lofty aim which has inspired his own life. Besides his work as a teacher, he has given many courses of public lectures, both at the Institute and in connection with the extension department of the University of Chicago. He is a busy man in his own studio, with his classes and doing the various kinds of literary work which claims his attention.

Among his pupils he is a great favorite, for while they know that nothing less than their best effort will satisfy him, they realize that he recognizes merit and honest endeavor, and never withholds the word of deserved commendation. Mr. Taft is most conscientious in his work, painstaking in every detail, striving for perfection in the finish of all he undertakes, and yet there is the greatest freedom in every curve, and almost the touch of vitality in every poise.

His professional work has been largely in portraiture and military monuments, and by his success in these efforts he has established a most enviable national reputation.

Those who attended the Columbian Exposition will recall, with great pleasure, the groups which he contributed—" The Sleep of the Flowers " and " The Awakening of the Flowers," on the Horticultural Building.

Among his most recent works are " Despair," done in 1898; " The Solitude of the Soul," 1900; " Knowledge," 1902, and " The Fountain of Lakes," 1903. A military group called " The Defense of the Flag," which was designed and executed for Jackson, Michigan, was also done in 1903. While ambitious and zealous in his efforts for the highest degree of attainment, Mr. Taft is a man of modest bearing, free from the arrogance which mars so many successful artists.

That his will be an enduring and world-wide reputation is conceded by those whose judgment is unquestioned.

William Vernon.

William Vernon.

The art-life of the Middle-West is becoming more and more recognized as each year makes history, and those associated with its advancement are also becoming known as men of artistic taste and literary and art research.

Possibly the Columbian Exhibit gave an impetus to art and developed connoisseurs and critics along art lines to an extent not admitted then, perhaps not fully realized even now.

Few men have been more closely associated for the past twenty years with this art-life of the Middle-West, particularly as existing in Chicago, than Mr. Wm. Vernon, who, during the greater part of that time, has been the manager of the art department of A. H. Abbott & Co.

During the "World's Fair period of Chicago Art," Mr. Vernon was Secretary of the Chicago Society of Artists.

Those who were in Chicago at that time will recall the vast number of distinguished people who, in various ways, were entertained by the city. The local Artists' Club, during the fair and for many months before, was the "rendezvous" of some of the world's most famous artists. Well-known painters from Holland, France, Spain, Italy, England and the Scandinavian Peninsula, and practically all of the best-known American artists, were guests of this club. Upon Mr. Vernon devolved the entertainment of these men of many climes and many tastes. That he discharged this duty to the delight of those who were fortunate enough to be recipients of this hospitality was attested many a time most eagerly and enthusiastically during that eventful time.

At about this time, Mr. Vernon secured for the club the Yerkes' prizes of $500 for the best collection of paintings by Chicago artists at the annual exhibition of the society. Chas. T.Yerkes, the donor of the prizes, gave them not only that year but annually for five years, or until the disruption of the society, in 1896.

Since the organization of the Vernon Gallery, Mr. Vernon has made yearly pilgrimages to the various shrines of art in Europe. He has been a student of art as well as an ardent admirer, and has achieved a wide reputation for rare discernment in the selection of works of art, particularly of the Barbizon and modern Dutch schools.

Mr. Vernon is well known as a most potent friend of aspiring artists who possess real talent. While he is, of necessity, a critic whom nothing escapes, no one more quickly recognizes real genius under the errors of inexperience, and thus he has earned the distinction of "bringing out" some of the most successful western painters. Mr. Vernon is a man of wide literary research, and wields a ready pen. He writes frequently on various subjects connected with art, and for a number of years was art critic for the *Chicago American*.

Charles Francis Browne.

One of the artists in Chicago, who has won for himself a reputation which places him, without question, in the very front rank of the best in his profession, is Charles Francis Browne. We speak of the vastness of the West, its wonderful resources, its varied scenery, and this and more is very true. After all, however, in the comparatively small confines of New England, we find the picturesque, the grand and the beautiful so combined, and so close the environment of the people, that we cannot wonder that many an artist has found development there.

Mr. Browne was born in Natick, Massachusetts, May 21, 1859, but the family soon moved to Waltham, where he received his early education. He began his art studies at the Boston Museum of Fine Arts, and prosecuted them later at Pennsylvania Academy.

In both of these art schools his work gave abundant promise of what the later years have accomplished. He was not only an enthusiastic and earnest student, but had that decided originality of conception and skill in execution which have characterized his more mature work. In 1883, he went abroad, and studied for several years with Gérome in L'École-des Beaux Arts. In 1892, he came to Chicago, and soon became connected with the Art Institute, where he has taught for the past eight years, and, as artist and teacher, has achieved a most gratifying success.

Oregon, Ill., where so many artists have their summer homes, has afforded Mr. Browne subjects for many pictures which have been exhibted at the Art Institute or found a place among the treasures of some art-lover. He is a landscape painter, and most exquisitely does he reproduce nature's most glorious coloring and her daintiest tints. It seems almost impossible to select from so many a few of his pictures for mention. In 1900, he exhibted at the Art Institute the following—" Summer Sky," " River Road," "A Hillside " and " The Yellow Pond;" in 1902, "Afternoon on Rock River," at Grand Detour, Ill., and " Harvesting Wheat," Oregon, Ill.

There is never a meaningless stroke of the brush in Mr. Browne's pictures. Every detail is most carefully given, and the results have made his pictures great favorites and widely known. He is a true lover of nature, and paints *con amore,* an important element in success. His wife is the sister of Lorado Taft, the sculptor, and the artist atmosphere is most delightfully felt in their home. He is at present (1903) abroad, and is planning to remain there the greater part of a year. This experience will be of value to him, for he is as indefatigable a student as in the days when he had reputation and success in his profession still to achieve. He will, no doubt, on his return, add many to the laurels already won.

Charles Francis Browne

Miss Christia M. Reade.

Coralie M. Reade —

Miss Christia M. Reade.

A most talented and versatile artist is Miss Christia M. Reade, a Chicago girl, who owes much of her artistic training to the Chicago Art Institute. Some years ago, she entered the institute life and color class, with no thought of attempting the work of an artistic designer. Some wonderfully clever designs, submitted quite casually to a designing and decorating firm in Chicago, decided the question. Miss Reade was importuned, and consented to become one of the staff of designers employed by this firm, devoting herself almost exclusively to designs for stained glass execution. She remained with this firm for some years, carrying her work through every stage from the initial sketch to the installed window, following this training by two and a half years of European study.

Returning to Chicago, she established a studio, and finds a ready market for the exquisite work which is designed and executed by her. It is her ambition some day to have a " shop " of her own, in which all sorts of beautiful things shall be made, and where she can devote herself even more than now to the stained glass work, so interesting and unusual. Among the better known examples of her extensive work along this line is the memorial window dedicated to Judge Drummond, recently placed in the Episcopal Church at Wheaton. " The Worship of the Wise Men " has been pronounced by competent critics as wonderfully artistic in design and creation. Conventionalized lilies and the half-unfolding scroll of another memorial window, designed in loving commemoration of a young girl, are exceedingly lovely and delicate in form and basic idea.

In the way of medals, brooches, buckles, fobs, clasps, chains, and all manner of artistic feminine belongings, Miss Reade has produced some most unique and effective results, especially in old silver and copper with semi-precious stones. In iron she also does excellent and original work, fashioning hinges, decorations, shields, crests and other finishing touches for the wood and furniture designs made by herself. In working both copper and brass, Miss Reade finds great pleasure and most satisfactory artistic expression. The originality and beauty of the thoughts she has wrought into metal place her in the highest rank among the comparatively few workers in this realm of art. Water colors and book plates also appeal to this gifted, artistic nature most strongly, and specimens of her book-plate art are in demand all over the country.

It is the wide scope of research and artistic delving, as well as the genius of originality and beauty-worship, which render Miss Christia M. Reade's wonderful achievements peculiarly her own.

Ralph Clarkson.

Ralph Clarkson

Ralph Clarkson.

In that beautiful building, the home of some of Chicago's best artists, Mr. Clarkson, widely recognized in the world of art, has his studio. New England has furnished a large proportion not only of the scholars, authors and orators of the day, but its artists as well. Among them no one has achieved more in his profession than has Ralph Clarkson. He was born in 1861, at Amesbury, Essex County, Mass., a near neighbor of the beloved Whittier, who was a friend of the family, and whom Mr. Clarkson knew and loved as a boy and until the death of the famous poet.

He first studied art in the Boston Art Museum, and later in the Julien Academy, in Paris, where he obtained the honor of being an exhibitor in the Salon.

For six years he lived abroad, traveling extensively in Spain, Italy, Germany, Austria and the Netherlands. These years were wonderful years to him in the opportunity they afforded to study the works of the great masters of various schools, and familiarize himself with what lay back of results attained, and, in a degree, with the secret of inspiration. That this experience is still of value to him is evidenced by his work, into which he has put the multifold and valuable gleanings of these years. Mr. Clarkson's special line of work is painting portraits, a work in which he has won a most enviable reputation.

almost mobile lip, being among their chief characteristics. Among the portraits he has painted may be named Judge Palmer and Miss Peck, of Milwaukee, Wis.; Mr. and Mrs. W. J. Bryan, of national fame; Carter Harrison, Mayor of Chicago; the late Governor Altgeld, and many members of the Studebaker family, of South Bend, Ind.

Mr. Clarkson is a member of the New York Color Club, President of the Art Commission, Chicago; Vice-President of the Municipal Art League (in which he has been very active); Treasurer Chicago Society of Artists, and member of the " Little Room." He was a member of the American Art Jury, Paris Exposition, 1900, and is a member of the Art Jury, St. Louis Exposition, 1904. Mr. Clarkson is an enthusiast in his profession, with high appreciation of its peculiar demands and a conscientious endeavor to meet his own lofty ideals. Comparatively a young man, his success is unquestioned, and his position assured in the foremost ranks of his profession.

Frederick Warner Freer, A.N.A.

FREDERICK WARNER FREER, A. N. A.

Frederick Warner Freer, A. N. A.

Frederick Warner Freer, A. N. A., was born in Chicago, Ill., in 1849, and has lived there most of his life, except when absent studying. He is a portrait and genre painter, who has achieved for himself a more than excellent reputation, and is a teacher of painting in the Art Institute, of Chicago. Among his most important and best known works may be mentioned "A Lady in Black," owned by the Boston Art Club; " Jeannette," owned by the National Academy of Design; " Consolation," " The Young Mother," owned by F. S. Coffin, of Boston; " The Old Letter," owned by the Detroit Club; " Thoughts of the Future," " In Ambush," etc., etc.

As a portrait painter, he has won a wide fame. His portraits are most satisfying in that they preserve the individuality of the person. Those who have been bitterly disappointed, as is often the case, in the picture from which they hoped much will appreciate this rare gift. The work is most exquisitely done, every detail is carefully given, the coloring is natural, the finish is perfect, and yet the pictured face is eloquent with the expression and the character of the original. That this fact is recognized is easily seen by a partial list of important works in this line which have been committed to him, and which he has done most admirably:—The late Dr. E. L. Holmes, President of Rush Medical College, the property of the college; the late Dr. Oliver Marcy, property of the Northwestern University; Dr. Angell, President of Michigan University, owned by the University; the late.Charles W. Fullerton, owned by the Art Institute, of Chicago; Judge G. S. Robinson, owned by the Supreme Court of Iowa, and others. He has had many honors given him in recognition of the excellence of his work. He received a medal at the World's Columbian Exposition, Chicago, 1893; a bronze medal at the Pan-American Exposition, Buffalo, 1901; a silver medal at the South Carolina Inter-State and West Indian Exhibit, 1901-02, and the Marten B. Cahn prize, from the Art Institute, Chicago, 1901. He has the title A. N. A. (Associate Member National Academy of Design), and is a member of the American Water Color Society, also of the Society of American Artists, of the Salmagundi, etc.

As a teacher Prof. Freer is enthusiastic, conscientious and inspiring. Ambitious and successful himself, he expects his pupils to have the highest aims and be willing to work for their realization. As an artist, his has been a rarely successful life, and he has made for himself a name in which he may well feel a pride. Many of the pictures which have been named have a national fame, and Chicago and the Art Institute congratulate themselves that Prof. Freer has identified himself with the art ambitions and interests of this city.

M. Inez Lee.

M. Inez Lee.

M. Inez Lee.

" The art of fencing, in this century, is learned and taught.as an elegant accomplishment, developing gracefulness and activity, while it imparts suppleness to the limbs, strength to the muscles and quickness to the eye.''

It is an art which has been improved and perfected during the past centuries, until of the two recognized schools— French and Italian—the French is considered by far the more scientific, embracing a more beautiful foil-play. For women fencing is rarely adapted, and from maid to matron only sheer love of the art induces its practice. In one of the large, handsome studios in the Fine Arts Building, Chicago, is an enthusiastic teacher of the art, and the keynote of her success has been careful, painstaking thoroughness.

In a pleasant country home, near Plainfield, Iowa, was born, March 4, 1874, M. Inez Lee. Of good old New England stock, by nature buoyant and hopeful, her childhood and youth were spent amid the flowers and the birds until she grew up a strong, self-reliant, superbly-developed young woman, passionately fond of outdoor sports and enthusiastic in her love of animals. Almost from babyhood she has ridden, and, at an early age, was an expert horsewoman. Out of doors from morning till night, now with her brothers, now out for a long ride alone, except for her horse and dog, she passed her childhood.

493

licitation of the neighbors, she commenced to give music lessons to their children. Tiring of this, at the end of two years, she went to college to prepare herself for teaching in the public schools, but before completing her course was teaching in a country school, studying nights to keep up with her classmates. ·

Later she went to Des Moines for further study, and from there to Chicago, where she has spent the greater part of the time since.

During all this time she has been an enthusiastic devotee of all kinds of athletics, and soon after reaching Chicago she took a thorough course in foil and broadsword work, including the regular United States Army cavalry practice, with Capt. F. E. Yates, fencingmaster of the Chicago Athletic Association. After teaching a year, she further perfected herself for her vocation by studying with the best instructors to be had in New York and Boston. She also spent some time at West Point studying the manœuvres and tactics as employed there.

Tall, with a wealth of red-gold hair, an erect and graceful carriage, she is a familiar figure on Michigan Ave., and her hosts of friends predict for her a brilliant success in her chosen work.

Rudolph Lundberg.

Rudolph Lundberg

Rudolph Lundborg.

An artist, devoting years to careful preparation for bis lifework, a delightful singer, a conscientious teacher and a well-known musical conductor; Rudolph Lundborg has achieved a merited success.

He was born July 25, 1870, in Trollhätten, Sweden, where he spent his early childhood. When twelve years' of age, he was sent to the College in Gothenburg, Sweden, where he remained five years. In 1887 he entered the Royal Musical Academy in Stockholm, from which he was graduated in 1892 in voice culture, piano, organ and harmony. The following two years were devoted to study under the private tuition of Prof. Ivar Hallström. For three consecutive years, 1894-97, he was elected organist and choirleader at Lindesberg, Sweden. But Rudolph Lundborg was not satisfied with what presented itself to him for achievement in his native country. He longed for larger fields of usefulness, and, in 1897, came to America. He very soon came in touch with musical effort in the middle-west, and was appointed the Musical Director at Burlington Institute College, in Burlington, Iowa.

Here he remained for two years, achieving a marked degree of success. At the end of that time he received a call which he accepted to become the Musical Director at Lombard

College, Galesburg, Illinois, where he has remained for nearly
five years.   In Galesburg he had opportunity for other than
the routine work of his school position.   He became most
favorably known, not only as a teacher and conductor, but
as a singer.   He gave many recitals and concerts in Galesburg and vicinity, which were successful to a most gratifying
extent, and was also the choir-leader in the First Lutheran
Church of Galesburg.   As a teacher, Mr. Lundborg has
given to those under his care the same excellence of method
and careful training which were his own during the years he
devoted to study.   Painstaking and persevering himself, he
exacts a like attention to detail from his pupils, and the results he attains are most satisfactory.   His whole life has
been spent in the atmosphere of study, and he is devoted to
the profession for which he is so well equipped, and in
which (although comparatively a newcomer in this country)
he has made an enviable reputation.   Feeling the need of
rest, wishing to revisit the scenes of his childhood and spend
some time with members of his family, Mr. Lundborg is at
present in Sweden.   He does not, however, expect to remain
here permanently.   His heart is in his work in America,
and, although the months of vacation have passed   most
pleasantly, he is planning to return to America in the near
future.

Katharine V. Dickinson.

KATHARINE V. DICKINSON.

Katharine V. Dickinson.

Among the music lovers and music teachers who are do-
extensive work along the most approved lines, none de-
ves more cordial recognition than does Miss Katharine V.
:kinson, whose home for the past eleven years has been in
.on, Ill. Her native city was Penn Yan, Yates County,
w York, her parents being Charles F. and Martha Cole
kinson.

Her education was obtained in New York City and in
ston, Mass. She received preparation for her special work
the New England Conservatory of Music, Boston, Mass.,
l from such eminent teachers as Mr. J. Harry Wheeler and
ne. Lena Doria Devine, of New York, both of whom were
pils and certified exponents of the principles of the old
lian school of singing as taught by the great Maestro Fran-
co Lamperti. Miss Dickinson is, therefore, thoroughly im-
d with these principles, and in her teaching adheres strict-
o them. Her piano study was under the direction of Prof.
o Bendix, Florence Keer and, later, Mr. Carl Lachmund,
v of New York. Theory and harmony were studied under
of. Louis Elson, the eminent author, critic and lecturer, and
late Stephen A. Emery, author of standard text-books.
:h preparation has been supplemented by further study
years of experience in teaching.

501

In 1891, she became director of the Voice School of Shurtleff College, Upper Alton, Ill., and, in 1893, was connected with the Alton Conservatory, which position she held until September, 1899, when she opened her own studio, where she is beginning her fourth season, having achieved unusual success. She was the founder, and is the director, of the Camerata Chorus, a chorus of fifty ladies, and for five years has been director of the choir of the First Presbyterian Church.

The work undertaken by Miss Dickinson in her present location is laid upon lines of broad musical culture. To that end she supplements her personal individual work not only with studies, in classes, directly essential to musical understanding and feeling, but with those broadening studies in literature and history necessary to a fine culture. Her abundant success in this method lies not only in the knowledge of her subject, but in that special gift of sympathy, rarer than knowledge, which marks the ideal teacher.

Miss Dickinson's influence in the field of public school music has been particularly felt. She has not only labored assiduously to place music in the required course of studies of every public school, but has carefully and earnestly trained many of the teachers, fitting them for the regular school work of that study. Numbers of her pupils are occupying lucrative positions as Supervisors of Music. Miss Dickinson's work has been so largely among teachers that she may fitly be called a teacher of teachers.

Henry Lake Slayton.

HENRY LAKE SLAYTON.

Henry Lake Slayton.

The name of Henry Lake Slayton is known all over this country as the name of the founder of the Slayton Lyceum Bureau, one of the oldest and largest entertainment bureaus in America. He was born in Woodstock, Vermont, May 29, 1841, the son of Stephen D. and Lucy Maria (Kendall) Slayton. The family in America is descended from Capt. Thomas Slayton, a native of Scotland, who came to Massachusetts in 1690. A large number of his descendants took part in the Revolutionary and Civil Wars.

Mr. Slayton's boyhood was passed on his father's farm, and after attending the district and High School in Lebanon, N. H., he took a three years' course at Kimball Union Academy and a special military course at Norwich University, Vermont. His father was a staunch Abolitionist, and the son, at an early age, became imbued with a like spirit. In 1861, at the beginning of the Civil War, a meeting was held in his native town, and an earnest call was made for volunteers, and various young men in the audience were invited to speak. Henry L. Slayton responded in words which, in the light of subsequent events, proved to have been almost prophecy. He promised to aid in every way at home by drilling companies and speaking, but he felt the time for him to enlist had not yet come, and said, in substance: " Success will not be ours till the colored people are armed.'' Declining offers to go into the field as an officer, he waited till September, 1863, when he was commissioned First Lieut. in the Second U. S. Colored Infantry, the first colored regiment armed by the U. S. Government. He served during the next two years, principally in the Gulf States and Florida, where no quarter was shown officers of colored regiments and where hardship and peril daily confronted him. He was repeatedly appointed on court-martials, and was a member of the Military Commission for Florida.

When mustered out of service, in 1866, he was commanding officer of company '' K ''. The following autumn he began the study of law, graduating from the Albany Law School in 1867. He began practice in Chicago, Ill., and was at once very successful, particularly as a criminal lawyer, and remained there until the great fire of 1871. By that calamity he lost his library, and barely escaped with his life. Those who were in Chicago at that time will remember the attempts made to burn the city, and the excitement prevalent as a result. Every or anyone unfortunate enough for any reason to attract attention was at once branded a '' fire-burner,'' and with difficulty escaped the fury of the mob. Walking on South State St. one day, Mr. Slayton, by some peculiarity of dress, thus excited the attention of those in the streets, and it was only after a most perilous experience that he was rescued from the furious crowd. At one time six revolvers were leveled at him, and it was only the fear of shooting others which saved him from the bullet. Almost immediately after the fire he accepted the position of Superintendent of Public Schools in Texas, and entered with enthusiasm upon his work.

His efforts in behalf of colored schools occasioned much ill-feeling, and as a result several schools were destroyed and his life was threatened. He remained in Texas two and a half years, managing and editing a newspaper in addition to his other duties. Ill health compelled his resignation, and after a brief visit to New Hampshire he returned to Chicago.

March 19, 1873, he was married to Mina E., daughter of John Gregory, a Universalist clergyman, of Northfield, Vermont. Mrs. Slayton was a talented elocutionist, and the desire to give her the coveted opportunity to appear in the right way before the best people led to the establishment, in 1873, of the Slayton Lyceum Bureau. From the beginning it was a success in furnishing and directing lecturers, readers, singers, dramatic and concert troupes in all parts of the country.

During a period of thirty years ending May 1, 1903, the Bureau negotiated over 65,000 lecture and concert engagements. Many noted representatives of artistic professions have received their first start under its auspices. This Bureau has branches in most of the large cities, while its agents are everywhere all over the country, busy with preparations for the coming season.

Mr. Slayton has a keen personal interest in the success particularly of those who have begun their public career with him, and is an inspiration to those too easily discouraged. As a manager, Mr. Slayton is enterprising, yet sufficiently conservative to avoid the mistakes and dangers so often incurred in the management of public entertainments. He is a ready and fluent speaker, and has written many newspaper articles. He is a man of strong convictions, and has the courage of these convictions. At the time of the Presidential campaigns

seemed as if his was a charmed life.

Mr. Slayton is planning to go, with his wife, to Ca
to live, at least during the winter months, and enjoy cc
tive rest.   Wherever he goes he will still be in touch v
work with which he is so wholly identified, and may
enjoy what he has provided for the pleasure of others.

John Franklin Stacey.

John F. Stacey

John Franklin Stacey.

John Franklin Stacey was born, March 16, 1859, in Biddeford, Maine. He first studied art in the State Normal School, Boston, Mass., graduating in 1881. The autumn of the same year he secured appointment as supervisor of drawing in the public schools in the towns of Pittsfield and North Adams, Mass. At the end of two years he resigned and went to Paris, there to further pursue his studies in art. For three years he was in the Julian Academy, under the direction of Boulanger and Le Febvre. Returning to America, he went West and became Director of the Kansas City Art School, which position he held for three years. At present he is the art instructor in the R. T. Crane Manual Training School, Chicago. For the past ten years he has been a constant exhibitor in all local exhibits and in numerous other exhibits, both East and West.

He paints landscapes exclusively, and has received most complimentary press notices. In 1900, he visited the Paris Exposition, and painted in the village of Anvers-sur-Oise during the summer. Another summer he spent in Mystic, Conn., where, out of the meadows and rolling hills of that New England country, he evolved pictures of which an art critic has written—" They are good, strong, clear pictures." In fact, some of his very best pictures have their origin in the " hilly highways, stone fences, Yankee farmhouses and neglected meadows of New England.'' Several clubs are the fortunate possessors of some of Mr. Stacey's paintings. '' Overlooking the Valley of the Mystic '' was bought by the Union League Club, of Chicago, at the February exhibition of 1902, and is recognized as one of the very best of his pictures. Mr. Stacey is at present the Vice-President of the Arts Club, of Chicago. Possibly one of the most marked characteristics of Mr. Stacey's work is its pronounced individuality. Others have painted like meadows and streams, but no one has presented them just as he has done. He has his own way of doing things, he sees from his own standpoint, and after looking at some landscape from his brush there comes an appeal to the heart which says none have done better. An enthusiast in his art, happy in almost an ideal way with his talented wife, success is his already. His untiring perseverance and his originality, his bold, strong touch and delicate comprehension of his subject, are winning him public notice and commendation which will enroll his name among the Chicago artists of the twentieth century.

Mr. and Mrs. Stacey both maintain studios in the Studio Building, a favorite retreat for beauty-loving souls, for the charm of home life, as well as artist life, is there.

Mrs. Anna L. Stacey.

Anna L. Stacy

Mrs. Anna L. Stacey.

Mrs. Anna L. Stacey was born in Glasgow, Mo., and educated in the Pritchard School Institute, of that State. As a child she enjoyed drawing, and received a few lessons from a teacher who observed her ability. After some years she availed herself of the opportunity to enter the Art School in Kansas City. One of the teachers in this school was a young man, John Stacey. He, too, noticed the ability of the fair-haired student, and persuaded her to move " her easel to his studio, and become his life-pupil." This was ten years ago. The young couple came to Chicago, and Mrs. Stacey entered the Art Institute and became a pupil of Leonard Ochtman, in the fall of 1893. While still a pupil, she received a prize for the best water-color at the West End Woman's Club Salon, of February, 1896. From that time she has exhibited at all local exhibitions, and, in the February exhibition of 1900, received honorable mention from *Young Fortnightly* on "A Gray Day on the Mystic River," Conn. In the February exhibition of 1902, she received the prize for the best picture exhibited. The picture was the head of a little red-haired girl, painted out-of-doors, and entitled " Florence." Of it an art critic wrote the following—" ' Florence ' portrays a child's head against a shadowy background of green foliage. The face is partly turned; long, reddish, golden-brown curls fall on the shoul-

ders, and eyes and complexion are painted in rich tones usually seen with that peculiar shade of hair. The brush work is
exquisitely done; there is something subtle and indefinable
which gives a charm to the beautiful creature. She seems
alive behind the glass, and to be elfin in her nature. This picture has been purchased by the Klio, and a picture of a young
woman meditating, ' When all the World Seems Fair,' was
bought by the Woman's Aid. Other pictures are owned by
the Nike, Union League and Arché Clubs. Mrs. Stacey paints
both figures and landscapes, intending to combine the two.
She attributes her success to perseverence and hard work,
rather than to any unusual ability.''

Her friends, however, are not prepared to ignore the fact
that she has wonderful talent.

She has become a leading painter among Chicago artists,
and bears her honors lightly, though proudly, always modestly
unassuming, happy in her life with her artist-husband. In
November, 1902, she won the Martin B. Cahn prize for a picture called " Village at Twilight." While Mr. Stacey was
painting meadows and farmhouses at Mystic, Conn., she wan-
dered to the wharves and boats, which gave her opportunity
to draw picturesque forms and use color freely. Besides these
are life-sized heads and two-thirds length figures, drawn out
of doors, in an old-fashioned garden.

They are pretentious, but well done, and quaint enough to
win her an enviable reputation.

Mrs. Stacey certainly has before her a brilliant career in
her chosen profession.

Mr. Jules K. Mersfelder.

Jules R. Mendfelder

Mr. Jules R. Mersfelder.

Mr. Jules R. Mersfelder was born in Western California, a fitting birthplace for the artist nature. One not conversant with the bewildering beauty of the California landscape, with the Italian softness of her skies, the loveliness of her waters and the grandeur of her seacoast, cannot possibly estimate the influence which these have upon a poetic nature. The influences of climate, of all this mystery of nature in her glory, this fullness of beauty, is potent in the development of the artistic impulse and in stirring ambitious inspirations.

So it proved in the case of Jules R. Mersfelder. He became an art student at the age of nine years, and until he went abroad Inners and Wyant were his preceptors. While a student in France, the Barbizon painters were of the most intimate interest to him, and to them he devoted many, many hours. This attraction was a strong proof of the impression made upon him, during his childhood and earlier years, by the California forests and their atmosphere.

Mr. Mersfelder has painted in many climes, striving to capture the beauties of each, no matter how elusive, and imprison them on canvas.

His is a restless spirit and, much as they may wish he would be contented to remain, even for a comparatively limited time, in one place, his friends have long ceased to be surprised at his erratic movements. One may see him painting quietly in San Francisco, chatting with his many friends in the Bohemian Club, with apparently no thought other than remaining around such pleasant surroundings, and in less than a fortnight find him as snugly ensconced in a studio in New York as if he had never known any other environment. He paints with great nervous energy, his restless spirit showing itself in every stroke of his brush, and he frequently finishes a picture at one sitting.

Yet this rapidity of achievement is not in any way suggestive of careless work. Rather, it is the impulse of genius, which will not permit rest till result is accomplished. Whatever he does, wherever his restless impulses lead him, they have never marred the work which has won for him honorable fame. His touch has ever a sort of forceful strength, and into all his work is woven an indefinable, luring grace of poetic charm and artistic mystery, which is entirely his own. His pictures have great variety of subject, but on each he has left the impress of his beauty-loving nature.

Although a native of California, Mr. Mersfelder has exhibited for the past twenty years in New York city, in the Society American and the Academy, and, much of the time, has had a studio in that city. His pictures have been favorably received at some of the most exclusive exhibits in this country, and connoisseurs everywhere find them full of rare charm.

Mrs. Jules R. Mersfelder.

MRS. *JULES R.* MERSFELDER.

Mrs. Jules R. Mersfelder.

Among the earnest students and most promising young artists at the Chicago Art Institute, probably no one is better or more favorably known than is Mrs. Jules R. Mersfelder. However honorable a pride Mr. Mersfelder may feel in his own attainments, none who know him but will say that his greatest pride and delight are in the achievements and possibilities of his girlish wife. Louise Wilcox was born in Chicago, and has received her education here. She is by nature a thorough student, and whatever interests her receives the most systematic investigation from her. This habit, which is one of her dominant characteristics, has made her well and widely informed on many and differing subjects. Her art studies have been pursued at the Art Institute under the direction of Ralph Clarkson and Mr. Vanderpool, both of whom predict a brilliant future for the persevering and talented student. She is particularly fond of painting children among the most attractive out-of-door environment, but she also paints general portraits and landscapes most effectively. One of the youngest exhibitors at the Art Institute, she has been represented by her work in some of the most prominent local exhibits, and has received very complimentary notices from some of the best art critics. Very ambitious, with lofty ideals and conceptions of possibilities, Mrs. Mersfelder is modest and unaffected to a remarkable degree.

While her beauty wins admiration wherever she goes, she seems absolutely unconscious of it, indifferent—absorbed in one thought, to achieve success in the work to which she is devoting her life. The atmosphere of earnest endeavor which is ever about her, the absence of anything like affectation, have won her many friends among artists of more established reputation, who rejoice in her successes as if they were their own. Her work, somehow, has the stamp of her own individuality, and there is a sweetness in the thought of the artist which reveals itself in a daintiness of coloring and a grace in execution which appeal to the heart. She has been to California with her gifted husband, and anticipates, with keen pleasure, other trips to the land of sunshine and flowers. Their studio (which has in it but little of their work, for their pictures find ready sale) is artistic and eloquent of the taste of its occupants. Rare hangings, curios of many a sort, cover the walls and lie about the room. If their plans materialize, and they should remove to New York, where Mr. Mersfelder has spent many years, Chicago will lose much. Wherever they may be, the progress of the young artist will be followed with keen interest, while Mr. Mersfelder adds to the laurels already his.

Harriet Lydia Warner.

HARRIET LYDIA WARNER.

Harriet Lydia Warner.

It is interesting to observe how a true artist will impress a community and obtain recognition as such. This is singularly true of Miss Harriet Lydia Warner.

She was born in Wilmington, September 4, 1875. Her father was Asa Pomeroy Warner and her mother Eliza Gould Warner. She was always exceedingly fond of music, but it was not until 1894 that the opportunity to begin her vocal studies presented itself.

Coming to Chicago in 1895, she accepted a position as stenographer, but pursued her studies evenings, graduating with high honors from the Chicago Musical College. Her instructors have been Ortengren and Barabini. Her voice is a soprano, of rich quality, clear tone and wide range.

To her work as a student she brought a vast deal of determination to win success, perseverance which knew no flagging, real love for music of the highest excellence, and the beautiful voice which reveled in giving utterance to the choicest gems of the song-world. Thus equipped, it was only to be expected that success would crown her efforts. She obtained a position as soprano in the Union Park Congregational Church choir, one of the most desirable choir positions in Chicago. Later she connected herself with a company which was giving the opera " Il Trovatore," and gained much popularity by her rendering of the soprano part.

527

Although the company was amateur, yet competent critics from St. Louis and Chicago gave Miss Warner credit for having taken the difficult role of Leonora with a cleverness and finish worthy of the best among high-class professionals. Everywhere, when this company appeared, the papers were most enthusiastic in their praise of Miss Warner, and many have predicted for her most brilliant success as a prima donna within the next few years.

Her home has been for some time past, and is now, in Joliet, Ill., and there she has done much towards inspiring and preserving interest in music and musical enterprises. She is the leader of a church choir in Joliet, and has proved herself not only a fine teacher but a most successful leader as well. Those know best who have had experience how many and apparently insurmountable are the difficulties which present themselves to the leader of a church choir. Not only is a knowledge of music necessary but a vast deal of tact, the inborn gift of leadership and a magnetic presence, are quite as essential to insure success. That Miss Warner holds this position to the delight of her audiences is a most complimentary tribute to her ability as a musician and her genius as a leader. As a singer, as a teacher and in her connection with this choir she has proved herself both talented and generally capable.

Wm. Dawson Armstrong.

WM. DAWSON ARMSTRONG.

William D. Armstrong.

William Dawson Armstrong, possibly best known to the
ic as a musical composer, was born February 11, 1868, in
n, Ill., where he still resides.   He received his education
e schools of his native city, but early began the study of
c, which he prosecuted zealously under many teachers.
ng them may be mentioned Mr. Charles Kunkel; E. R.
ger, of St. Louis, Mo.; Clarence Eddy, of Chicago; the
Dr. G. M. Garrett, of Cambridge, England.   His has been
ιy life.   He was instructor in the Forest Park University,
ouis, Mo., 1891-1892, and at present is Musical Director
hurtleff College, Upper Alton, Ill., and Professor in
ge of the music of the Western Military Academy, of the
ə place, 1892-1903.
He was organist of the Church of the Reedemer, St.
is, Mo., 1894-1898, and also organist of the Church of the
ty, St. Louis, Mo.   From 1900-1902 he was President of
Illinois State Music Teachers' Association; from 1901-
President of the musical section of the Illinois Teachers'
ciation, at the same time State Vice-President for Illinois
he National Music Teachers' Association.   He has ap-
ed with success both as concert organist and pianist, and
made a specialty of teaching.
While he is widely known as a musical composer, he has

also contributed literary articles to the leading musical magazines. He has written in nearly all the smaller and larger
forms of composition, for orchestra, piano, organ and the
voice. Most of the larger works are in manuscript, including " The Spectre Bridegroom,'' an opera first presented in
St. Louis, Mo., with Grace Studdiford in the title role, an
overture for orchestra, " From the Old World,'' also string
quartettes, trios, etc.

His works have been published by every leading music
house in the United States, by Breitkopf & Hartel, Leipsig,
Germany, and Novello, Ewer & Co., London, England; but
only a very incomplete list of them can be given here.

Among his sacred compositions we find "A Choral Evening Service in A,'' " I Will Not Leave You Comfortless '' and
" Resurrection.'' For the organ, "A Pastoral Prelude,''
" Contemplation,'' " Slumber Song,'' and many others. He
has also written for the piano and violin, piano duetts, quartettes for mixed voices, and, in fact, every variety of musical
composition. From a long list of piano solos which have received flattering notice from eminent authors, we mention
"A Night in Venice,'' " To the Spring,'' "Elegy,'' " Souvenir
of Verona,'' " Gavotte in B flat,'' "An Evening Song,''
" Polonaise '' and " Nocturne.'' His songs are of infinite
variety, gay and sad, dramatic and descriptive, with many of
the sweetest ballads ever written. We give the names of a
few—" Waiting,'' "A Life's Lesson,'' " Tell Me, Dearest
Maiden,'' " The Return,'' etc.

Mr. Armstrong's compositions are sure to find recognition everywhere among the lovers of true music.

Edward Baker.

EDWARD BAKER.

Edward Baker.

Brierly Hill, England, was the birthplace of Edward Baker, but when he was quite young he came to America, and has spent so much of his time on this continent that he can be really accounted an American.

Very early in life he showed decided talent for musical achievement, and received his first training on the piano and organ from teachers in Joliet and Chicago.

In his playing, even in the beginning of his life as a student of music, were found the same delicacy of coloring and wonderful comprehension of theme which characterize his later work. This is intuitive. The teacher's realm, however well equipped that teacher may be, is to a certain extent circumscribed. He can impart knowledge and technique, he can direct musical tastes, but this peculiar artist-touch is born, not taught.

This Mr. Baker possesses in a pre-eminent degree, and it is the potent charm of his work as a pianist. For several years he was the organist of Christ Church, Joliet, which position he filled to the delight of his audiences. He enjoyed organ playing, but feeling that to achieve the success he coveted he must make a choice of instruments, he has for years devoted himself to the perfecting of his piano work.

Recently he returned from an extended trip in Europe,

where he studied under most eminent teachers. Among them may be mentioned Pauey, the renowned pianist, and L. Emil Bach, who was a favorite pupil of the immortal Liszt, and Kullac, and was on terms of close friendship with Luigi Ardetti, the eminent conductor and composer, and Joseph Hollman, the well-known 'cellist. After devoting some time to study, the most rigorous and exacting, Mr. Baker began a concert career. His first success as a pianist in England, the land of his birth, was in London. Among other concerts at which he played with most gratifying result was one in Windsor, which was patronized by royalty. Wherever Mr. Baker has played he has obtained most pronounced recognition as a pianist of rare promise.

As before intimated, the great charm of his playing lies in the peculiar coloring of tone, the beautiful effects of light and shade, the sympathetic touch, which bring him at once *en rapport* with his audience, however critical. Possibly as marked a characteristic of Mr. Baker is his absolute ease of manner at the piano. No matter how difficult a number he plays, it is played with a freedom from mannerism and an ease of manner which have their own charm for any audience. Mr. Baker has a most excellent testimonial from Mr. Bach, whose requirements of his pupils are most severe. Mr. Bach characterizes him as an earnest pupil, a brilliant pianist and a most conscientious teacher.

John B. Barnaby.

JOHN B. BARNABY.

John B. Barnaby.

For some years past Springfield, Ill., has been the home of John B. Barnaby, an accomplished musician, a fine singer and a most successful teacher.

Mr. Barnaby was born in Halifax, Nova Scotia, in 1863. His education was received in Nova Scotia, although he lived for some time in Philadelphia, Pa., and in Annapolis, Nova Scotia. Music had always great charm for him, and he determined not to be satisfied until he had had the advantages of study not only with the best masters at home but with those abroad.

His voice is a baritone, of great richness and sweetness of tone, and he has conscientiously improved the rare opportunities he has had of cultivating and developing it. He sings so exceedingly well that he might have made a great success in the concert-room. This, however, was not his aim in devoting years to musical study.

Realizing how many voices are ruined by lack of proper treatment, he was ambitious to excel as a teacher, and devoted himself with enthusiasm to gleaning the best ideas from various methods for his own use.

He began his musical studies in his native city, and then went to Philadelphia, Pa.; afterward to Italy; later to London, and last to Paris. Wherever he was, he was never satisfied with anything but the best instruction, and the years devoted to study with the great teachers of the day are among the most cherished memories of his life. Among his vocal teachers may be named the following—Lacey Baker, of Philadelphia, Pa.; William Shakspeare and Signor Alberto Randegger, London, England; Signor Cortesi, Florence, Italy, and Mons. Jacques Bonby, Paris, France. About ten years ago he went to Springfield, Ill., where he still resides. He is a teacher of voice culture and the art of singing, and has been eminently successful in his work. He has started in their career and encouraged in their ambitions several well-known public singers, and has as great pride in their successes as if they were his own.

In addition to his work as a teacher, he is organist of Christ Episcopal Church, of Springfield, and has always a most excellent choir of mixed voices, which he leads, feeling great satisfaction in the work which they do. He has gathered about him a large class of students, not only from Springfield but adjacent towns as well. The enthusiasm of his pupils is a most eloquent testimonial to his popularity as a teacher.

He usually spends his summers abroad, sometimes devoting the months to study, for he is still an earnest student and anxious to take advantage of everything new in his chosen profession. Often, however, he finds needed rest and great pleasure in spending the months in travel, always returning with added zeal to his work.

Francis Campbell.

FRANCIS CAMPBELL.

Francis Campbell.

Francis Campbell, basso cantante, conductor and teacher of singing, received his first musical education in his native city, Detroit, Mich. From Detroit he went to London, England, entering there the Royal Academy of Music, and becoming a pupil of Duvivier and Holland. He also studied harmony and counterpoint with the late Sir George MacFarren. Ambitious for further opportunity for musical culture, he next became a pupil of Vannuccini, in Florence, Italy, and spent the following year in Bologna, devoting his time to voice culture with Briganti-Mobilé, and composition with Busi. While in Italy Mr. Campbell sang with success in many concerts and recitals. After returning to America he settled in Grand Rapids, Mich., where he has been a most successful singer, teacher and conductor. Throughout the Middle-West, both in concert work and oratorio, he has become very favorably known, and has been continuously engaged in church choirs. His pupils are the most eloquent testimonials to his success as a teacher, many of them being professional singers, and several of them on the operatic stage. As a conductor he has proved his marked efficiency. The Schubert Club, a male chorus of sixty voices, has become, under his direction, one of the finest mannerchors in the West. At its semi-annual concerts some of the finest artists on the

beautiful songs, and has also composed work in larger forms, notably two cantatas, " Saint Brandan," for baritone solo and male chorus, the words being the striking poem of Matthew Arnold, and Kipling's " The Bell Buoy " for men's voices.

The autumn of 1902 found Mr. Campbell located in Chicago, where he is rapidly gaining for himself a place in the foremost rank as both singer and teacher. His studio work has obtained recognition as honest and of the very highest endeavor. The results of this effort are being daily exemplified in the healthy progress made by his large and constantly increasing class in vocal culture.

Mr. Campbell may be called a many-sided artist, since in few are united a fine conductor, a delightful singer and an able composer. As a teacher he wins the confidence of his pupils, as a conductor he is an inspiration to his chorus, as a singer he charms his audience, and as a composer he is winning his way to fame. While ambitious in his own special lines of work, laudable public musical enterprises and work interest and appeal to him.

Already, though his residence in Chicago is comparatively brief, he has become identified with them to some extent. This will be shown by the fact that Mr. Campbell is one of the faculty of the Bush Temple Conservatory.

Mrs. Haswell T. Bonfield.

MRS. *HASWELL* T. BONFIELD.

Mrs. Haswell T. Bonfield.

This is an age when women are making history as never before. Identifying themselves enthusiastically with uplifting effort in every direction, music and art are receiving an impetus never before felt, and that the results will be far-reaching and satisfactory none can doubt.

Kankakee has been for the past twelve years intermittently the residence of Mrs. Haswell T. Bonfield, and to her influence owes much of the progress made in that time in its musical status. Mrs. Bonfield was the daughter of Mr. and Mrs. A. M. Brobst, and was born in Knoxville, Iowa.

Her early education was recived at the Knox Conservatory of Music, in Galesburg, Ill., from which she was graduated under Prof. Wm. F. Bentley, Director. She has also had the advantage of being under the tutelage of William H. Sherwood and Eleanor Sherwood, of Chicago, and further studied under Hambourg, the father of Mark Hambourg, in London, England. Teaching, organ-playing and co-operation with musical clubs and various musical enterprises have absorbed the time and energies of this talented and cultivated musician.

She lived in Kewanee, Ill., where for two years she played the pipe organ in the Congregational Church, and for a time lived in Cambridge, Ill. In both Kewanee and Cambridge, in

additon to her other work, she was supervisor of music in public schools.

For three years she resided in Burlington, Iowa, where
she played the pipe organ in the Congregational and Baptist
churches, and was prominent in the Woman's Musical Club.
The years 1899 to 1902 found her Director of the Burlington School of Music, and her departure was recognized as a
great loss in musical circles. Since her residence in Kankakee
Mrs. Bonfield has not only devoted herself to her special work
as a teacher and to local musical enterprises, but has taken a
keen interest in State and national musical affairs. She is a
member of the National Music Teachers' Association as well
as of the State Association in Illinois.

During the years 1896-97 she taught in the Kankakee
Conservatory of Music, and at the same time was organist for
the First M. E. Church. In 1897, as Vice-President for Kankakee County, she secured for Kankakee the meeting of the
Illinois State Music Teachers' Convention. She is a member
of the Euterpean Club and the Woman's Club, taking an active interest in the work done by both of these clubs. In the
Euterpean Club she holds the office of Grand Matron. In the
Woman's Club she is chairman of its Musical Department,
and, bringing to this work the results of her experience, cultivation and the advantages accruing to her from residence
abroad, she is stimulating this department to work with highest ambitions and advanced ideals.

ames Courtland Cooper.

JAMES COURTLAND COOPER.

James Courtland Cooper.

James Courtland Cooper was born in Antioch, Ill., in 1855, the gifted son of Wm. and Julia Farnsworth Cooper. He early began the study of music under the old Italian master, Leo Kofler, who was a pupil of Charles Otto. After seven years of study with Kofler he began teaching in New York. He was eminently successful as a teacher, and his wonderful voice soon gained him a most enviable reputation as a singer. Mr. Cooper has that most rare of gifts, a pure robusto tenor voice. His voice has remarkable power, and at the same time most enchanting sweetness of tone, and the range of his voice is extraordinary. Three octaves are within very easy compass for him. With this wonderful voice he felt that he had much to expect when he should decide to appear in opera, a life which appealed to him most strongly. After teaching a few years he had partially completed a contract for the grand opera when his throat began to trouble him. On examination a tumor was discovered on the right vocal chord, being the fourth case of the kind mentioned in medical history and the first ever known in the throat of a singer. Thwarted thus in the beginning of what promised to be a most brilliant career, he was in the hands of the most eminent scientists of the day—the wonderful voice was silenced and cure seemed the impossible.

marvel and delight to those who hear him sing as ever. These years, however, had been years of study and research, and the ambitions of life were changed as the result of this experience. Sympathizing with those who from any cause might find their voices leaving them, knowing from his own experience how overwhelming was such a calamity, he decided to devote his life in connection with teaching to the restoring and building of voices, and in this he has had a wonderful success. He came in 1901 to Chicago, and has remained there, being at present located in Steinway Hall, in that city.

Enthusiastic in his profession, full of sympathy and possessed of most magnetic presence, Mr. Cooper is making himself a power in the musical circles of Chicago. He has been very successful as a teacher, having prepared for light opera several singers of note. He uses the old Italian method, and he has achieved wonders in the treatment of those whose voices seemed utterly to have left them.

Miss Maud Chappelle.

MISS MAUD CHAPPELLE.

Miss Maud Chappelle.

Of a musical family, endowed with a beautiful voice and charming personality, Miss Maud Chappelle has made for herself a place among the very first young musicians of Chicago.

She was born in Wisconsin, and received her education at the Seminary of the Sacred Heart, in Chicago, afterwards studying with the best vocal instructors in New York and Boston. Miss Chappelle has traveled extensively, and is well known as a most delightful contralto soloist in the leading cities of the United States, especially in New York, Chicago and San Francisco. In the latter city she occupied, for some years, the position of soloist in the Temple Emanuel and in St. Paul's Episcopal Church. After leaving San Francisco, she was engaged in concert work in New York and various cities in the East. Chicago became her choice as her field for teaching, and she has attained great success. Her graduate pupils are in demand among operatic managers, by whom her method of inculcation is highly commended. In addition to her work as an instructor, she is largely engaged in church solo work and concert tours. Her Alma Mater claims a portion of her time as a vocal teacher. From the press, wherever she has sung, she has received the most flattering notices, from a few of which we quote. The

Musical Courier, of New York, said: " Miss Chappelle has a voice of excellent quality, of true contralto character, vibrant and powerful, with great carrying capacity. It is trained with the utmost care, showing in its effect thorough schooling and a method that produces gratifying results. She sings with intelligent comprehension of the subject, giving poetic interpretations, aided by a clear enunciation, and having temperament, she gives an interesting account of herself in songs of the highest standard. Singers of that calibre are rare, and there is a great chance for Miss Chappelle." The *New York Herald* said: " Miss Chappelle is gifted with a marvelous contralto voice, pure in tone and wide in range." The *New York Journal* gave this notice: " The solo work of Miss Chappelle won the warmest applause. She possesses a phenomenal contralto voice and a charming personality." The *San Francisco Town Talk* wrote of the " immense popularity of Miss Chappelle " and " her sweet and silvery voice." An Oakland (Cal.) paper, *The Times,* said: " Miss Chappelle's singing was a splendid ensample of sustained dramatic work, delivered in a broad style, with an organ of great power, well phrased and with perfect enunciation. Her reception was a genuine ovation." This endorsement from the two coasts is supplemented by that of every audience before which she has appeared, and she is daily adding to her laurels in her studio and her varied work before the public.

Grace Elliott Dudley.

GRACE ELLIOTT DUDLEY.

Grace Elliott Dudley.

A Chicago girl, who is slowly but steadily winning her way to recognition in the best musical circles and work of Illinois, is Miss Grace Elliott Dudley, who was born in Chicago, February 7, 1879, and has made this city her home most of her life. She received her education and musical training in her native city, and is an example of the fact that real talent need not go away from Chicago to find development. Her first teacher was Noyes B. Minor, of the American Conservatory, in Kimball Hall, in which school she has received her entire musical education.

On account of his failing health, she continued her work with Karleton S. Hackett, with whom she studied from 1896-1900. She also studied the piano with Mrs. Gertrude H. Murdough, and harmony with Mr. Adolph Weidig. In 1896 she won the second medal in the Academic Department of the Conservatory, and in 1898 the highest gold medal in the Collegiate Department. Since 1897 she has sung in choirs and given recitals in Chicago and other cities. In 1901 she went to Jacksonville, Ill., to take charge of the Vocal Department in the Illinois Conservatory of Music in connection with the Jacksonville Female Academy, the oldest women's school in the West.

For two years she has held this position, and this fall, as

the Conservatory and Academy have been merged into the Illinois College, in Jacksonville—an affiliated school of the University of Chicago—she returns to take charge of the music in the college, a great compliment to one of her years. She has been the soprano in the Presbyterian church during her residence in Jacksonville, and returns to take a similar position in the Congregational church the coming year. Her hope is that in the early future she may be able to discontinue teaching and devote herself entirely to oratorio work, for which she is peculiarly well fitted. We cull a few lines at random from the many flattering press notices which she has received whenever she has sung: " Miss Dudley's voice is a soprano of wide range and beautiful quality, brilliant, but not at the expense of sympathy;" " The more frequently Jacksonville people hear Miss Dudley's voice the more are they wedded to it in admiration. Power, sympathy and exquisiteness of tone characterize her voice."

Miss Dudley seems to have music in her soul, and when she sings there are beauty and grace in every note. She sings with the confidence and ease born of thorough ability. At recitals given at Lake Forest, Champaign, Springfield and Decatur, Ill., she made herself at once a favorite. Perhaps Miss Dudley has no greater charm than the modesty with which she accepts the honors showered upon her in her short musical career. This bespeaks the true artist, in its way, as much as do the beautiful voice and musical taste.

Francis J. Haynes.

FRANCIS J. HAYNES.

Francis J. Haynes.

Francis J. Haynes is a musician of unusually wide culture, and is distinguished not only as a vocal teacher of merit but as a fine conductor, and the composer of some most excellent music. He was born in Hudson, Michigan, October 26, 1867. His parents were Orlando W. and Ursula A. Haynes.

Most of his life has been passed in his native State, where he obtained his education. Hillsdale College, in Hillsdale, Mich., is his Alma Mater, and M. W. Chase, of Hillsdale, one of his earliest teachers in music, to which he was devoted from an early age. He also studied music with John Murray Merrill, of Lansing, Mich., and later with Signor A. Marescalchi, of Chicago, Ill. Besides his native town, he has lived at various times in Morris, Ill., and in Warren and Youngstown, Ohio. For the past three years his home has been in Streator, Ill., where he has most thoroughly and satisfactorily identified himself with the best musical life and effort of the city.

Mr. Haynes has charge of the vocal department in the Streator Conservatory of Music, giving his attention not only to voice culture but to the teaching of the theory of music and composition. His success as a teacher has been most decided, and his services as conductor have also been in requisition.

The Ladies' Lyric Club, of Streator, is a musical society

creditable manner. They count themselves fortunate to have been able to secure the services of Mr. Haynes as their director. In his method of teaching Mr. Haynes is in many ways original. He does not believe in being imitative, but rather in encouraging pupils to think for themselves and gain knowledge by hard work and persistent effort. His own career is an example of the possibilites which such work can achieve, as he has always been not only an enthusiastic but an earnest and thoughtful student.

As a composer Mr. Haynes has made a success, of which he is justly proud. He has written a number of compositions, nearly all vocal. They are songs, part-songs, quartettes for male and female voices and chorus anthems.

Although still a comparatively young man, Mr. Haynes has always influenced the best musical circles wherever he has lived. He has given not a little time and attention to conducting choruses, a line of work for which he has great aptitude. The fact that Mr. Haynes' education has been entirely received in this country proves that it is possible for an American who is devoted to his art to attain success in the highest degree by embracing the opportunities which his own land affords for a musical education.

Frederic Henke.

FREDERIC HENKE.

Frederic Henke.

One of Aurora's best-known musicians is Mr. Frederic Henke, who, while still in his early twenties, gained for himself an enviable reputation as a violinist. He inherits his musical talents from his father, Mr. William Henke, who, in his younger days, was an organist and violinist of more than ordinary ability.

Mr. Frederic Henke was born in Aurora, Ill., in 1878, and has always lived in that city lying so picturesquely by the Fox River.

He was educated in the public schools of Aurora. Always passionately fond of music, he determined to perfect himself, as far as possible, as a violinist. Early he felt the necessity for instruction such as he could not receive in Aurora. He sought the best methods, the most thorough discipline; he wanted to listen to artists and have the inspiration of their presence and tuition. He studied with Earl Drake, T. Spiering and with Max Bendix, who will accept no one as a pupil unless he possesses exceptional talent and ability. After his work with Max Bendix, Mr. Henke's musical friends noted great improvement in his work, and felt he was truly proving himself an artist. His playing is a delight to all who hear him. His tone is broad as well as delicate and musical. His bowing is smooth, strong and graceful; his fingering steady, yet free and flexible. In additon to his strength and smoothness of execution there is a masterly conception and interpretation of whatever theme he renders, which assure his success as a musician.

He began to teach when only eighteen years of age, and his ambition was to found, in his native city, a musical school which should win for itself a reputable place among like schools in the State. At length the opportune time came, and he had the coveted pleasure of aiding in the founding of the Aurora School of Music. For four years he was its principal instructor for violin pupils, and made for himself, not only in that connection but among many pupils outside of the school, a most enviable reputation for his excellence as a teacher.

While his playing indicates under what artist he has studied, he still preserves his own individuality in the interpretation of themes. This characteristic he endeavors to maintain in his pupils, believing it an absolute necessity to produce the best results.

Mr. Henke is a valued member of the Dorthick Club, of the Alice L. Doty Trio, the Symphony Club and the Chicago Musical Club, and is gaining favorable comment in both concert and recital work.

Those who know Mr. Henke best in his work, both as an artist and as a teacher, predict large things for him in the line of his chosen profession.

Katherine Howard.

KATHERINE HOWARD.

Katherine Howard.

Nothing marks more definitely the progress of music and art in America than the fact that in the ranks of those who have had no educational advantages, except those obtained in their native land, are found some of our best artists. Talent, which is not the gift of any one country, developed by American teachers who are not surpassed anywhere, and aided by indomitable American perseverance, is achieving results which obtain recognition for American musicians, painters and sculptors everywhere.

Katherine Howard, who was born in Aurora, Ill., and who has received her education along all lines entirely in her native State, is a very notable example of such success. Her early training was received in the schools of West Aurora, where she graduated from the High School. Fond of music, she began the study of both the piano and organ, and has had the advantage of tuition from the best teachers in Illinois. With Clarence Eddy, she devoted four years to the study of the organ, taking subsequent lessons and doing some coaching with Harrison M. Wild. Mme. Fannie Bloomfield-Ziessler was her piano teacher, and, under the direction of this wonderful pianist, she made excellent progress. The late Frederick Grant Gleason, a scholarly musician and composer, opened to her the mysteries of harmony and fugue, so that her musical education has beeen conducted on the most thorough and comprehensive basis.

Miss Howard has had flattering offers to go on the road with various companies, but she has preferred to remain in her native State, and all her work, as organist and accompanist, has been done in and near Chicago. For the past two years her home has been in this city or vicinity, and she has become well known to its musical public. Before the Chicago Woman's Club she has frequently appeared, both as soloist and accompanist, and usually accompanies Mrs. Jennie Osborne Hannah, Frances Cantdell and other favorite vocalists. While her reputation as an excellent accompanist is established, possibly her greatest success is as an organist. Wherever she has played she has taken rank with the best organists, and has gained reputation as one of the world's most accomplished women organists. She has assisted at the dedication of several organs, for nine and a half years was organist for the People's Church, in Aurora, later of the Unity Church, Chicago, and is at present organist of the First M. E. Church, Evanston, Ill. As a teacher she has been popular and successful, having large classes and maintaining the highest standard of excellence in all their work. Her studio has been located in Kimball Hall, and her classes have averaged at least twenty-five pupils.

With definite ambitions and constant, conscientious endeavor for their attainment, Miss Howard has obtained coveted recognition in the best musical circles.

alter Howe Jones.

WALTER *HOWE* JONES.

Walter Howe Jones.

It is a fact which claims recognition that the West is giving to this country more and more men and women of culture and of talent. We used to speak of Eastern culture and Western enterprise, but while the West has lost none of its enterprise, it is also giving to the world some of its best and most successful artists.

Walter Howe Jones was born October 8, 1862, in Hastings, Minn., where his parents, Roys and Hannah S. Jones, had their home. His general, as well as his musical, education was received for the most part in Chicago, Ill., and Berlin, Germany.

When he began the study of music he aimed to have none but the very best teachers in this country and abroad, and the result is shown in the excellence of his work. He has studied with Clarence Eddy, in Paris; Amy Fay, in New York City; Ludwig Deppe, H. von Herzogenberg and Teresa Carreno, in Berlin, Germany. Since his return to this country he has lived in Clinton, Iowa; Chicago, Ill.; Champaign, Ill.; Greencastle, Ind., and for the past two years in Jacksonville, Ill.

Wherever he has lived he has been connected with the best musical enterprises of the place. He has been engaged as a teacher in the conservatories of music connected with the De Pauw University, Greencastle, Ind.; the University of Illinois, at Champaign, Ill and in the Conservatory of Music at Jacksonville, Ill.

575

He is connected with the Wednesday Musical Club, at Jacksonville; is director of the Jacksonville Choral Society and Opera Club. He had the honor of being elected the first President of the Choral Society of the University of Illinois and County Vice-President of the Illinois Music Teachers' Association.

He has earned for himself an enviable reputation as a successful teacher, fine director and an intelligent musical critic.

His superior educational advantages compel him to be satisfied with nothing less than the best, and his connection with the various musical organizations of Jacksonville has given them an impetus and ambition which has been **greatly** to their advantage. He leaves Jacksonville for **New York** City to accept a position with Hinds & Noble as editor **and** chief critic for their musical publication department. It is a position for which he is well qualified, and from which he can wield a coveted influence over the musical affairs of the country.

He will be greatly missed in Jacksonville, and the prospect of his departure is the occasion of deep regret. The position to which he goes is one in which he will, no doubt, win deserved reputation among the best musical critics of the day.

His practical experience as teacher, director and leader will give him insight into the real merits of musical effort and realization of result hardly possible to one who has never had the benefit of like tuition.

Mr. Jones is to be congratulated upon this new departure, an honor richly deserved,

Phebe Jefferson Kreider.

PHEBE JEFFERSON KREIDER.

Phebe Jefferson Kreider.

Miss Phebe Jefferson Kreider was born in Jacksonville, Ill., her father being Ed. C. Kreider and her mother Mary W. Kreider, of that city. Most of her life has been spent there, except when absent pursuing her musical studies. She has had exceptional opportunities to study with the best teachers not only in this country but abroad, remaining so long in both Dresden and New York that she counts those cities as places of residence. She has done a great deal of most excellent concert work, and has achieved an enviable reputation not only in that work but as a soloist in church choirs. She has been an ardent student in both vocal and instrumental music, beginning her studies in her native city. Among the vocal teachers with whom she has studied may be named the following—Melita Otto-Alvsleben, at Dresden; Albert Gérard-Thiers and J. Harry Wheeler, in New York. Her piano teachers have been Henri Johannesson, Wallace P. Day, of Jacksonville, Ill., Gustav Ehrlich, Frau Ballard-Dittmarsch and Theador Mueller-Reuter, in Dresden. She has the gift, which is a sort of genius, of accompanying well, and in connection with her work as a teacher and a member of musical clubs she has given most genuine satisfaction as an accompanist.

While enjoying the success which her appearance in public ever brought her, she felt that her rare training under so

teacher, and to this work she is mainly devoting herself. She is a vocal teacher at the Illinois Woman's College and College of Music, located at Jacksonville, Ill. This school has a fine reputation even in that educational center, and Miss Kreider has made for herself a reputation second to none in her profession as an enthusiastic, able and conscientious teacher. An artist herself in both vocal and instrumental music, she gives to her pupils most thorough instruction from the best methods, and the benefit of illustration, that most potent of teachers.

She does not, however, permit her work in connection with the school to engross all her time or attention. She is a most valuable member of the Wednesday Musical Club, of Jacksonville, and has been very efficient in stimulating the work of that club to the highest possible standard. She has been a member of its Executive Board and also one of the Program Committee. Her long residence abroad and the many opportunities she has had to meet great artists and to come in touch with many musical organizations make her valuable in both her club and school work, and she is happy in the appreciation shown her efforts.

rederick Locke Laurence.

FREDERICK LOCKE LAURENCE.

Frederick Locke Lawrence.

Frederick Locke Lawrence was born January 19, 1869, in Springfield, Vermont, the son of Merrill L. and Kate Locke Lawrence.

As a boy he was exceedingly fond of music, playing at his first church service when only twelve years of age. He was given rare opportunities to develop his wonderful talent, studying with some of the best masters in America and Europe.

In 1887 he was graduated from the Northwestern University Conservatory of Music in Evanston, and afterwards studied the piano in Boston with B. J. Lang before going abroad. In Leipsig his teachers were Carl Wendling, Julius Klengel, Gustav Schreck and Carl Reinecke.

Under Clarence Eddy he prosecuted his organ study, and with his various masters he proved himself a conscientious and talented pupil. It was his ambition to become a pianist, and his playing while but a youth was considered phenomenal.

A severe attack of rheumatic fever so ruined his technique that he was compelled to abandon this hope, and has devoted his time to teaching and composing. He has gone deep into the theory of piano technique, and prides himself on being an expert in that line.

His home for the past two years has been in Urbana,

Ill., but he has lived in Claverack, N. Y., Northfield, Minn., and in Evanston, Ill. As an instructor in piano he taught in Evanston for three years, was for five years director of the Claverack Conservatory of Music, Director of the Carleton College School of Music for three years, and of the University of Illinois School of Music for three years.

For many years he has been engaged as conductor of various musical societies and orchestras, and in this work has achieved an excellent reputation. As a publisher, he has met with gratifying success, writing some songs and quite a little for orchestras. One of his songs, " Go, Lovely Rose," is in its third edition, and others have been quite successful. He has just completed a book, " The Rationale of Piano Technic," which he expects to publish within a year,* (and is composing a set of studies preparatory to the Bach Little Preludes and Fugues which will soon be given to the public) and which will be used in the regular course in the musical school in Urbana.

While disappointed in his choice of a career which he hoped to make brilliant, Mr. Lawrence has accomplished much in the world of music both as a teacher and a composer, for he has given to his work enthusiasm and the results of true culture.

Although obliged to a great extent to abandon piano-playing, he has played the organ all his life—since his first public appearance as a boy in the church service.

He plays it not only with skill but *con amore,* and his gift for improvising is a source of delight to those who are fortunate enough to hear him.

---

* "Bach Preparatory Studies" are just out. Published by the Geo. B. Jennings Co., Cincinnati, O,

The Lyceum Bureau.

Among the products of the present age probably none is more potent in result or more far-reaching in beneficence to the world than is the Lyceum Bureau.

Some forty years ago a few great orators, such as Edward Everett and Wendell Phillips, began to illuminate our public lyceum and commencement rostrums with their perfectly-wrought, powerful and glowing orations and lectures. The idea was in time developed that men and women of genius would do well to devote themselves to this lofty effort for the platform of the lyceum, and at the same time the thought took form under an organizing head, or Lyceum Bureau. The amount of good accomplished by these institutions is hard to estimate. They supply the people with an inexhaustible storehouse of knowledge, art, literature and music where other sources of learning are circumscribed.

The most noted lecturers, readers and musicians place their services at the command of some bureau. Not only celebrities, but men and women heretofore unknown, have become famous under this direction. There are three or four lecture and concert bureaus that do four-fifths of the lyceum business of the country, which amounts to not less than a million of dollars annually. Among them may be mentioned the Redpath Bureau, of Boston; the Lyceum, in Rochester, N. Y.;

the Brockway Bureau, of Pittsburgh, which is associated with the Slayton Bureau, and the Slayton Lyceum Bureau, of Chicago, besides smaller like organizations.

Twenty years ago nine-tenths of the bookings were made by correspondence, but since then the advance agent has taken the field, under the direction of the bureau, thereby greatly increasing this special field of education and entertainment. This is all conducted in such a quiet and unpretentious way that the general public, even the metropolitan press, know little of its magnitude. While difficulties and financial embarrassments have often beset both the bureau and local committees, hope for better days has appeared with the establishment here and there of an endowed lecture course. No man can put his money to better use. The lecture course is the most potent educator of the people; it is their school, their recreation, their college.

It is simply impossible in any ordinary review to give any idea of the wonderful work done by these bureaus. Suffice it to say that most of the greatest lecturers of our land, its most delightful entertainers of various lines, magicians, characterists, etc., its musicians, soloists, both vocal and instrumental, and musical attractions, such as bands, concert and opera companies, orchestras, quartettes and musical clubs, are all under the management of some Lyceum Bureau.

In spite of many obstacles, difficulties and, at times, discouragments, the Lyceum Bureau has become a permanent institution, inseparable from an advanced civilization and colleges of learning.

Mrs. Lillian Morgan=Miller.

MRS. *LILLIAN* MORGAN-MILLER.

Mrs. Lillian Morgan-Miller.

Among the most ambitious and successful of Illinois' younger pianists few give greater promise than Mrs. Lillian Morgan-Miller. She is the daughter of Henry B. and Jeannette W. Morgan, of Peoria, and was born in that city January 12, 1882. Except when absent for the purpose of obtaining the best musical instruction, she has lived all her life in her native city. She began the study of music with Mrs. E. D. McCullough, of Peoria, and later came to Chicago. She studied harmony and the theory of music with Adolph Weidg and Frederick Grant Gleason, and the piano with Fannie Bloomfield Zeisler, all of Chicago. The talent which she displayed called forth such hearty commendation from her instructors, and her enthusiasm and application as a student were such, that it seemed as if she merited not only the best which this country could offer but that she should have the advantages of travel and study abroad. She therefore went to Germany, that home of music, where she received instruction from some of the best professors of music in Berlin.

Leopold Godowsky, whose reputation places him among the finest living pianists, and Xavier Scharwenka, a pianist and composer of world-wide fame, were among her teachers. Miss Morgan proved herself equal to the demands even of such exacting teachers, for it is well known that they accept as pupils only those who evince remarkable talent. Since her return to her home she has proved the benefit received from their tuition.

She was much interested in the success of the twentieth Sangerfest, of the Northwest Sangerbund, of 1902, and won high encomiums from those whose good fortune it was to hear her play at that time. Anxious still to keep in touch with a musical center, she is a member of the Lake View Musical Club, of Chicago.

Mrs. Miller is of most pleasing personality, ambitious, thoroughly imbued with the spirit of musical endeavor.

At a concert given in Peoria she played most delightfully, winning from a musical critic, through the press, the following notice: " Miss Lillian Bruce Morgan, who had a double number on the programme, was by no means the least of the soloists. Much has been heard by Miss Morgan's friends in regard to her playing, and yesterday the young lady's performance proved that half had not been told. Miss Morgan's playing would make friends for her anywhere. Her technique is remarkable for so young a player, her touch is charmingly graceful, and the tone produced clear and singing. Her interpretation of the Chopin Nocturne showed real musical feeling, and her playing of the Moskowski waltz was a brilliant achievement. The ' Music Box,' given as an encore, was delightfully done. Peoria has reason to be proud of Miss Morgan, whose future is full of golden promise."

rs. Lillian Wiley Orebaugh.

MRS. *LILLIAN WILEY OREBAUGH*.

Among th
strating the a
with any of t
achieved a ma
position in tl
Wiley Orebau
Mrs. Ore
lineage from
tire life in I
Wiley, a me
Linn County
Missouri Ai
able place in
of this sket
Blessings,
leading law
At an
est and gra
struction
death in tl
its most k

Mrs. Lillian Wiley Orebaugh.

Among the younger native pianists who are daily demonstrating the ability of American musicians to hold their own with any of the foreign teachers and artists, none have achieved a more substantial success or gained a more enviable position in the music circles of Illinois than Mrs. Lillian Wiley Orebaugh, of Watseka.

Mrs. Orebaugh is of pure American stock, tracing her lineage from Revolutionary ancestors and having lived her entire life in Illinois. Her father, now deceased, was John S. Wiley, a member of one of the prominent families of Mc-Lean County, and veteran of the Civil War. Her mother was Missouri Arnold, whose family has long occupied an honorable place in the annals of McLean County, where the subject of this sketch was born, and who lived in and near the city of Bloomington until her marriage to David A. Orebaugh, a leading lawyer of Watseka.

At an early age Mrs. Orebaugh displayed remarkable talent and great enthusiasm for music. Her first systematic instruction was from Albert Beuter, of Bloomington, whose death in the morning of his career deprived music of one of its most brilliant votaries. Later she entered the Illinois Wesleyan College of Music, and finished the course of that institution with the class of 1894. Since her graduation she has

taken post-graduate instruction from some of Chicago's most
famous teachers, being at present a pupil of Emil Liebling.

Mrs. Orebaugh has been actively engaged in concert work
and teaching for a number of years.

In the fall of 1895 she was elected director of the Watseka
Conservatory of Music, which position she has since held un-
interruptedly to the entire satisfaction of management and
patrons.

The high standard of musical attainments achieved by
her pupils, who are scattered over Central and Eastern Illinois, attests the splendid success which Mrs. Orebaugh has
enjoyed in her work.

Mrs. Orebaugh's attainments are not by any means confined to the realm of music. She is a lady of rare literary culture and a writer of more than ordinary ability. At the 1902
convention of the Illinois Music Teachers' Association she delivered an address of characteristic strength and vigor of
thought, which stirred the interest of the profession at large
and attracted the attention of the leading daily papers and
music journals throughout the country. In this address Mrs.
Orebaugh vigorously advocated the competitive examination
and licensing, under State supervision, of music teachers.

Following up her idea with characteristic energy, she procured the introduction in the Legislature of a bill embodying
the suggestions made by her before the convention, which, notwithstanding its novelty, narrowly escaped being enacted into
a law.

As a progressive, modern, wide-awake musician, with an
assured future, Mrs. Orebaugh ranks well among her *con-
freres* in Illinois.

Katherine Schuster.

KATHERINE SCHUSTER.

Katherine Schuster.

Musical environment, many excellent instructors and her own persistent effort have combined to give Katherine Schuster a most desirable position among Chicago's musical artists. She was born in Chicago, April 30, 1864, and lived in that city till 1891, when she removed to Oak Park, where her home has been ever since. She was educated at St. Patrick's Academy, a convent school, where her love for music was stimulated by the beautiful music she heard sung at the masses and festivals. While a schoolgirl she studied the piano for a few months with Pauline Weishaar, and later with Rose Dugan. It was not, however, till she was twenty years old that she pursued her musical studies at all seriously. She then began voice culture, sight singing and the study of harmony with Mrs. Sara Hershey Eddy, director of the Hershey School of Music, and remained under her tuition for about two years. She has always felt that Mrs. Eddy laid an excellent foundation for future work.

She resumed her piano study at the Chicago Musical College under Mrs. Clara Osborne Reed, and at the end of three years obtained a teacher's certificate, and was awarded a diamond medal for her excellence in harmony. In 1894-5 she studied vocal music with Miss Eleanor Smith, 1899 with Miss Fannie Root and in 1901 with Mr. Frank Baird. She studied

technique with A. K. Virgil and Miss Alma Rose.   The study
of harmony seemed to possess a wonderful fascination for her,
for later she studied it with Mrs. Jessie Gaynor and Thos.
Tapper, of Boston, and others.   She has since herself evolved
a method for teaching harmony which her pupils find very
practical and easy of comprehension.

Besides obtaining a teacher's certificate from the Chicago
Musical College, she has devoted time to the system of teaching music in the Chicago public school (Mr. Tomlins') and to
Parsons' Kindergarten Method.   For years she has attended
regularly the Thomas' Orchestra Concerts, and feels that this
has been a great factor in her musical education.

As will be seen by this hasty review of her student life,
she has been and is a most earnest, conscientious and thorough scholar.   Since 1890 she has had under her instruction classes in vocal culture and piano study, and for the past
few years has been connected with the Columbia School of
Music, of which a former teacher, Mrs. Clara Osborne Reed, is
the Director.   In this school she is teaching ear-training,
sight-singing, elementary harmony and harmonic analysis.
She has been a member of the Chicago Apollo Club for years,
and is also a member of the Schumann Club.   A busy woman,
bent on self-improvement, enthusiastic in her profession, Miss
Schuster is a most conscientious teacher of the art of music in
its three branches, hearing it, reading it, and interpreting
it either through the voice or piano with equal understanding.

Franklin L. Stead.

FRANKLIN L. STEAD.

Franklin L. Stead.

One hardly realizes, unless circumstances suggest research, how many earnest students and how many real artists there are who, devoting themselves to the teacher's work, are pursuing their chosen vocation in every part of our country.

Ambition, stimulated by talent, has made opportunity; and opportunity improved has been followed by results which justify pride. Possibly in no State are there more men and women who, after achieving real success in the concert-room, have given themselves to the teacher's work than can be found in Illinois, and a recognition of their success is always a pleasure.

Franklin L. Stead, whose home for the past four years has been in Jacksonville, Ill., was born September 29, 1864, at Marseilles, Ill. His general education was received at Ottawa, Ill., and Boston, Mass. Early, however, his love for music asserted itself, and he began to devote himself especially to preparation for his lifework.

He was a pupil in the New England Conservatory of Music and in the Boston College of Music, in Boston, Mass., and both in Boston and Chicago studied with some of the best teachers this country has known. Among them may be mentioned Henry Dunham, George Whiting, Otto Bendix, George

601

Chadwick, Louis Elsen, Carl Faeleten and Frank Hale, of Boston; Harrison Wild and Emil Liebling, of Chicago.

He has held several fine positions as church organist, and and has done with success a large amount of concert work.

For ten years he was the director in the Conservatory of Music in Yankton, South Dakota, and for six years Professor of Music in the Yankton College, teaching harmony and counterpoint as an elective in the regular college course.

For the past four years he has held the position of director in the College of Music in Jacksonville, Ill., a position of responsibility which he fills with great credit to himself, and where he has endeared himself to the many pupils who have had the advantage of his training.

As a student, ambitious, painstaking and conscientious, the same characteristics have marked his career as a teacher and made him eminently successful.

Having studied only with the best teachers this country knows, he has had only the best to offer to his pupils, and he has the tact and skill in imparting knowledge which are the birthright of but few.

While his work in the concert room won for him many laurels, and his success was a source of pride to him, yet he realized that to achieve the reputation as a teacher which could satisfy his ambition he must make that his lifework, devoting to it all his energies.

Results have proved the wisdom of this decision, and he occupies a foremost place among the music teachers of Illinois. He is a member of the State Music Teachers' Association, and keeps in touch with the best musical effort of the day.

Mary Brown Tanner.

MARY B. TANNER.

Mary Brown Tanner.

Situated in the heart of Illinois is Jacksonville, one of the oldest towns in the State, and for many years a center of literary, musical and art activity. The seat of colleges and academies of high standard, it possesses that subtle intellectual atmosphere so characteristic of college towns.

In this city, and into an environment conducive to best effort, Mary Brown Tanner was born. In her home she was peculiarly fortunate. Both father and mother were deeply interested in all things educational and literary, her father, Edward Allen Tanner, being, until his death, President of Illinois College.

Her musical education, begun in Jacksonville under the tutelage of Mrs. Adelaide Freeman, was continued later in Boston, New York, Munich, Dresden, Paris and London, under the able leadership of such teachers as Madam Hall, of Boston; Madame Anna de la Grange and M. Leon Jancey, de l'Odeon, of Paris, and Frederick Walker, of the Royal Academy of Music, in London. Not only has she come in contact with great masters, but she has heard great artists and known the broadening influence of residence in musical and art centers.

For eight years Miss Tanner has been teaching in her native city. She has given much time to organizing choral societies for the presentation of cantatas and oratorios; has marked success in concert work. Realizing, as time passed, that a successful teacher cannot give herself to the public and, at the same time, call forth the highest development from her pupils, she has for the past five years devoted herself almost exclusively to what may be considered teacher's work. Having made the highest ideals her own, she endeavors to inspire like ambitions in the minds of those under her care, insisting always that the best general education is absolutely necessary for the fullest musical growth. Into her work she carries a conscientious desire for her pupils' advancement; that enthusiasm which made her own work while a student so successful; the power of adapting herself to individual needs; a knowledge of many methods gained from various teachers, and, above all, that indefatigable energy so essential to success. As the inevitable result of such training, many of those who have gone out from her tuition are occupying with great credit responsible positions as teachers and singers in this and other States.

Robert Walter.

ROBERT WALTER.

Robert Walter.

In a little village in Thuringia, near Erfurt, Saxony, which gave to the world the famous Bach family and other famous musicians, Robert Walter was born, May 22, 1859. The first music which reached his ears, aside from his mother's lullaby, was the chorus of anvils from his father's blacksmith shop. He was endowed with an intense love for music, and recognizing the fact that he possessed real talent, at an early age his father placed him in the hands of a private instructor, and he began the study of the violin.

Soon the boy eclipsed his master, and was sent to the city by his father, where he received more advanced instruction, and where he later took up the clarinet in connection with the violin.

Mr. Walter came to America in 1877, and spent two years in Wisconsin, after which he accepted an offer from a dramatic company to play the clarinet in the band and orchestra. After three years he became the leader of the band and orchestra, and remained with them some time in this capacity.

In the summer of 1886 he was solicited to direct the Goodman Band at Decatur, Ill., but he had already signed a contract with his old manager. At the close of the season, however, he accepted the invitation, which was still open to him,

made wonderful progress under his leadership.

When Mr. Walter became its director the reed section consisted of one clarinet player, and he a beginner. Now the section has ten B flat clarinets, a quartette of saxophones and a bassoon. The band has acquired a reputation, not only in Illinois but several adjoining States, as a concert band. Their repertoire has become extensive and varied, including many standard overtures and operas, which are rendered in a manner to reflect great credit on the organization and its director. Mr. Walter's ability as a soloist has been a great advantage to him, for it has enabled him to be not only a director but an instructor as well.

He has become very enthusiastic in his work, and has inspired those associated with him with the laudable desire for the best achievement. Mr. Walter has made a special study of the arranging of programs, and in this, as well as in his work as a director, he has made a great success. Few people realize that it is an art to be able to arrange a successful program that there shall be suitable variety even where all is of the best grade of music.

Mr. Walter may congratulate himself on the reputation he has as a thorough musician, a fine director and for his skill in arranging programs. Two diamond medals, which he wears, are expressions of the appreciation and regard felt for him by the people of Decatur.

illiam Frederick Bentley.

WILLIAM FREDERICK BENTLEY.

William Frederick Bentley.

This country of ours, in which we feel so just a pride, is making itself felt in the world of music, art and literature, as well as in matters of finance and questions of international interest. Our schools of learning are everywhere, and our conservatories of music take rank with the best of other lands. These conservatories not only offer advantages to those who desire to study, but also afford opportunity for those who are ambitious to make for themselves a place and a reputation in the musical world.

Enterprise, advancement, are America's watchwords, and are as marked characteristics of musical effort as of all other. Among aspirants for such musical fame is William Frederick Bentley, of Galesburg, Ill. He was born in Lenox, Ohio, September 12, 1859. His father was Cyrus Augustus Bentley, his mother Harriet (Prentice) Bentley. His musical education has been thorough and from the best instructors he could command. He is a man of executive ability, and enjoys the work of a conductor—a work in which he excels.

His father was one of the early musicians of Northeastern Ohio, a singer and a choral conductor, and the son inherits this ability of leadership.

In 1883 he was married to Miss Julia A. Webster, of Geneva, Ohio. In 1885 he moved to Galesburg, Ill., and became the director of the Knox Conservatory of Music, in that city, an office he still holds. As a teacher, Mr. Bentley has met with very great success. His standard is high, he never admits discouragement, and he has won the confidence of his pupils to a degree so remarkable that it has been helpful in result. The fact that he has retained his position in connection with the conservatory so many years furnishes abundant proof of his success, and he has now become so identified with the work there that he counts the interests of the conservatory his own. The work which is achieved by this college of music is well known, its graduates commanding fine positions as soloists and teachers. Perhaps comparatively few recognize the quiet, untiring, masterly work of the director in the satisfactory results attained. In addition to his work as director of the Knox Conservatory of Music and a teacher of singing, Mr. Bentley is also the conductor of the Galesburg Musical Union, a choral society of over 100 voices, which is attempting difficult work with excellent results. It is a source of encouragement to those who are really interested in the musical progress of this country that scholarly, musical men are willing to devote time and talent to the tuition of the youth in our colleges and schools.

Musical standards are thus being raised, and that such faithful artists play a leading part in what is of vital importance to the musical future of this land is beyond doubt.

Morris Rosenfield.

The business men of any city or State are its hope and strength in many important ways. Their success makes possible the cultivation of what is most beautiful in art, the most enjoyable in music, the most elevating in the realm of literature. Sometimes this influence is underestimated, and the maxim " honor to whom honor is due " passes quite out of life's daily practice, if not wholly out of thought.

No man has left his imprint more indelibly on the business history of Mcline, Ill., than Morris Rosenfield, who, as a shrewd financier and intelligent manufacturer, and prominently identified with political affairs, made his influence felt in all directions. He was born in Germany, December 18, 1841, his parents, Jacob and Ellen Rosenfield, being natives of Germany. He came to America when young, and in the early sixties became interested in a farm wagon manufacturing company located in Moline, Ill. As a result of his influence, the business was organized into a corporation, which was known as the Moline Wagon Co. He was elected the first President, and held this position without interruption until his death in Germany in 1899. Under his wise administration, the business developed rapidly into one of the largest institutions of the kind in America. It is practically the most important factory in this country devoted exclusively to the manufacture of farm wagons.

He was a very firm Republican, and actively interested not only in State, but in national political issues. For six years he held the position of Chairman of the Rock Island Republican County Committe. He was delegate to the National Conventions which nominated Blaine and Logan, Harrison and Reid.

His calm judgment and keen insight into matters of finance made him a most valued advisor, and he was always ready to give to others the benefit of his experience. He was, until his death, Director of the First National Bank, and Vice-President and Director of the People's Savings Bank of Moline, Ill.

Nothing which was indentical with the business or social advancement of the city in which he lived was unnoticed by him. He was a man of broad sympathy and generous impulses, interested in literary enterprises and the development of the best intellectually, morally as well as financially, that lay within the possibilities of those about him.

He was married in 1874 to Julia Ottenheimer, of Cinnnati, Ohio. Into his domestic life he carried the same integrity, the same lofty purpose, which marked his career in other directions. In his death Moline and Illinois lost a honored citizen, a valuable counsellor, a man of unerring business instinct, and one who was second to none in his achievements for manufacturing interests which had come under his control. Mr. Rosenfield was a man who enjoyed the social side of life and affiliation with men of affairs. He was a member of the Union League Club, of Chicago, and also of Masonic and other fraternal societies.

Mrs. Richard P. Yates.

MRS. *RICHARD P. YATES.*

Mrs. Richard Yates.

One of Illinois' daughters now occupies the position of first lady of the State, and the grace and dignity with which she is filling that place, so full of varied and often perplexing demands, have made her a most enviable reputation among those with whom she has been brought in contact. Illinois' daughters are making their impress on all the higher walks of life, and, as artists and singers, composers and writers, as well as in positions of honor and trust, are proving themselves equal to every sort of attainment.

Helen Wadsworth was born, September, 1865, in Jacksonville, Ill. Her father is Archibald C. Wadsworth, her mother Delia A. (Witherbee) Wadsworth. The history of her ancestry links itself with that of the Revolution, as is evidenced by the fact that she is a member of the Daughters of the American Revolution.

In October, 1888, she married Richard Yates, an ambitious, talented young lawyer, and during almost sixteen years has been his helper in every possible way—a womanly woman, a home-lover, a devoted mother, yet discharging, in gracious manner, the many public duties which have devolved upon her. She was educated at the Illinois Woman's College, at Jacksonville, Ill., and is an earnest, devoted patron of music and art. In a very quiet, unassuming way, she helps those who are struggling for recognition in the world of fame to help themselves, and in the success of their achievements finds her compensation.   One well-known composer, in speaking of those who had encouraged and aided her, said—" But, first of all, I must always mention my dear Mrs. Yates, who has given me the opportunity to make possible what seemed the impossible."

So manifold have been the duties connected with life at the Executive Mansion, that Mrs. Yates has not been able to identify herself with the work of the various clubs in Springfield, as she would have been glad to do under other circumstances.   Not contented with being a nominal member, the many social obligations resting upon her have made anything else impracticable.   Eight hundred calls paid during the past three years is an item which indicates her busy life, and surely furnishes abundant reason for her not attempting what she knows she could not accomplish.

Governor and Mrs. Yates have two lovely, bright little daughters, Catherine and Dorothy, aged twelve and eight years.   Mrs. Yates is a member of the M. E. Church, and anxious for success in all lines of church work.   Although, to a great degree, unable to actively participate in the work done by literary, social and philanthropic clubs, her interest in their achievements is very great, and she has a keen and intelligent appreciation of what is being accomplished by the women of our own and other lands.

Of most charming presence, full of genuine hospitality, genial and courteous, sympathetic and helpful, Mrs. Yates will always be remembered most lovingly by those who have best known her life in the position she is filling so well.

Miss May F. Carpenter.

MISS MAY F. CARPENTER.

Miss May F. Carpenter.

While claiming the sunny South as her birthplace, Oak
Park, Ill., for the past ten years, has been the home of the
rarely talented young artist, Miss May F. Carpenter. She was
born in Kentucky, March 21, 1878, but obtained her education
in Indianapolis and Chicago. Both vocal study and the study
of the piano have received from her most unflagging attention, and in both she is making a fine reputation, a circum-
stance so rare as to merit special comment. She has studied
the piano with Militzer, of the American Conservatory of
Music, and with F. Bush. For eight years she has been a
pupil of W. C. E. Seeboeck, whose reptuation as a pianist is
national, and under his tuition achieved such success that
for years she has been his assistant teacher of piano. No
greater endorsement could possibly be given her than this association with Mr. Seeboeck, and he does not hesitate to voice
his opinion of her talent and success in very emphatic terms.
He said of her—" Miss Carpenter has, for a number of years,
been a most earnest worker with me, and is now a thorough
and enthusiastic musician and teacher." In vocal music, she
has studied with Jessie L. Gaynor, Nelson Burritt, Edward
Nell, of Indianapolis, and Mrs. C. Trimble. With these
teachers, she has also made an exceptionally fine record, and
when she has appeared in many recitals she has won laurels

both as a pianist and vocalist. Besides the work she does in
assisting Mr. Seeboeck, she has met with great success in her
own class, which she teaches in her studio in the Fine Arts
Building. Concert work also engrosses much of her time, her
most recent appearance being with Prof. Seeboeck, at Oak
Park. This concert was a great success, and received the
most flattering notices, not only from local papers but from
the Chicago press as well. While she delights in her work
both as a vocalist and pianist, it is safe to predict that she will
eventually concentrate her efforts in one direction, and present indications are that it is her greatest ambition to excel as
a pianist. Possibly recognizing this fact, a Chicago paper
wrote—" Miss Carpenter's musicale last night brought to the
front a pianist of unusual merit. She scored a great tri-
umph, and it is predicted she will make a brilliant career as a
pianist."

While busy in her studio, in her work as a teacher elsewhere, and with her concert work, Miss Carpenter still finds
time to identify herself with some of the leading clubs of Chicago and vicinity. She is a member of the Schumann Club,
of Chicago, and the Beethoven Club, of Oak Park. Miss Carpenter is a notable example of what real talent, supplemented
by enthusiasm and perseverance and stimulated by ambition,
can accomplish. Such success should inspire to like effort
every ambitious young artist, in spite of many discouragements, which possibly seem almost insurmountable.

Mrs. Florence R. Magnus.

MRS. FLORENCE R. MAGNUS.

Mrs. Florence R. Magnus.

Chicago is becoming each year more and more a center to which ambitious, earnest men and women come, and where they do most creditable work. The Fine Arts Building is a wonderfully busy hive, where sculptors and painters, singers and pianists, writers and artists, flock, and from which goes out an influence, refining, uplifting and educational, through the whole community. Among those who have a home in this pleasant building is Mrs. Florence R. Magnus, a conscientious and successful teacher, as she was an enthusiastic and earnest pupil. Mrs. Magnus was born in New York City, February 24, 1856, the daughter of Phœbe and Edwin Reynolds. Aside from New York, she has lived in St. Louis, Hamburg, Germany, and, for the past twenty years, has had her home in Chicago, identifying herself with its musical growth and interested in all its musical effort. She was educated at first in her native city, and began singing in concerts there at the very early age of five years, and from that time till she was thirteen appeared many times and became a great favorite. Her ambition was to educate herself for the grand opera; for which her beautiful voice and charming presence seemed preeminently to fit her. Signor Severini, of New York, was her instructor in singing, and she studied the piano with Henry Maylath, of the same city. Under these teachers, she made

progress which seemed almost phenomenal. Her friends
cherished for her the highest ambitions, and she looked forward to a distinguished career.   Ill health, which has doomed
many a young aspirant for fame to disappointment, compelled
her to abandon a career which was so full of promise, but she
still desired to pursue her studies, so she decided to go to Germany to study piano.   She made Hamburg her home, and
strove, in her devotion to art, to forget in a measure that
which had so changed all the plans of her life.   Her earlier
tuition and the habits of study formed almost in babyhood,
aided by her talents, made her a most apt and satisfactory
pupil, and her advancement was quite beyond the usual.   Her
teacher was Prof. Degenhardt, and she remembers the time
she spent as his pupil with the greatest pleasure.   Some time
after her return to America she came to Chicago, and, in 1893,
began teaching in this city, a vocation she still follows most
successfully.   She is not, however, so entirely occupied with
duties within her own studio that she ignores the claims of
others.   She is a valued member of the Amateur Musical
Club, of Chicago, and there are few musicians so full of sympathy for students trying to fit themselves for a professional
career as is Mrs. Magnus.   Her methods are the best, and
from her own experience she is able to give to her pupils much
of value to them which cannot be found in any text-book, the
result of a life in which ambitions have had to be surrendered,
and yet the years all laden with usefulness and real achievement.

Louis Lehman.

LOUIS LEHMANN.

Louis Lehmann.

Louis Lehmann was born in Muehl am Neckar, Kingdom of Wurtemberg, Germany, May 1, 1851.

His father, Joel Lehmann, was a school-teacher. Early he began the study of music under the most able tutelage. He was educated at Esslingen, Kingdom of Wurtemberg, Germany, and, later, in this country. He first studied the piano, organ and harmony under the direction of Prof. Christian Fink, of Royal Seminary, Wurtemberg. After coming to America he still pursued these branches of musical study with Prof. Louis Ritter, of Vassar College. His vocal teachers have been M. S. Downs and C. G. Buck, of Poughkeepsie, N. Y., and J. B. Barnaby, of Springfield, Ill. He has been not only an indefatigable student, but has also been ambitious and successful in his achievements.

Springfield, Ill., has been Mr. Lehmann's home for the past twenty-three years, and he has thoroughly identified himself with all the musical enterprises of that city. Since living there, he has twice given the " Creation "—once with an orchestra and once without—the Farmer's Mass in B flat in concert, " Belshazzer's Feast " (Butterfield) in costume, Mendelssohn's " Hymn of Praise," and Sullivan's " Prodigal Son " twice.

All his life he has been to some extent before the public

wherever he has lived.   While in Cooperstown, N. Y., he was organist of the Presbyterian church.   In Poughkeepsie, N. Y., he was director of the Twenty-first Regiment Band and also of Morning Musicales, on Saturdays, at Eastman's National Business College.

For four years he was organist of the Baptist Church, and of St. Paul's Episcopal Church for one year.   Since residing in Springfield, Ill., he has conducted several societies, among them the former Mendelssohn Society, the Oratorio Society, Choral Union, and, for twelve years, was the director of music at the Chatterton Opera House.

For six years Mr. Lehmann was organist of St. Paul's Pro-Cathedral, for one year at the Congregational Church, and for the past fifteen years has held, and still holds, the position of organist in the First Presbyterian Church.

For twenty-three years he has been the director of the Illinois Watch Company Band, an organization in which he takes the deepest interest.   From this little sketch of his busy life, his versatility of talent and enthusiastic devotion to his profession are easily recognized.   For years he has especially interested himself in the best success of band and orchestral music, particularly as represented by the band of which he so long has been the director.

Mr. Lehmann has contributed the greater part of his entire income to keeping this band in the very foremost rank, and his unselfish devotion has been rewarded by the success attained.   It is such self-sacrificing artists who are an uplift and inspiration to all musical effort.   The name of Louis Lehmann will always be inwrought into the musical history of the city which he so long has called his home.

anor Wilhelmina Marie Scheib.

ELEANOR SCHEIB.

Eleanor Wilhelmina Marie Scheib.

Eleanor Scheib, although a young artist, has had so brilliant a career that she is well known to the music-loving public of Chicago. Born in Chicago, October 15, 1878, and educated almost entirely in the city of her birth, those who are interested in noting the progress of young American artists feel peculiarly gratified at her success. Her parents, John Adam and Antonie Amalie Scheib, recognized the talent of their little daughter, and she began to receive instruction on the piano when not quite six years of age. Her first public appearance was made in Brooklyn, N. Y., where she played before an audience of two thousand. Her teachers in Chicago have been Wm. A. Fuhring, Miss May Lucine Potvin and Mrs. Regina Watson in piano study, and A. J. Goodrich, now of New York City, Herbert Wrightson and Adolph Weidig, the latter of the American Conservatory, in harmony.

She made her professional début in Chicago, at Music Hall, Fine Arts Building, in recital, February 13, 1900, although she had done a great deal of excellent work for three or four years previous to that time. She is a member of the Amateur Musical Club, of Chicago, and is very enthusiastic in all musical work. Miss Scheib has been recognized for years as one of the leading pianists in Chicago. She has appeared in concerts in Brooklyn, Boston and other Eastern cities, and has made extensive tours through the West. Through her artistic work at the George Hamlin concerts, during the past two seasons, she has received most complimentary notices from the daily papers and various musical publications. The Strauss music accompanying the recitation of " Enoch Arden " has been rendered repeatedly by Miss Scheib with most notable success.

As every pianist knows, this music requires an artist, and an accomplished artist, at the piano, or the beauty of the composition is absolutely lost. Miss Scheib's rendition has combined technical accuracy with most intelligent interpretation, the dramatic, poetic and sympathetic requirements of this difficult composition being so admirably met that she stands without a peer in the execution of this exceedingly difficult music. Her technique is excellent, and she plays with a delicacy of expression and an intelligence which make her a favorite with those who appreciate the true artist.

Miss Scheib has most charming presence, freedom from affectation, a genuine musical temperament, and merits the place she has made for herself among the best pianists of the day. More and more the fact that the pupils of our American teachers may achieve success second to none is obtaining recognition, and their career is a source of pride to those interested in the progress of music and artists in Chicago and Illinois.

Nellie Hobbs Smythe.

NELLIE HOBBS SMYTHE

Nellie Hobbs Smythe.

Few have attained as enviable a reputation along so many lines of musical work as has Mrs. Nellie Hobbs Smythe, who was born in Terre Haute, Ind., November 12, 1865. Early her musical tastes were decidedly developed, and when but fifteen she was playing an organ in church.

In 1884, she was granted a diploma from the Mt. Carroll, Ill., Female Seminary for proficiency in piano, organ, harmony and composition, history and vocal music. The following year she received an especial medal for a postgraduate course, and remained in the school for three years as one of the instructors in music. During this time she came regularly to Chicago, receiving instruction from the best teachers, and also devoted some time to concert work. Her parents removed to Benton Harbor, Mich., and in 1888 Mrs. Smythe established the music department of the " College " of that city. The season of 1889-90 was spent in Europe visiting the conservatories of Leipsic and Dresden, and studying with the best masters in Berlin. Among Mrs. Smythe's teachers may be named Wm. H. Sherwood, of Chicago; Prof. Karl Klindworth, Berlin; Frau Melvina Bree, Theodore Leschetizks and Prof. Edward Gärtner, both of Vienna.

Upon her return to America, the work of teaching in the " College " was continued, with some concert work, until her

639

marriage in 1892. After this time, for four years, her home was in Wichita, Kan., where she acquired a State reputation as a musician.

In the summer of 1896, Mrs. Smythe with her husband (also a musician—a tenor singer), went abroad, where, for three years, they both devoted themselves to the study of music, with headquarters at Vienna, Austria.

Returning to America, after a short concert tour in the West, they located in Chicago. Here Mrs. Smythe at once engaged in teaching, accompanying and concert work, and was secured as the soprano in the quartette in the People's Church (Dr. H. W. Thomas'), at McVicker's Theatre.

During the seasons of 1900, 1901 and 1902, Mrs. Smythe traveled as soprano with the Madrigal Club, the last season under the management of the Central Lyceum Bureau. In the fall of 1902, she again assumed charge of the Music Department of the " College " at Benton Harbor, Mich. In addition to this, she maintains a studio in the Fine Arts Building, Chicago, and prosecutes her special line of work in the illustrated musical lecture field, which has developed rapidly the past few seasons and calls her to all parts of the country.

The press everywhere is unanimous in its commendation of this special line of work as done by Mrs. Smythe.

Her stage presence is magnetic, her repertoire varied and large, her accompaniments translate and emphasize the very soul of song, and a most brilliant future is predicted for this versatile artist.

Mrs. Estelle B. Davis.

MRS. ESTELLE B. DAVIS.

Mrs. Estelle B. Davis.

Litchfield, Ill., was the birthplace, June 11, 1867, of Miss Estelle Beach, and has been her home all her life.

Her father was a prominent manufacturer and business man of that city, having been connected with the Litchfield Car and Machine Co., with Beach, Davis & Co., bankers, with the gas and electric plants, and other enterprises. She was graduated, in 1884, from the public schools of the town, and spent a year at the Academy of Jacksonville, Ill. Her musical education was begun at the age of nine years, with local teachers, but, owing to ill health, her studies were much interrupted. At the Academy she began violin lessons and commenced her piano study. In 1885, she went, with her parents, to California and Colorado, continuing her violin work while in Colorado. She made her first appearance at a Sunday concert at the penitentiary at Cañon City, it being the custom to invite all visitors to the city who were musical to sing or play at the Sunday service. Her health being now fully restored, she resumed her musical studies, on her return home, by going to Jacksonville once a week. Miss Alice Rhoades was her violin teacher and Mrs. Freeman her vocal instructor. The next two years she studied the violin with Prof. Lehmann, of Springfield, Ill.

Subsequently Prof. Waldauer, of the Beethoven Conservatory, in St. Louis, Mo., was her teacher, and she was graduated from this conservatory in 1895. Since then she has studied the violin with Wm. Elterich, of New York, and for the past two years piano with Mrs. J. A. Gerhard, who is a resident of Litchfield.

On February 16, 1893, Miss Beach was married to Mr. David Davis, who was captain in the Fourth Illinois during the Spanish-American War. During 1892-93-94, she was leader and first violin in a small orchestra, which was organized for study and pleasure. She is a charter member of the Woman's Club, which was organized in 1890, and was its President for three years—1897 to 1900. Through her efforts a musical department was added to the club, and they took up the study of musical history, using a text-book by Fillmore. The programs were from American composers. In 1900-02, they studied a few of the early composers and discussed various musical forms, using Apthorp's " Opera, Past and Present," as a text-book, and giving musical illustrations from the operas. In 1902-03, Mrs. Davis was elected chairman of this department, an office she still holds. Under her direction they have continued their study of opera, and used Folk songs and national music of various countries in their programs.

Last winter, a ladies' chorus was organized, with Mrs. J. A. Gerhard as director, and the hope is to make the organization permanent.

A most gifted musician, with rare executive ability, Mrs. Davis is a wonderful help and a constant inspiration to those about her, and that she is appreciated is shown by the positions which she so ably fills.

Mrs. Anna Groff=Bryant.

MRS. ANNA *GR*OFF-BRY·ANT.

Mrs. Anna Groff-Bryant.

With the spirit of perseverance which distinguishes the worker of the West, Mrs. Anna Groff-Bryant has made a place for herself among American teachers, which shows how true merit can command success.

Born, thirty-six years ago, on a Wisconsin farm, she spent her childhood years in a wholesome, out-of-door life, storing up the energy which has made it possible for her to endure the strain of her later work, under which a less rugged nature must have broken.

The father, Michael Groff, was a sturdy German; in fact both mother and father came of German stock, and up to the child's twelfth year English was unknown to her. At this age she was sent to the Milwaukee Female Seminary, where her first study in English branches began. After two years at Milwaukee, she entered the academic course at Northwestern University. The several years following found her deeply engrossed in college work. Sciences and subjects involving research appealed most strongly to her.

It was during her work at Evanston that her musical study began. From the completion of her academic work her whole energy was devoted to the study of music, particularly to the voice, with a singer's career in view.

Later the study of the voice from the deeper, the scien-

tific standpoint, interested her. She saw in every human being the possibility of vocal development. She made a thorough investigation among musical authorities in a search for
the truth. She studied with various teachers, analyzing, com-
paring and contrasting vocal methods.

Beginning her own work as a teacher, results demonstrated her theories from the first. The work became so en-
grossing that it demanded the sacrifice of her own public career. In less than ten years she has attained a success which,
though it may seem remarkable, is purely legitimate, and
traces back to natural causes.

A day spent in her studios in the Fine Arts Building
finds her dealing with every variety of condition, from the
crudest tone to the most advanced.

She studies each student from the individual standpoint,
bringing to each the remedy for his special condition. Of as
great interest to her as the musical side of her art is the study
of the human voice as an instrument. All the crudities and
defects of tone are dealt with, as well as diseases of the throat,
even loss of voice being successfully treated.

Mrs. Bryant believes that every voice has range and compass and volume as truly as any other instrument. If a
voice is of limited range it is the fault of the trainer.

Mrs. Anna Groff-Bryant is an untiring student, an ardent worker in the cause of voice development and artistic
singing, and her success is the natural result of earnest effort.

Katherine Spear Cornell.

KATHERINE SPEAR CORNELL.

Katherine Spear Cornell.

Mrs. Katherine Spear Cornell, known in musical circles for her beautiful voice and her thorough musical education, is the daughter of Mary R. and Wm. H. Spear, and was born in Hinsdale, Ill., October 28, 1872. Except when away for the purpose of studying, she has always lived in or near Chicago, and for the past fourteen years has made this city her home. Early in life she had a keen desire to devote herself to the study of music, of which she was passionately fond. Most gratefully does she remember Mrs. Ellen S. Crosby's helpful influence at this time in directing her towards the study of the best music and the reading of choice literature. Those who know Mrs. Crosby's enthusiastic devotion to the study and interpretation of the choicest in the realm of music can imagine how great an inspiration she could be to this gifted young girl, on the threshold of life, hardly knowing how to attempt the achievement she thought possible. She began her musical studies in Chicago, and prosecuted them later in Boston and London. While in Boston, she studied with Signor Augusta Rotoli, and became imbued by him with the ambition to fit herself for work in grand opera. With this in view, she studied most unremittingly under excellent teachers, and her wonderful voice, as it matured, gave promise of magnificent results. In Chicago her teachers were Frederick W. and Miss

651

Fanny Root, Varasi, Wm. Nelson Burritt and Max Heinrich. These teachers all encouraged her to persistent effort, for nature had endowed her with a voice of fine range, great sweetness and remarkable power, and she felt its cultivation might mean much to her in many ways. After the year of study in Boston, of which mention has been made, she went abroad and studied under Wm. Shakspeare and George Henschel. Her concert work has been most successful, and she has sung in some of the best churches in Chicago. For two years she sang in Dr. Thomas' church (while the services were held at McVicker's Theatre), at Trinity M. E. Church, and through Philip Hale's influence secured a position in Dr. De Normandie's church, in Boston. After leaving Boston, Philip Hale wrote repeatedly to her, urging her to return to that city and make her début there with the Boston Symphony Club. About this time her sister, Edna, died. This young girl was, like her sister, very fond of music, and when but sixteen was an accomplished violinist. This sad event exerted a great influence upon the older sister. She gave up her plans to become a singer of grand opera, and, although no less a lover of music, has enjoyed it in her home, and has sung only in churches, sometimes in concerts or in private social circles. In June, 1892, she married John Evans Cornell, of Hyde Park. Although as much interested as ever in music, Mrs. Cornell is most happy at home with her three little ones, and, unless some entirely unforeseen emergency should render it necessary, the public will probably only hear this gifted singer in the most limited way. Mrs. Cornell is a most devoted mother, and feels no regrets that earlier ambitions were relinquished.

Frank Croxton.

There is no career where the results of good, early training are more evident, or in which the right foundation is more essential to success, than in that of the professional musician. The fallacy of the old belief that almost any sort of a teacher will do for a beginner has been so often proved, that wise parents and those having charge of pupils who desire to study music realize how gross an error it is to permit any careless teaching or imperfect method to enter into the commencement of a musical education.

Frank Croxton, one of the most promising young musicians of the day, does not fail to acknowledge the fact that to his splendid early training he owes much of his unusual success. He was born in Paris, Kentucky, October 7, 1877, the son of Chester and Mary Henderson Croxton. His father was not only a fine singer but a thorough and accomplished musician as well, and was his son's first instructor. Thus the boy had ever about him the influence of a true artist, and it stirred his ambition and stimulated effort. After studying with his father, he was placed successively under the tuition of Frank Herbert Tubbs and Oscar Saenger, of New York City, and Frank Barton Webster, of Chicago. His voice, which is a rare basso, has thus had the advantage of the best culture, and this has often won for him positions over older and more experienced singers.

653

tion to his choir and concert work. He is the basso soloist at the Kenwood Evangelical Church and in the Jewish Temple, Chicago.

To him has also been accorded the honor of being soloist with the Thomas' Orchestra on Festival trips for two seasons.

He has a large repertoire of operas and oratorios, and spent three years singing operas in the very best companies.

For the past three years Mr. Croxton has been a resident of Chicago, and teaches in connection with the Chicago Conservatory of Music, where the success of his pupils is a source of great pride and gratification to him. In this work he shows the excellence of his early training, and aims to give to those under his instruction the advantages which have been of such value to him.

Mr. Croxton's voice and stage presence adapt him particularly for the most difficult oratorio work, a work he greatly enjoys. Such has been his success, that to-day he is considered one of the best oratorio bassos now singing in America. This is a distinction rarely accorded to one of his age, and the future should hold no limit to the musical possibilities before this ambitious musician.

Mabelle Crawford.

Possessed of a rich and beautiful contralto voice, with a charming personality and sunny disposition, Mabelle Crawford is a favorite in musical and social circles. Perhaps it is her own freedom from the little jealousies too often apparent among singers that has won her the friendship even of those who, like herself, are striving to win the favor of the public. It is about twelve years since she made her début in Chicago, and since that time she has sung almost constantly in Chicago churches, as well as in other musical work. For years she was the contralto soloist at St. Paul's Church, and also at the Kehilath Anshe Mayno Synagogue. She has sung in the most important cities throughout the United States in opera, concert and oratorio work. Her magnificent voice particularly adapts her for the work in the larger roles of operas and oratorios, and she has grown steadily in favor since her first appearances. She is remarkably conscientious in her work, and shows in every branch of it the intellectuality which is one of her dominating characteristics. As a student, she has always evinced the most artistic tastes and genuine refinement in all her thought, and her singing shows the results attained by this sort of devotion in the acquiring of knowledge. Her stage presence is not only pleasing, but at once impresses her audience with the feeling that an ambitious and refined artist is before them.

The excellence of her achievements has found endorsement from those with whom she has appeared, representing the best in musical circles. Among them may be named Wm. H. Sherwood and Max Bendix, who stand in the foremost ranks of Chicago's artists. Twice she sang at the International Exposition, and won from those immense audiences the greatest applause, and added many to the laurels already hers. At the great New York Chautauqua, for some years she was the contralto soloist. There she not only delighted the public, but won the highest encomiums from members of the faculty. From their expressions of satisfaction we quote— "No singer has ever achieved greater success upon the Chautauqua platform or given better satisfaction than has Miss Mabelle Crawford."

Miss Crawford's voice is not only a large voice and of wide range, but it is a voice of the most exquisitely sympathetic quality. Whether interpreting the themes of oratorios or the arias from operas or singing sacred anthems, which she greatly enjoys, the same intelligence is apparent in her rendition, and her voice most wonderfully answers to each shade of thought. Her ballad singing is a delight, for every variety of song finds pleasing interpretation by this young artist's rich, sweet voice. Miss Crawford's career is so full of promise that her future is fraught with interest not only to the Chicago public but to music-lovers all over the country.

Lightning Source UK Ltd.
Milton Keynes UK
UKHW020959031218
333381UK00014B/2005/P